Football Research in an Enlarged Europe

Series Editor
Albrecht Sonntag
ESSCA School of Management
EU-Asia Institute
Angers, France

This series publishes monographs and edited collections in collaboration with a major EU-funded FP7 research project 'FREE': Football Research in an Enlarged Europe. The series aims to establish Football Studies as a worthwhile, intellectual and pedagogical activity of academic significance and will act as a home for the burgeoning area of contemporary Football scholarship. The themes covered by the series in relation to football include, European identity, memory, women, governance, history, the media, sports mega-events, business and management, culture, spectatorship and space and place. The series is highly interdisciplinary and transnational and the first of its kind to map state-of-the-art academic research on one of the world's largest, most supported and most debated socio-cultural phenomenona.

Editorial Board:

Richard Giulianotti (Loughborough University, UK)
Kay Schiller (Durham University, UK)
Geoff Pearson (Liverpool University, UK)
Jürgen Mittag (German Sport University Cologne, Germany)
Stacey Pope (Durham University, UK)
Peter Millward (Liverpool John Moores University, UK)
Geoff Hare (Newcastle University, UK)
Arne Niemann (Johannes-Gutenberg University Mainz, Germany)
David Goldblatt (Sports writer and broadcaster, UK)
Patrick Mignon (National Institute for Sports and Physical Education, France)

Arne Niemann • Alexander Brand
Regina Weber

Football Fandom and Identity in the 21st Century

Europe on Their Minds

Arne Niemann
Department of Political Science
Johannes Gutenberg University Mainz
Mainz, Rheinland-Pfalz, Germany

Alexander Brand
Faculty of Society and Economics
Rhine-Waal University
Kleve, Germany

Regina Weber
Faculty of Society and Economics
Rhine-Waal University
Kleve, Germany

Football Research in an Enlarged Europe
ISBN 978-3-031-40630-0   ISBN 978-3-031-40631-7   (eBook)
https://doi.org/10.1007/978-3-031-40631-7

© The Editor(s) (if applicable) and The Author(s), under exclusive licence to Springer Nature Switzerland AG 2024
This work is subject to copyright. All rights are solely and exclusively licensed by the Publisher, whether the whole or part of the material is concerned, specifically the rights of translation, reprinting, reuse of illustrations, recitation, broadcasting, reproduction on microfilms or in any other physical way, and transmission or information storage and retrieval, electronic adaptation, computer software, or by similar or dissimilar methodology now known or hereafter developed.
The use of general descriptive names, registered names, trademarks, service marks, etc. in this publication does not imply, even in the absence of a specific statement, that such names are exempt from the relevant protective laws and regulations and therefore free for general use.
The publisher, the authors, and the editors are safe to assume that the advice and information in this book are believed to be true and accurate at the date of publication. Neither the publisher nor the authors or the editors give a warranty, expressed or implied, with respect to the material contained herein or for any errors or omissions that may have been made. The publisher remains neutral with regard to jurisdictional claims in published maps and institutional affiliations.

Cover illustration: © Fans holding EU flag / photo by Kathrin Reichert

This Palgrave Macmillan imprint is published by the registered company Springer Nature Switzerland AG.
The registered company address is: Gewerbestrasse 11, 6330 Cham, Switzerland

Paper in this product is recyclable.

Acknowledgements

As Bertolt Brecht once remarked, the "pains of the plains" are what awaits those who have successfully overcome the "pains of the mountains", suggesting that everyday routine politics of implementing a plan might be even more burdensome in comparison to see an idea advancing to become a plan, and a reality in the first instance. In 2017, the German Research Foundation (DFG) awarded us research money for a project, which set out to investigate the Europeanisation of identities through football more thoroughly. From 2018 to 2021, we implemented this research in our project "EUFOOT: The Identity Effect of Europeanised Lifeworlds - Becoming European through Football". Doing so often was in many ways an exciting and illuminating experience despite the fact that the Covid-19 pandemic also affected our research as described in our concluding chapter.

This book contains the results of our research project in a comprehensive form. During the process of preparing this manuscript we had to pass through some "pains of the plains": writing, revising and polishing nine chapters alongside normal work duties is no trifling matter. However, given our very rich empirical material, excellent writing team-spirit and great assistance from various corners, composing and completing this book has been very rewarding and enjoyable indeed!

This book has hugely benefited from two decisions. The first one seems rather coincidental and trivial (although at first glance only). In late summer 2004, Arne Niemann had to wait in front of his former PhD supervisor's office at Pembroke College, Cambridge because Geoffrey Edwards' meeting with one of his then PhD supervisees was surpassing the already generous 90 minutes (usual for him—very unusual otherwise) bracket. Arne decided to use the opportunity to peek into Chris Young's office door across that was open. Chris invited him in and during the 15-minute conversation, they discovered their joint passion for football. As Chris was still short of a chapter on a co-edited book on German football, he did not greet Arne good-bye without asking him to think about contributing a chapter from a political science perspective. Back at the University of Dresden, Arne reported the issue to Alexander and they came up with their first paper idea on the Europeanisation of German football that was also later included in Thomlinson and Young (2006). The second decision was made in the summer of 2018 when Alexander and Arne decided to hire Regina as the main researcher for EUFOOT. Without her structured way of working, diligence, methodological know-how and foresight—all at an extremely high level of professionalism—the project would probably have failed miserably.

We would like to thank Tobias Heck, Johannes Muntschick, Friedrich Plank and Vincent Reinke for co-authoring two chapters and their brilliant contribution thereto. Many thanks also to Florian Koch for carrying out part of the research and for his input to some earlier drafts of our work. We would also like to express our gratitude to Bertus de Jong and Alexandra Bumcke for conscientiously proof-reading the chapters with eagle eyes, and Maria-Cristina Garcia-Marin, Tilman Luca Menzel, Yannik Suhre, Svenja Budde, Laura Hähn and Felix Schönbach for their competent research assistance.

A research project needs not only committed researchers and assistance, but a community that critically discusses, questions and stimulates one's work. We could build this project on the shoulders of several communities in football research and in European integration research. We thank the numerous colleagues who contributed to discussions and improved our work. Especially the community around the previous EU-FP7 project Football Research in an Enlarged Europe (FREE), which lives on in the 'Football in an Enlarged Research book series', has been a constant support. We thank especially the Series Editor Albrecht Sonntag who has been a benevolent companion to our endeavour. Many thanks also to Palgrave Macmillan's Publishing/Commissioning Editors Sharla Plant and Liam Inscoe-Jones for competently accompanying the publishing process.

Last, but definitively not least, we also wish to thank the many football fans who took the time to share their impressions and views during the interviews, alongside the survey on social media, as well as during field work and conferences. Without your time, interest and openness, this project would not have been possible.

Finally, we want to thank our friends and family who have been a great source of support and encouragement through the entire process!

Mainz, Kleve and Berlin in the summer of 2023

Arne Niemann
Alexander Brand
Regina Weber

Reference

Young, Christopher, and Alan Tomlinson, eds. 2006. *German football: History, culture, society.* London: Routledge.

Contents

1	**Introduction**		1
	1.1	Research Question and Context	1
		1.1.1 The Europeanisation of Football	3
		1.1.2 (Football) Fan Research	5
		1.1.3 Identity Research and the Europeanisation of Identity	9
	1.2	Relevance of the Book	11
		1.2.1 Academic Relevance	13
		1.2.2 Socio-Political Relevance	14
	1.3	Approach and Selected Key Findings: Varying Europeanisation of Identifications	16
		1.3.1 Identity Work in Online Fan Forum Discussions	18
		1.3.2 Survey Analysis: Cosmopolitan and Communitarian Fans	20
		1.3.3 Interviewed Fans' Narratives of Europe and the Game	21
	1.4	Plan of the Book	23
	References		25

2 Europeanisation of Football — 31
2.1 Introduction — 31
2.2 Sport/Football in the Context of European Integration Since the 1990s: Theories and Concepts — 32
    2.2.1 The Concept of Europeanisation — 35
    2.2.2 The Europeanisation of Football — 40
2.3 A Europeanisation of Football Fan Identities? — 50
References — 53

3 Football Fandom Research — 63
Tobias Heck, Alexander Brand, Arne Niemann, Regina Weber, and Vincent Reinke
3.1 Introduction — 63
3.2 Considerations on the Notion of Fandom — 64
3.3 (Multi-)disciplinary Approaches to Football Fandom — 68
    3.3.1 Football Fan Typologies—Construction Principles — 71
    3.3.2 Thematic Clusters of Fan Typologies — 76
3.4 Instead of a Conclusion: Which Gaps Do Exist in Fan Typologies? — 80
References — 83

4 Identity Research and the Europeanisation of Identity — 87
4.1 Introduction — 87
4.2 Social Identity Theory and Identity Approaches in Sport — 89
    4.2.1 General (Social) Identity Theory — 89
    4.2.2 Research Linking Identity and Sport — 94
    4.2.3 The Europeanisation of Identities: Measures and Blind Spots — 97
    4.2.4 The Europeanisation of Identities Through Leisure Time Activities and Lifeworldly Experiences — 104
4.3 Concluding Remarks — 110
References — 110

5 Analytical Framework and Research Approach   121
5.1 Introduction   121
5.2 Analytical Framework and Operationalisation of Football Fan Identity   122
    5.2.1 Communities of Belonging   123
    5.2.2 Frames of Reference   125
5.3 Eight Fan Scenes Across Europe: Case Selection and Description   128
    5.3.1 Case Selection Logic   130
    5.3.2 Short Description of the Eight Club Cases   136
5.4 A Three-Step Approach to Study Europe on Fans' Minds   141
    5.4.1 Qualitative Analysis of Online Message Boards Discussions   142
    5.4.2 Online Survey Among Football Fans in the Four Leagues   144
    5.4.3 In-depth Interviews   145
5.5 Conclusion: Reflections on the Benefits of the Mixed Methods Approach   146
References   147

6 Identity Work in Online Fan Forum Discussions   153
6.1 Introduction   153
6.2 Structured Paired Comparisons of Football Fan Discourses   154
    6.2.1 The Europeanisation of Player Markets as a Conditioning Factor   159
    6.2.2 The Level of Participation in European Club Competitions as a Conditioning Factor   169
    6.2.3 Public Attitudes Towards Europe/the EU as a Conditioning Factor   179
6.3 Further Analysis, Discussion and Conclusion   186
References   191

xii Contents

7 Surveying Football Fans: Cosmopolitans and Communitarians   193
- 7.1 Introduction   193
- 7.2 Typology of Football Fans   194
  - 7.2.1 Cosmopolitans and Communitarians   194
  - 7.2.2 A New Typology of Football Fans: Making Europeanisation Visible   197
- 7.3 What Shapes the Fan Typology: League, Club and Individual Level Influences   203
  - 7.3.1 Assumed Logics of Influence   203
  - 7.3.2 Analytical Model   205
  - 7.3.3 Results   210
- 7.4 Conclusions   215
- References   217

8 Football Fans' Narratives of Europe and the Game   221
Johannes Muntschick, Friedrich Plank, and Regina Weber
- 8.1 Introduction   221
- 8.2 Database and Methodology   222
- 8.3 Description of Interview Findings Across Six Clubs   226
  - 8.3.1 FC Bayern München: Dahoam in Europe   227
  - 8.3.2 Hannover 96: Playing National, Dreaming Europe   231
  - 8.3.3 Manchester United: Local at Heart—International in Ambitions   235
  - 8.3.4 Newcastle United: Local Working-Class Identity with Interest in Europe   239
  - 8.3.5 Sturm Graz: Regionalised Europeanisation and Embedded Within Europe   243
  - 8.3.6 Wacker Innsbruck: A Flagship for the Region, an Eye Towards Europe   246
- 8.4 Paired Comparisons of Results   250
  - 8.4.1 Assessing the League Level   251
  - 8.4.2 Assessing the Club Level   254
  - 8.4.3 Assessing the Country Level   256
- 8.5 Key Findings and Conclusions   257
- References   259

9	**Conclusions**		**261**
	9.1	Introduction	261
	9.2	Results	263
		9.2.1 The Smaller Role of Fandom Intensity	264
		9.2.2 Spatiality: Between the Local and Europe	265
		9.2.3 How to Deal with Inconsistent/Conflicting/ Contradictory Results?	267
		9.2.4 Fan Criticism of an Increasingly Inaccessible European Football	272
		9.2.5 Sport and Politics?	273
	9.3	(Further) Lessons Learned	276
		9.3.1 The Football Fan: An Elusive Object of Study	276
		9.3.2 The Covid Pandemic as a Big Disruptor	278
		9.3.3 Super League Dreams and Nightmares	279
	9.4	Further Research	281
	References		283

Index 289

Notes on Contributors

Alexander Brand is Professor of Political Science/International Relations at Rhine-Waal University in Kleve, Germany. His research focuses on sport/football and politics, the politics of development, (US) foreign policy and media and international relations.

Tobias Heck holds a Master's degree in Urban and Cultural Geography. He is working as a political advisor for the Cologne Chamber of Trades (HWK) and has a fascination for socio-political research, identity studies as well as research on gentrification.

Johannes Muntschick is a researcher and lecturer at the Department of Political Science at Johannes Gutenberg University Mainz, Germany. His research interests include regional and international institutions, regionalism and external influence, conflict (management) and politics in sub-Saharan Africa. His research has been published in (edited) books with Palgrave and in various international and national journals.

Arne Niemann is Professor of International Politics at Johannes Gutenberg University Mainz. His research focuses on European Integration. Niemann's publications include *Explaining Decisions in the European Union* (CUP 2006) and have appeared, amongst others in the *Journal of European Public Policy*, the *Journal of Common Market Studies*,

International Relations, International Migration Review and the *International Review for the Sociology of Sport*.

Friedrich Plank is a post-doctoral researcher at Johannes Gutenberg University Mainz. His main research interests include EU foreign and security policy, EU energy policy, peace and conflict studies, comparative regionalism, and Africa–EU interregionalism.

Vincent Reinke is a researcher at Johannes Gutenberg University Mainz. He is part of the FANZinE project which deals with football as the basis for social cohesion in Europe. His research is especially concerned with the political and sociological dimensions of sport.

Regina Weber is head of the department of industrial transition at the Stiftung Arbeit und Umwelt in Berlin and an adjunct lecturer at the Faculty of Society and Economics at Rhine-Waal University in Kleve, Germany. Her research covers social identifications, expressed in everyday activities, and their implications for political behaviour. Her work appeared, amongst others, at *Sport in Society*, *Party Politics* and the *Journal of Contemporary European Studies*.

List of Figures

Fig. 5.1	Sequence of methodological steps in the mixed-methods research design	142
Fig. 6.1	Coded fan articulations, emerging argumentative patterns in our software-based analysis, and the non-random choice of representative examples (here: articulations of ManU fans on a European frame of reference)	158
Fig. 7.1	Frequencies of the indicator items for the latent class analysis. N=2950, missing values for the whole data are imputed with the R-package mice	196
Fig. 7.2	Fan types: Classes of the latent class analysis, group characteristics and sizes. N=2950	200
Fig. 7.3	Decisive differences between fan types: predicted answer probabilities of the decisive items at given group membership. Graphs show the answer probability of a certain item conditional on group membership for the four types of fans. N=2950	201
Fig. 7.4	Graphical overview of the analysis and illustrated procedure of constructing the dependent variable	206
Fig. 7.5	Average Marginal Effects of the covariates in the combined regression model. Graph shows the change in predicted probability of cosmopolitan attitudes as the covariate changes by a 1-unit change	213

List of Tables

Table 1.1	Selected clubs and respective values of key variables	17
Table 3.1	Football fan typology research overview	81
Table 5.1	Analytical framework with the two dimensions' communities of belonging and frames of reference	128
Table 5.2	Overview of selected cases and data on selection criteria. Club and league data from transfermarkt.de. Internationalisation and Europeanisation of player market are calculated as the 5-year-average 2013/14–2017/18. Participation in European club competition (any stage, any competition) during the seasons 2008/09–2017/18	129
Table 5.3	Survey responses, per league and total as well as mean return per club	144
Table 6.1	The analytic grid for online discourse analysis: categories of comparison	156
Table 6.2	Degrees of Europeanisation among clustered fan communities across Europe	187
Table 7.1	Indicators for the quality of different models, the null model (1-class-model) to a 7-class-model	199
Table 7.2	Distribution of the types of football fans, dependent variable for the regression analysis	207
Table 7.3	Overview and distribution of the independent variables. Tables shows exp.(coeff). N=2950	209

Table 7.4 Regression coefficients and performance indicators for the logistic regressions. Reference group of the dependent variable: communitarian fans; shows exp(coeff) and SE in brackets. Reference category: Bundesliga (AT) — 211
Table 8.1 List of pseudonymised interviews — 223
Table 8.2 Three clusters of paired comparisons — 251

1

Introduction

1.1 Research Question and Context

This book seeks to explore the importance of lifeworldly[1] activities—more precisely, of football fandom and spectatorship—for the formation of a European identity. Research on European identity has paid scant attention to lifeworldly, sport-related and supposedly non-political activities. This is remarkable given that the governance structures in some sports, especially in football, have been strongly Europeanised in recent decades. Fans and the public had come to assign football a unifying role in 2014: some 76% of football supporters and more than 61% of the general European public agreed with the idea that football unites Europeans (FREE 2014).

In this study, we examine the extent to which a Europeanisation of football fans' perceptions and identities has taken place alongside the Europeanisation of player markets, competitions and football governance

---

We thank Florian Koch for his comments and suggestions on a previous version of this chapter.

[1] 'Lifeworld' is used in this text not in the strong Habermasian sense, but largely synonymous with everyday life/non-political spheres of action.

structures. In particular, we explore whether and to what degree the mindsets and perceptions of football fans, followers and spectators have been shaped by the changes that the game has witnessed since the 1990s. Here, we refer to the normalisation of squads and training staff originating from all over Europe, and player transfers across European borders in what is a common professional area characterised by free movement; the growing profile of the UEFA Champions League as a European tournament of top-tier clubs, both in terms of air time and aspiration, becoming the place of dreams (as well as repudiation) in the eyes of millions of football fans; the resulting transnational patterns of fan travel to matches abroad, the fascination with "going Europe" when a football match becomes an occasion to spend time elsewhere across the continent; and, last but not least, the emerging structures of transnational fan culture, organisation of fan networks and shared agendas among organised fans throughout Europe. Wouldn't all these phenomena also suggest that the transformation of European football has left its mark on the perspectives and attitudes of football fans towards Europe?

In a research project funded by the German Research Foundation (DFG) from 2018 to 2022, we set out to investigate the level and extent of such a Europeanisation of identities among football fans in Europe. Based on a four-country-eight-club case rooster (on case selection: see Sect. 1.3), we tackled two main research questions: To what extent are identities of football fans across Europe "Europeanised"? What factors condition the level of Europeanisation of football supporters' identities across different contexts? Distinguishing between club-level (top performer vs. relegation battler), league-level (high vs. medium or low level of Europeanisation of the respective player markets) and country-level context (differing degrees of Euroscepticism within the respective societies), we compared articulations, opinions and self-identifications of fans following German, English, French and Austrian teams in an effort to elucidate the impact of such different factors on the Europeanisation of identities.

Our approach took three research contexts as points of departure. They need to be briefly introduced at this stage before we sketch out the added value of the book in more detail, summarise our approach and key findings and provide a short overview of subsequent chapters. These research contexts concern (1) the Europeanisation of football, (2) (football) fan research and (3) identity research and the Europeanisation of identity.

1.1.1 The Europeanisation of Football

Europeanisation can be broadly defined as the process of change in the domestic arena driven by change at the European level of governance (Schmidt 2002). The past quarter-century has seen a significant degree of Europeanisation in the governance structures of football, although the process has not been purely top-down. While domestic actors are subject to European-level pressures, they also affect the policies at the European level to which they have to adjust at a later stage (Börzel 2002). Such a broader notion highlights the interdependence between the European and domestic levels that shapes and conditions the process of Europeanisation in football (Brand and Niemann 2007, 4). Our earlier work distinguished between three different dynamics of Europeanisation (Brand and Niemann 2007; Brand et al. 2013; Niemann and Brand 2018). The first encompasses the top-down pressure from the European level, that is rulings by the European Court of Justice (ECJ) or investigations by the European Commission—processes commonly referred to as "downloading". Second, these pressures are matched by various attempts to influence such measures on the part of domestic actors and contexts, commonly defined as bottom-up Europeanisation or "uploading" (Börzel 2002). These reciprocal processes must be distinguished from a third strand of Europeanisation dynamics that is fed by transnationalising processes, like the development of transnational lobby networks (e.g. the European Club Association) or the formation of a de facto pan-European football league, the Champions League. We call this dynamic "crossloading" (Brand et al. 2013).[2]

---

[2] The term "crossloading" itself has been introduced into Europeanisation debates by Howell (2004), albeit in a slightly different manner. We use the concept in order to highlight the cross-boundary activities of societal, subnational actors and their agency alongside conventional European politics.

Four developments that have shaped the game across Europe since the mid-1990s stand out for their significance: the regulation of player markets after the ECJ's Bosman ruling, increasing coordination of clubs on the European level, the Europeanisation of broadcasting rights and the growing prominence of the Champions League. Of these, the Bosman ruling and the subsequent lifting of caps on overseas players has had the most visible effect on the game in Europe (Niemann et al., 2011). However, behind the scenes, the European-level broadcasting rights debate has furthered coordination and lobbying structures between some clubs and associations, and eventually made the Commission backtrack on its initial goal of decentralising this domain. Intense coalition-building and lobbying following the broadcasting debates also helped to bring about the Commission's "White Paper on Sport" (2007) that, to some extent, enshrined peculiar exemptions of football *as a sport* from systematic competition regulation. These examples show that EU-level pressure may sometimes spur only partial adjustment in football governance, whereas core policies remain intact notwithstanding their potential friction with EU legislation (Niemann and Brand 2008, 100–101).

As a consequence of such EU-level pressures, though in part also pre-dating them, transnational coordination among clubs has intensified since the early 1990s. While football associations such as UEFA emerged as umbrella organisations of national football associations, individual clubs stayed sidelined for much of the twentieth century. As a counterweight, several "top clubs" from several European countries formed what became known as the G14, seeking to influence UEFA (and FIFA) by leveraging their individual power positions as "best-selling" clubs in European football (Mittag 2018). Although the G14 eventually dissolved in 2008, transnational club coordination stayed intact—now in the more encompassing form of the European Club Association (ECA) which, despite boasting nearly 200 ordinary and associated members, still acts principally on behalf of the top clubs and their particular interests (Keller 2018).

The development of the previous European Club competitions—European Champions Cup, the European Cup Winners' Cup and the UEFA Cup—into a de facto European league system in the form of the Champions League (CL), the Europa League (EL) and now also the

Conference League is perhaps the most obvious sign of Europeanisation in football. Over time, the consistent qualification of largely the same set of clubs has yielded a relatively stable pattern of recurrent participation that is functionally near-equivalent to a truly pan-European "league mode" (Pawlowski et al. 2010; Niemann and Brand 2018). Unsurprisingly, the CL has been coined "an engine that supposedly makes Europe hang together more closely", but also a "political myth" that may contribute to more Europeanised attitudes and to the European idea more generally (Niemann and Brand 2018, 2, 2020).

Hence, we had more than enough reason to believe that the Europeanisation of football described above had affected not only the structures and governance of European football but its fandom, too. The evolution of the CL into a de facto European league regularly exposed—and continues to expose—fans to competition among foreign clubs and clubs from "their" league. In addition, the increasing prevalence of foreign-born players on team rosters across the continent may not interfere with fans' ability to identify with "their" team (Ranc 2012). The Europeanisation of the structures and governance of football might thus have prompted a normalisation in the perceptions of football fans of certain (initially game-related) aspects of "Europe" (such as freedom of movement) and arguably impact on whether they are "becoming more European".

1.1.2 (Football) Fan Research

Our second point of departure has been the literature on football fans as well as fandom's implications for wider societal dynamics. We found specific merit in four aspects of this broad-ranging debate spearheaded by Sociologists and Sport Studies researchers: (1) considerations on the notion and definition of fandom, (2) the attempt to classify and distinguish between different types of fans and fandom, (3) the pioneering foray (especially of British scholars) into transnationalisation effects of football (and the English Premier League in particular) and (4) the seminal insights generated through the FREE-research project ("Football Research in an Enlarged Europe", 2012–2015, funded by the EU under the FP7-scheme) (FREE 2015).

First, our concept of a "football fan" includes all those who articulate an interest in a football team or (club) competition, be it infrequently or regularly, passively watching or actively following (cf. Redhead 2003). Under this broad definition, only a basic emotional, monetary or temporal investment is necessary to qualify as a fan. However, communality and a collective sense of belonging are of principal importance (e.g. Clcland et al. 2018; Porat 2010). Although their engagement need not be of any particular intensity, fans must be engaged with football in their everyday life. "Fandom" refers to a generalised commitment that must not be confused with representing one's team to the outside world, for example by wearing merchandise (nor with being a member of an organised fangroup). It rather encapsulates the idea that being a fan can find various expressions in everyday life.

Second, it has been widely acknowledged that there are now a large number of fan typologies (e.g. Fillis and Mackay 2014, 344). Insofar as most typologies address fans' values, attitudes and behaviour, one might have expected them to be immediately useful for our purposes. However, the specific focus of most such classifications is of rather limited value in light of our research interests. A case in point are the early studies of Clarke (1973), Critcher (1973, 11ff.) and Taylor (1972, 364). Their approaches centre around a dichotomy between traditional post-war male working-class fans with close ties to their local community clubs versus genuine middle-class spectators choosing their preferred team like consumers from a wide variety of options. Even though spatial arguments (local vs. translocal orientations) featured significantly in such classifications, they did not really aim at transnational phenomena. These works, however, did kick-start a decade-long debate on both the level of engagement (participatory vs. passive, cf. Redhead 2003) and fan intensity (supporters vs. flâneurs, in Giulianottis' (2002) coinage).

It has been these two cleavages, in conjunction with an effort to classify different attitudes towards violence among fans, that have drawn the most attention in the literature on football fans. In the German context, Heitmeyer and Peter (1988, 32ff.) proposed a three-tiered typology differentiating consumption-oriented from football-centred and experience-oriented fans, with the latter category reserved for those who seemed to take football matches only as an occasion to engage in brawls and incite turmoil. Mixing such an account with aspects of commercialisation and (hyper-) commodification, Grau et al. (2016) set out to develop a typology based on differing subjective perceptions of the "ideal stadium experience". Unsurprisingly, these and similar studies have been conducted in various country and league contexts, each producing their own slightly differing set of classifications (e.g. Pearson 2012).

More recently, García and Llopis-Goig (2019) took such typologisation efforts to a new domain. Their five-type classification scheme is geared towards the question of how European fans respond to the complex new (governance) structures in modern football. It reveals substantial divisions: while those fans classified as *moderns*, *critics* and *club-militants* (standing for about two-thirds of European football fans) mistrust international football bodies, *institutionalists* distrust football club authorities and *globalists* distrust national bodies. In addition, unlike institutionalists as well as critics, and especially club-militants, globalists and moderns doubt that their personal engagement—for instance as a member of the club and/or fan community—will have a (substantial) impact on club governance. As their well-crafted categories make clear, fandom has morphed into a post-national phenomenon.

Third, this was likewise the point of departure for the seminal studies of King (2000, 2003, 2004), Millward (2006, 2009) and Levermore and Millward (2007). By means of ethnographic research, King explored ideas of a growing "European consciousness" among a group of locally based Manchester United F.C. (Football Club) fans in the late 1990s. He argued that these fans are beginning to see themselves as more European and that two main mechanisms are propelling this change. First, increased opportunities for travelling across Europe brought about by the increase of Champions League games made supporters progressively identify as "European" in a cultural sense (King 2000, 424–426). Beyond that, King (2000, 2003) suggested that the growing coverage of all European leagues on British television made fans more aware of other European national leagues, cities and countries and that this familiarity was also building up a European consciousness. Millward listened to the voices of Liverpool F.C. and Oldham Athletic F.C. supporters, seeking to establish whether these were identifying with an idea of Europe. He found that Liverpool

F.C. fans had developed a loose identification with football-related notions of Europe as a consequence of their team competing at the European level and their experiences while following it through Europe (Millward 2006, 2009, 106–171). In contrast, Oldham Athletic A.F.C. supporters—by following a team that remained in the lower divisions of English football—exhibited only local and national patterns of identification (ibid.). Similarly, Levermore and Millward (2007, 159) set up a framework to explore the roots of a newly found "European sense of belonging" among fans. Last but not least, in his path-breaking book on the internationalisation of the English Premier League (EPL), Millward (2011) also alluded to elements of fan culture and fandom emerging from transformations at the structural and organisational levels, with the phenomenon of "foreign fandom" (i.e. following and supporting a team in a foreign country) becoming more common.

Fourth, building on this work, the trans-European research project FREE, funded by the European Commission (2012–2015), also included a track on identity-related research among football fans (FREE 2015). This track focused on two specific aspects: first, a foray into feminisation and identities (from an anthropological perspective), and second, an examination of the relationship between football and feelings of Europeanness against the background of the possible emergence of a European public sphere of football (with shared memories and communication channels as well as agendas to link fans across societies). Not by chance did the publication output of FREE build important bridges into fan research: in a more historical vein, into collective memories of a European football past (Pyta and Havemann 2015); in ethnographical terms, into fan experiences and expressions in select places throughout Europe (Schwell et al. 2016); and in a more sociological understanding, into fan activism as a particular type of social engagement on behalf of football fans as a distinctively shaped subpopulation of the European citizenry (García and Zheng 2017).

1.1.3 Identity Research and the Europeanisation of Identity

Finally, our research effort also links up to the more Political Science- and International Relations (IR)-driven effort to capture the elusive phenomena lumped together under the label of "European identity". From the outset, we found that European identity research of the Political Science and IR type (as opposed to a more sociological understanding) has thus far restricted itself to analysing very specific aspects. First, it seems primarily geared towards elite discourses on Europe. Second, where it opened up towards the wider European publics, it remained rooted in rather narrow understandings of Europe as a political entity, or the assessments of respondents on more narrowly cast *political* issues. It did so for well-intentioned reasons: for instance, when it asked questions about people's knowledge of Europe in global politics or the European Union and its symbols, it did so both with an eye to the function of a possibly emerging collective identity for the political legitimacy of European integration in general and the EU's emerging polity in particular.

Starting from the assumption that the relationship between national and European identities cannot be cast in zero-sum terms (Carey 2002), such approaches limited their attention to the home turf of Political Science: commonly perceived political norms, levels of appreciation for the EU's institutions, attention paid to and evaluations of political action at the EU level. Consequently, when it was suggested that Europeans have multiple identities as both the nation and Europe are "imagined communities" (Anderson 1991) and individuals tend to identify, to varying degrees, with both communities (Duchesne and Frognier 1998; Checkel and Katzenstein 2009; Risse 2010), European identity research framed these communities as predominantly *political* in nature, outlook and orientation. From this standpoint, various approaches and studies have undoubtedly done important research, for example into the potential for a common European identity grounded on shared values, normative ideas and political convictions (cf. Kaelble 2009) or on shared ethical self-understandings (Kantner 2006).

Equally insightful, yet likewise restricted to traditional political concerns, were explorations of the public identification with Europe, or more specifically of the "identity potential" of the EU (Gillespie and Laffan 2006; Fligstein 2008), mostly on the basis of Eurobarometer data. Finally, examinations of the possible emergence of a European(-wide) public sphere (Vreese and Vliegenthart 2012) sprang from the debate, as such a transnational sphere could arguably serve as a base for a collective identity. Consequently, such and similar studies only looked into the convergence of *news agendas, political coverage and news frames* in mass media coverage throughout Europe (Trenz 2004; Koopmans 2007; Koopmans and Statham 2010; Risse 2010, 113–119, 127–156).

What has been conspicuously absent from these accounts, however, is what occupies the attention and draws on the resources of a significant number of European citizens: everyday and leisure-time activities, supposedly non-political identifications and subjective articulations on all sorts of things and doings,[3] among them, for instance, (football) fandom. Hence, at least in the Political Science and IR tracks on "European identity" research and investigations into identity in a wider understanding, there has been a distinct lack of studies into the everyday/lifeworldly, seemingly non-political dimensions of European identity formation.

Our ambition was thus to pick up on the more recent sociological interest in the relationship between the Europeanisation of everyday life (cf. Delhey 2005; Favell 2011), transnational mobility across Europe (cf. Mau 2010; Kuhn 2012) and resulting patterns of attitudinal and/or identity change. While these studies were undoubtedly ground-breaking in nature, they have left ample room for a further exploration of the identity dimension in particular. For example, Mau (and colleagues) sought to probe whether increased transnationality across Europe goes hand in hand with higher levels of identification with Europe. He noticed a strong correlation but, as he himself underlines, causality could run both ways: attitudinal change could be the result of increased transnationality, or a

---

[3] The single big exception here is the EUCROSS research project (cf. EUCROSS 2014). EUCROSS, however, had a decidedly sociological focus, even though Political Scientists contributed to its efforts. See also Recchi et al. (2019).

higher propensity to move across European borders could be supported by an already Europeanised mindset (Mau 2010).

We also took some inspiration from Kuhn (2012), who showed that top-down programmes of planned Europeanisation such as Erasmus may fail: they cater to an already Europeanised elite, while the larger population—the real target audience which largely lacks a broader Europeanised horizon—remains mostly unaffected (but see, in contrast, Mitchell 2015). Hence, "transnationalism from above" (Mau 2010), such as exchange programmes, may not provide the most fruitful testing ground for Europeanisation effects at the identity level. In contrast, non-elite fields of activity where transnationalism happens rather unconsciously, by default, and in a bottom-up manner—true "transnationalism from below" (Mau 2010) as, we argue, could possibly be found in football fandom across Europe—seems to be the more promising avenue. If patterns of identification among non-elite actors such as football fans exhibit transnational (here, Europeanised) qualities to a considerable degree, this would be a powerful argument for this hypothetical link between everyday activities and identity formation.

1.2 Relevance of the Book

The aim of this book is threefold. First, we want to inquire into Europeanised patterns of identification among football fans in a systematic, cross-societal fashion to elucidate whether the changing experiences of the game have also shaped the mindsets of fans and supporters. While this is often assumed and occasionally backed up with anecdotal evidence, we aspire to set this assumption on firmer evidential ground and determine the extent to which football fans across Europe have adjusted their identification patterns to the structures and overall organisation of the beloved game.

Second, even though this is an interesting topic in itself, we also aim to demonstrate that such a Europeanisation nurtured in a decidedly life-worldly context of activities also has profound political implications, and therefore should be included in discussions on the trajectories of "European identity". It is one thing to speculate whether significantly more people would invest ample resources and emotions in following their team up to the UEFA Champions League finals rather than tracking their representatives in the European Parliament. But demonstrating that all this fandom and identity work also (implicitly and indirectly) bears political relevance is a powerful argument in favour of paying closer attention to European citizens in their capacity as sporting and sport-watching people. Football fans are to be found on both sides of the Brexit debate, but to what extent has their fandom contributed to forming a specific political preference and vice versa? Most supporters might find merit in the idea of having many locally trained youths in their team, but how relevant is the players' country of origin really if one's beloved team was fielding a (near) all-European squad? These questions shall also be asked mostly from a Political Science (and IR) perspective.

Third, our project also brings politically relevant aspects to the table. While we would not claim that football is necessarily a cosmopolitan force shifting whole societies towards an appreciation of diversity across Europe, subliminal Europeanisation might nonetheless have the capacity to normalise "Europe" in the eyes of its citizens. Moreover, fandom as a vector of Europeanisation may be shown to create linkages and forge relationships subconsciously, as a form of bottom-up Europeanisation. This stands in contrast to "Europeanisation from above" schemes such as Erasmus+ exchanges, which openly and explicitly aim to foster a European identity. Vague talk about the Champions League providing a sort of "continental glue" where politics fails is perhaps better described as myth-making rather than as serious analysis (Niemann and Brand 2020). Besides, countervailing effects stemming from Brexit or rising populism might overpower the effects of sports, sport spectatorship and identity work for the moment. It nonetheless remains important to illuminate the potential for common sportive experiences within a largely shared framework of sport organisation, and against the background of increasingly transboundary communities to provide aspects of "European togetherness" to the people throughout Europe. In what follows, we will briefly detail the academic and societal/political relevance that might result.

1.2.1 Academic Relevance

This book adds academic value for several reasons. First, it contributes to broader European identity research (particularly in Political Science/IR). While the vast Europeanisation literature has been conspicuously silent about developments concerning everyday and leisure-time domains (but see Jacobsen 2003, EUCROSS 2014), Political Science research on European identity has tended, as noted, to focus almost exclusively on the perceptive and evaluative level of *strictly political issues*. This literature covers the development of conscious political identities, geared towards the institutions and the EU integration project, and towards Europe as a space emerging from shared normative convictions. In contrast, our book addresses the lack of studies into the lifewordly, seemingly non-political dimensions of European identity formation. We attempt to fill this gap by looking into the largely unconscious side-effects of activities, which nevertheless have an impact on the degree of familiarity with Europe, the normalisation of "going Europe", the appreciation of Europe as a space of action as well as in-group/out-group aspects of community formation (nationality, foreignness). Such issues lie at the heart of any analysis of current politics within Europe and are thus also at the core of Political Science, as particular identities privilege and legitimise particular actors, policies and polities.

Second, the book seeks to contribute to European identity work located in sociological and related research. Rather than focusing on selective participation in student exchange programmes (Kuhn 2012), or job mobility (Favell 2011; EUCROSS 2014) amid the more educated layers of society, we explore a *non-elite* context that allows for inferences about larger segments of European populations and the likelihood and forms of transnational identity formation therein. By concentrating on the mass phenomenon of football that reaches all spheres of society, we examine a group of people (fans and supporters) that are usually, and often for good reason, considered less cosmopolitan and mobile (King 2000).

Third, this book will further our understanding and insight in terms of more genuine football fan research related to European identity as initiated by Sport Sociology. While the work of King (2000), Millward (2006, 2009) and Levermore and Millward (2007) has undoubtedly been very useful, it is of rather limited scope due to its focus on developments in the UK, and around the EPL. Building on their insights, we significantly extend the *range of findings* (by studying several country, league and club contexts) as well as the *depth of findings* by examining aspects of continuously practiced football fandom through various methods.

This brings us to a fourth aspect of academic relevance: our book is innovative from a methodological point of view. We use a multi-method approach—including qualitative data analysis of fan forums, an online fan survey geared towards quantitative analysis, semi-structured interviews and paired comparisons across football clubs—that combines both qualitative and quantitative elements in order to produce empirical data in a systematic fashion. While elements of this approach have been on display in other analyses of football fans and similar objects of study, most notably in the already cited FREE-project and the works of Millward (e.g. 2008), we claim that the combination of these various methods (on their interplay, see Sect. 1.3 and Chap. 5) in a rigorous comparative design presents a novelty in this area of research.

1.2.2 Socio-Political Relevance

This book has societal and political importance in various respects. First, football—as a field of activities—seems to pose an especially hard case for the formation of a transnational, European identity, given its historically rather national outlook, structures and prevalent orientations among fans and supporters. Football has been considered as a carrier of national or local identities that tend to work in an exclusive rather than inclusive fashion (King 2000; Meier et al. 2019). In that sense, it presents an ultimate test case for elucidating whether transnational shifts in structural contexts (the organisation of the game, competition formats, composition of players markets, etc.) can have a formative impact on identities in what constitutes a parochial rather than a cosmopolitan context, prima facie.

Second, at the same time it has been suggested that sport as such presents an ideal carrier of identity change given the huge emotional investment of fans (Goodwin et al., 2001). Preliminary research indicates that football—socially, commercially and culturally the most important sporting activity in Europe—has a substantial sociocultural impact on individuals' perception and understanding of what constitutes Europe. FREE (2015) concluded that football has unique bridge-building potential to (positively) influence national stereotypes. If fans and spectators have become more used to, interested in and positive about football at the European level, this might also unconsciously challenge prejudices and stereotypes. This could be all the more significant given the large number of football fans and spectators in Europe.

Third, football might, in more subtle and indirect ways, indeed provide some ingredients for an integrative "glue" among the citizens of Europe in times of multi-crisis. Phenomena and developments such as the so-called European refugee crisis, the Eurozone crisis, Brexit and its emerging consequences, rising populism and perhaps also the economic, social and public health consequences of the COVID-19 pandemic—with Russia's war against Ukraine constituting another (potentially) divisive future issue—have arguably exacerbated divisions among European governments and Europeans alike. Quite certainly, they have left their (divisive) mark on European citizens' perceptions and evaluations concerning the *political* project of European integration as well as their attitudes towards each other. In times of multiple crises, football (though in crisis itself, not least due to the pandemic and its ensuing regulations) might be seen as a provider of at least some sense of "togetherness". If football supporters' identities, rather unwittingly, have indeed become more Europeanised through the game in the last two decades, this may, for example, mitigate negative stereotyping and stimulate positive mutual perceptions. In that restricted but not unimportant sense, football might thus help to indirectly foster cohesion in times of profound societal and political stress.

1.3 Approach and Selected Key Findings: Varying Europeanisation of Identifications

Our study provides a perspective on Europeanisation of fan identifications that vary across the different leagues and clubs but at the same time also exhibit some similar cross-national patterns. Without delving too deeply into our research design (see Chap. 5), we briefly state here which clubs and fan communities we selected as the basis for our work, and what methods were chosen for analysis. We expected three variables to act as relevant predictors of Europeanisation among football fans: the public attitude towards Europe in the respective society, the degree of Europeanisation of the player market (i.e. the share of non-domestic players) in the respective football league and the participation of the club in European competitions. While the public attitude in the host country captures the influence of wider societal opinion on the identity formation of football fans, the other two variables measure the specific exposure to Europe through football. Consequently, we chose four national leagues from four European countries: Germany, the UK (England), France and Austria. In each of the four countries, we selected two clubs: one top-tier club that regularly competes in European competitions and one club that can be seen as a relegation battler. The sample, as indicated in Table 1.1, was to ensure that we had included a variety of values concerning key variables in a systematic fashion.

Our research strategy employs a mixed-method approach, combining three techniques to assess the phenomenon from various angles. The methodological tools that we used for our triangulation consisted of (1) a qualitative discourse analysis of online message board discussions among fans, (2) an online survey of football fans and (3) semi-structured in-depth interviews with fans. Finally, structured paired comparisons were carried out to dig deeper into the role of the three influencing factors on our context levels (club, league and country).

The results of the study confirm the relevance of football-related exposure on fans' identifications: Both the state of the player market and clubs' participation in European competitions explain partly why fans

Table 1.1 Selected clubs and respective values of key variables

Condition/ context Club	League	Public attitude towards Europe/EU (*country* context)	Europeanisation of player market in the *league* (*league* context)	Participation in European club competitions (*club* context)
Bayern München	Bundesliga (DE)	Rather Europhile	Medium-high	High
Hannover 96	Bundesliga (DE)	Rather Europhile	Medium-high	Low
Manchester United	English Premier League	Rather Eurosceptic	High	High
Newcastle United	English Premier League	Rather Eurosceptic	High	Low
Olympique Marseille	Ligue 1	Rather Europhile	Low-medium	High
Toulouse FC	Ligue 1	Rather Europhile	Low-medium	Low
Sturm Graz	Bundesliga (AT)	Rather Eurosceptic	Low-medium	High
Wacker Innsbruck	Bundesliga (AT)	Rather Eurosceptic	Low-medium	Low

either associate themselves with a European space/sphere or not. Societal embedding, on the other hand, proved to be less useful for understanding differences across fan communities. Furthermore, we also see quite diverse patterns of identification with Europe *among fans of the same clubs*, thus not influenced by our expected predictors. This indicates that the Europeanisation of football does not only have the power to influence fans in the direction of "becoming European", but it might impact fans to differing degrees or in different ways. If Europeanisation in the realm of football is taken to be a proxy of, or hugely supporting, hyper-commercialisation, fans may feel increasingly alienated, protest or vote with their feet. In an interesting twist, though, this does not necessarily mean abandoning Europe: fans might coordinate their efforts against UEFA-style elitism on a continental level or even find other cross-boundary niches to pursue their love of the game. In sum, what we find is a quite fascinating mix of predictable, countervailing and ambivalent responses of fans towards the Europeanisation of football governance.

1.3.1 Identity Work in Online Fan Forum Discussions

The examination of online message board discussions among supporters of the eight selected clubs during a period of two seasons shows that the Europeanisation of football has left a mark on how fans understand the game and on what they identify as in-group and out-group. However, while we see indicators for a Europeanisation of fan identification across all clubs, the degree of exposure to Europe via football influences *how* fans attribute meaning to the European level of football in their debates. In particular, the club-level factor (participation in European competition) and, to a somewhat lesser degree, the league-level factor (Europeanisation of the transfer market) seem to matter decisively for fans' perspectives.

Even for a club far off from regular European competition, the very context of a Europeanised league might make a difference concerning how much attention supporters pay to the game abroad—as the case of Newcastle United fans demonstrates.[4] They frequently discuss other European leagues and players, despite the club's distance from European club tournaments. Leagues with comparatively less Europeanised player markets—such as the French Ligue 1 and the Austrian Bundesliga—have bred more appreciation for local and national talent, or regional orientations as in the case of Wacker Innsbruck. By far the greatest weakening of national ties and frames became visible in the case of Bayern Munich—an effect which is, however, *not* replicated in Hannover 96 fans, at that time competing in the same fairly Europeanised player market context of the German Bundesliga but with little chance of qualifying for European competitions. Frequent exposure to, as well as (successful) participation in, European-level club competitions seems to have instigated Europeanising tendencies among the respective supporters.

These tendencies have not been uniform. Still, most supporters of top-level clubs in European football defined their clubs as aspiring to be top-notch at the *European* level. Even though there were regional and local

---

[4] As opposed to our period of investigation, following the takeover by a consortium of the Saudi Public Investment Fund, Newcastle United's ambitions have increased and the club has qualified for the Champions League for the 2023–2024 season.

anchors in the cases of clubs like Bayern Munich, Manchester United and Olympique Marseille (narratives of regional bonds and hard work, not being dominated by "rich oil investors" from faraway places, having a glorious past as authentic domestic champions, cultivating local rivalries), most of their respective fan scenes had opened up to European-level developments and seemed to judge players from all over the continent on the basis of skill and merit rather than origin, as they also followed football throughout Europe more intensely.

By comparison, fans of relegation battlers did not worry much about Europe. There are simply too few points of contact linking their club's destiny to European-level football, and only in the case of the highly Europeanised context of the English Premier League was there a mild spillover effect of monitoring European-level developments observable in discussions of Newcastle United fans. An interesting side effect was that, at least occasionally, the Europeanisation of structures of *elite* football and the increasing gap between top sides and the rest were rather critically assessed—as a source of one's own club's misfortune and solidified barriers to entry into the top ranks. In that sense, the contours of a perception of two worlds of football materialises: the European level and their own below it.

Somewhat counterintuitively, the degree of support for or scepticism towards Europe and the EU in particular in the embedding societies did not play any substantial role. Even more strikingly, hardly any references to Europe, the EU, institutions or politics could be discovered in the identity-relevant online discussions under study. Where politics became an issue, as in the case of Brexit and UK fan forums, it was discussed in parallel and isolated from the game-specific aspects. In a final attempt to solidify and condense the data points gleaned from comprehensive online discourse analysis and the ensuing matrix of paired comparisons, we transformed our insights into numerical values in order to measure which factor had the highest explanatory value as regards the Europeanisation of mindsets and perceptions. Thus, we were able to demonstrate that exposure to European-level competition seems to carry the greatest power in this regard.

1.3.2 Survey Analysis: Cosmopolitan and Communitarian Fans

Our research also contributed to the aforementioned attempts at a classification of football fans. We were able to amend existing categories in order for them to make the varying impact of the current state of Europeanisation on different groups of fans visible. In this context, our survey of football fans from all clubs in the first leagues of the respective four countries (with close to 3000 participants) served as a data set for a quantitative corroboration of the complex Europeanisation tendencies among football supporters. Based on a solid battery of items measuring how fans react to the Europeanised structures and formats of the game, a 2 × 2 matrix of fans was identified using latent class modelling. The resulting four different types of football fans were thus distinguished by the intensity of their fandom and their assessment of the Europeanisation of the game. Regarding fandom intensity, we could distinguish between *frequent fans* and *occasional* fans. The former are frequent match attendees and have various connections to the club, that is via official membership or through organised fan-groups. The latter attend matches only occasionally and have few or no connections with the club. In terms of their assessment of the Europeanisation of the game, we were able to distinguish between *cosmopolitan* and *communitarian* groups among football fans. While both types emphasise the importance of the local connectedness of their respective club and also show appreciation for home-grown players in its ranks, the *cosmopolitans* attribute hardly any relevance to the national level—both in terms of competitions and as a primary selector for the composition of teams. *Communitarians*, on the other hand, ascribe importance to national belonging and value domestic players as an important ingredient of the game and a source of identification. It is worth noting that these different sets of attitudes towards the role of national belonging are prevalent both among intense fans and among the casual and occasional supporters. This shows that attitudes towards the Europeanisation aspects of football are not strongly linked to fandom intensity.

Examining the different levels of potential influence, we can identify factors at the club level as important aspects that distinguish between cosmopolitan and communitarian fans as well as between occasional and frequent fans. For the latter, the appearance of a club in European competitions is distinctive—the more successful a club is (i.e. the closer it gets to regular appearances at European competitions featuring top-tier teams), the more it attracts occasional fans, both from the cosmopolitan and the communitarian spectrum. The most relevant predictor of whether a fan is categorised as cosmopolitan or communitarian, in turn, is whether their club's first team has a high or a low share of foreign (non-native) players.[5] Clubs with many domestic players tend to draw a rather *communitarian* supporter base, while fans of clubs with a high share of non-domestic players seem to attribute less or no relevance to the players' national origin. These results corroborated the "exposure logic"—the more fans are used to seeing "their team" being composed of non-domestic players, the more they reject aspects of *national* belonging as important for them with regard to football. This tendency shows that the ongoing internationalisation of player markets, which has intensified in the recent past across the whole European continent (FIFA 2019), also has the potential to influence whether and to what degree fans attribute significance to questions of national belonging, and to what degree their minds have opened up to more Europeanised patterns of identification.

1.3.3 Interviewed Fans' Narratives of Europe and the Game

As a third methodological step, we conducted 63 semi-structured interviews with fans of Bayern Munich, Hannover 96, Manchester United, Newcastle United, Sturm Graz and Wacker Innsbruck. Interviews for the two French clubs could not be secured in a satisfying fashion, unfortunately, due to the situational context (Covid-19), the elusiveness of the French supporters in particular (see conclusions), and other project-specific circumstances. Still, the interviews we could conduct complemented the first two methodological steps in that they highlight fans' individual

---

[5] Our survey analysis further suggests that a combination of various factors—including the degree of internationalisation of a league, attitudes towards European unification and the degree of Europeanisation of a club's squads—provide most predicative power concerning cosmopolitan attitudes.

logics and perceptions, both regarding the Europeanisation of football and regarding their identifications vis-à-vis Europe. They showed in a more nuanced fashion how the Europeanisation of football has left a mark on fans and their appreciation of different aspects of the Europeanisation of the game, and how such lifeworldly experiences may interconnect with more political attitudes and identifications.

The analysis of our interviews revealed that the degree to which fans are exposed to regular and (successful) participation in European-level club competition does set in motion Europeanising tendencies among the respective supporters compared to fans whose clubs tend to be busy trying to stay in the highest national league. Even though fans generally display a high level of positive attitudes towards playing European, there is substantial evidence to suggest that the frequent exposure of Bayern Munich and Manchester United fans is key for the very positive view fans of these clubs have on European competitions. Fans of clubs that are less present in the CL and EL also highlight the relevance, quality and key role of the European club competitions, but at the same time they also tend to criticise their closed character and commercialisation.

Our analysis further suggests that differences in the composition of player markets have some effect on the way fans approach football, although to a limited extent. Overall, very Europeanised player markets create some divergences when compared to more closed markets. Finally, for the interviewed supporters, variation in public attitude towards Europe/the EU does not seem to play a considerable role for the perceptions of communities of belonging and frames of reference. Our findings based on semi-structured fan interviews largely mirror those of our examination of online discussion forums regarding the relevance of the three conditioning factors.

Interestingly, while our discourse analysis of online fan forums—and also, by and large, our semi-structured interviews—suggest that a club's participation in European-level competitions is the conditioning factor carrying the greatest explanatory power for Europeanised fan identities, our survey indicates that affiliation with a club competing at the European level does not increase the likelihood of cosmopolitan fan identities. Here, in contrast, the degree of Europeanisation of a club's squads was identified as the single most powerful factor in correlating with cosmopolitan attitudes.

1.4 Plan of the Book

In what follows, we provide a brief overview of the book's structure. Aside from this introduction, it comprises four parts. We begin with a discussion and analysis of the existing bodies of research and literature which have informed our investigation (Chaps. 2, 3 and 4). Chapter 5, provides a bridge towards our own efforts. It introduces our methodological apparatus and the project's research design. The following part contains our empirical analysis across methods (Chaps. 6, 7 and 8). Chapter 9, summarises the results and aims at solidifying our insights into overarching conclusions. In the remainder, we give a brief overview of the individual chapters.

Chapter 2 elaborates the main developments of Europeanisation in football since the 1990s and discusses its potential implications for football fandom and fan identification. Our main argument is that the structures of football have been significantly Europeanised in the past three decades (i.e. establishment of the European league system, a Europeanised transfer market). Following from that, exposure to Europe is the "new normal" for many football fans, with a potentially important impact on identity and their understandings of in-groups and out-groups in particular.

Building on that, Chap. 3 examines the current state of research in football fan-related work in greater detail. It starts with a discussion of the notion of "fan" and then proceeds with a contextualisation of fan identification research, covering the heterogeneous literature traditions in Sociology, Sport Studies and Sport Management research. We zoom in again on select typologies of fans in their capacity to relate to the issue of Europeanisation of fandom.

We take the debate on identity further in Chap. 4 by describing the state of the art in identity research within the context of Europeanisation. We further define core approaches of research and measurement towards Europeanisation in the realm of identities, mostly with reference to the works of Brubaker and Cooper (2000) and Eder (2009). We thus start from an identity concept resting on the tripartite structure of identification, self-understanding and communality, linking back to our ambition to carry out research in a realm of lifeworldly/everyday and leisure-time activities.

In Chap. 5, we describe our analytical framework, which informs our approach to both research and the design of our study. Based on the twin pillars of the concepts *communities of belonging* (COB) and *frames of reference* (FOR), we develop a more fine-tuned set of categories and coding schemes. This seems particularly warranted as the phenomena which we seek to study often belong to the realm of unconscious, subliminal identity work among fans who perceive themselves as fans, yet rarely reflect on their identities shifting along the way. In a second step, we introduce our comparative grid which allows us to study developments in four countries with the aim of generating more generalisable data. Finally, we briefly describe and justify the methods chosen as well as how they are interrelated and mutually supportive in our design.

Chapter 6 describes and analyses the main trends within discourses among fans in select online message boards. In particular, we evaluate discussions about rivalry, competitions and player transfers against the conceptual framework. Wrapping up the outcomes, this section concludes with the observation that the normalisation of Europe in football has left a visible mark on fan discourses, albeit to different degrees, across leagues and clubs.

Chapter 7 then provides the data from an extensive online survey of football fans in the four relevant leagues, both in a descriptive and analytical fashion. It establishes a new typology of football fans based on their attitude towards the visible Europeanisation of football. Distinguishing between cosmopolitan fans, who do not consider national belonging to be important in their fandom, and communitarian fans who attribute some relevance to such belonging, the analysis highlights how the Europeanisation of football has influenced aspects of fan identities differently across fans of similarly positioned clubs. In a second step, we analyse which factors influence who is a communitarian and who is a cosmopolitan, showing that individual-level characteristics as well as league- and club-level factors are important.

Chapter 8 completes our report of the study's main results. It is based on semi-structured, qualitative interviews with fans from six clubs and reveals the subtle identifications, self-understandings and communality patterns among fans within their own narration. The chapter highlights how the heterogeneous attitudes towards players and rivals from across the continent are rationalised by individual fans and how their football-specific attitudes relate to their wider political attitudes and understanding of the world.

Chapter 9 wraps our project up. We review our main findings and insights across the three analytical steps in which we investigated fan perspectives and identifications. In doing so, we also discuss the divergence of findings across methods and how to square those inconsistencies. Subsequently, we report some experiences and observations that go beyond our scientific results (strictly speaking), thereby highlighting some lessons learned from the project. Finally, the chapter discusses how our findings trigger new questions and research avenues that should be pursued to uncover the full potential of football and leisure-world activities more generally for European identity research.

References

Anderson, Benedict. 1991. *Imagined Communities*. revised. London: Verso Books.

Börzel, Tanja. 2002. Member state responses to Europeanization. *Journal of Common Market Studies* 40 (2): 193–214. https://doi.org/10.1111/1468-5965.00351.

Brand, Alexander, and Arne Niemann. 2007. Europeanisation in the societal/trans-national realm: What European integration studies can get out of analysing football. *Journal of Contemporary European Research* 3 (3): 182–201.

Brand, Alexander, Arne Niemann, and Georg Spitaler. 2013. The two-track Europeanization of football: EU-Level pressures, transnational dynamics and their repercussions within different national contexts. *International Journal of Sport Policy and Politics* 5 (1): 95–112. https://doi.org/10.1080/19406940.2012.665381.

Brubaker, Rogers, and Frederick Cooper. 2000. Beyond 'identity'. *Theory and Society* 29 (1): 1–47. https://doi.org/10.1023/A:1007068714468.

Carey, Sean. 2002. Undivided loyalties. *European Union Politics* 3 (4): 387–413. https://doi.org/10.1177/1465116502003004001.

Checkel, Jeffrey T., and Peter J. Katzenstein, eds. 2009. *European identity*. New York: Cambridge University Press.

Clarke, John. 1973. *Football hooliganism and the skinheads*. Birmingham: University of Birmingham.
Cleland, Jamie, Mark Doidge, Peter Millward, and Paul Widdop. 2018. *Collective action and football fandom: A relational sociological approach*, Palgrave studies in relational sociology. Cham: Springer.
Commission of the European Communities. 2007. *White Paper: White Paper on sport*. Brussels.
Critcher, Charles. 1973. *Football since the war: A study in social change and popular culture*. Birmingham: University of Birmingham: Centre for Contemporary Cultural Studies.
Delhey, Jan. 2005. Das Abenteuer der Europäisierung. *Soziologie* 34 (1): 7–27. https://doi.org/10.1007/s11617-005-0228-4.
Duchesne, Sophie, and André-Paul Frognier. 1998. Is there a European identity? In *Public opinion and internationalized governance*, ed. Oskar Niedermayer and Richard Sinnott, 193–223. Oxford: Oxford University Press.
Eder, Klaus. 2009. A theory of collective identity making sense of the debate on a 'European identity'. *European Journal of Social Theory* 12 (4): 427–447. https://doi.org/10.1177/1368431009345050.
EUCROSS. 2014. *The Europeanisation of everyday life: Cross-border practices and transnational identifications among EU and third-country citizens: Final report*. EUCROSS.
Favell, Adrian. 2011. *Eurostars and Eurocities: Free movement and mobility in an integrating Europe*. Malden: Wiley-Blackwell.
FIFA. 2019. *Global transfer market report 2019: Men professional football*. FIFA.
Fillis, Ian, and Craig Mackay. 2014. Moving beyond fan typologies: The impact of social integration on team loyalty in football. *Journal of Marketing Management* 30 (3–4): 334–363. https://doi.org/10.1080/0267257X.2013.813575.
Fligstein, Neil. 2008. *Euroclash: The EU, European identity, and the future of Europe*. Oxford/New York: Oxford University Press.
FREE. 2014. European policy brief: Football research in an enlarged Europe. *European Policy Brief* 1.
———. 2015. *Football research in an enlarged Europe – Project final report*. FP7 Project, Funding Scheme FP7-SSH-2011-2. Football Research in an Enlarged Europe (FREE).
García, Borja, and Ramón Llopis-Goig. 2019. Club-militants, institutionalists, critics, moderns and globalists: A quantitative governance-based typology of

football supporters. *International Review for the Sociology of Sport* 9 (3): 101269021986866. https://doi.org/10.1177/1012690219868661.

García, Borja, and Jinming Zheng, eds. 2017. *Football and supporter activism in Europe: Whose game is it?* Cham: Springer.

Gillespie, Paul, and Brigid Laffan. 2006. European identity: Theory and empirics. In *Palgrave advances in European Union studies*, ed. Michelle Cini and Angela K. Bourne, 131–150. Basingstoke/New York: Palgrave Macmillan.

Giulianotti, Richard. 2002. Supporters, followers, fans, and flaneurs. *Journal of Sport and Social Issues* 26 (1): 25–46. https://doi.org/10.1177/0193723502261003.

Goodwin, Jeffrey, James M. Jasper, and Francesca Polletta. 2001. *Passionate politics: Emotions and social movements*. University of Chicago Press.

Grau, Andreas, et al. 2016. Football fans in Germany: A latent class analysis typology. *The International Journal of Sport and Society* 7 (1): 19–31.

Heitmeyer, Wilhelm, and Jörg-Ingo Peter. 1988. *Jugendliche Fussballfans: Soziale und politische Orientierungen, Gesellungsformen, Gewalt*. Weinheim/München: Juventa-Verlag.

Howell, Kerry E. 2004. Developing conceptualisations of Europeanization: Synthesising methodological approaches. *Queen's Papers on Europeanisation* p0044. Queens University Belfast.

Jacobsen, Jens K. 2003. The tourist bubble and the Europeanisation of holiday travel. *Journal of Tourism and Cultural Change* 1 (1): 71–87. https://doi.org/10.1080/14766820308668160.

Kaelble, Hartmut. 2009. Identification with Europe and politicization of the EU since the 1980s. In *European identity*, ed. Jeffrey T. Checkel and Peter J. Katzenstein, 193–212. New York: Cambridge University Press.

Kantner, Cathleen. 2006. Collective identity as shared ethical self-understanding. *European Journal of Social Theory* 9 (4): 501–523. https://doi.org/10.1177/1368431006073016.

Keller, Berndt K. 2018. Sectoral social dialogue in professional football.: Social partners, outcomes and problems of implementation. *etui Working Paper* 2018.04. Brussels.

King, A. 2000. Football fandom and post-national identity in the new Europe. *British Journal of Sociology* 51 (3): 419–442. https://doi.org/10.1111/j.1468-4446.2000.00419.x.

King, Anthony. 2003. *The European ritual: Football in the new Europe*. London/New York: Routledge.

———. 2004. The new symbols of European football. *International Review for the Sociology of Sport* 39 (3): 323–336. https://doi.org/10.1177/1012690204045599.

Koopmans, Ruud. 2007. Who inhabits the European public sphere? Winners and losers, supporters and opponents in Europeanised political debates. *European Journal of Political Research* 46 (2): 183–210. https://doi.org/10.1111/j.1475-6765.2006.00691.x.

Koopmans, Ruud, and Paul Statham. 2010. *The making of a European public sphere*. Cambridge: Cambridge University Press.

Kuhn, Theresa. 2012. Why educational exchange programmes miss their mark: Cross-border mobility, education and European identity. *Journal of Common Market Studies* 50 (6): 994–1010. https://doi.org/10.1111/j.1468-5965.2012.02286.x.

Levermore, Roger, and Peter Millward. 2007. Official policies and informal transversal networks: Creating 'pan-European identifications' through sport? *The Sociological Review* 55 (1): 144–164. https://doi.org/10.1111/j.1467-954X.2007.00686.x.

Mau, Steffen. 2010. *Social transnationalism: Lifeworlds beyond the nation-state*. London: Routledge.

Meier, Henk E., et al. 2019. Fan identification and national identity. *Sport in Society* 22 (3): 476–498. https://doi.org/10.1080/17430437.2018.1504771.

Millward, Peter. 2006. 'We've all got the bug for Euro-aways': What fans say about European football club competition. *International Review for the Sociology of Sport* 41 (3–4): 375–393. https://doi.org/10.1177/1012690207077706.

———. 2008. The rebirth of the football fanzine: Using E-zines as data source. *Journal of Sport and Social Issues* 32 (3): 299–310. https://doi.org/10.1177/0193723508319718.

———. 2009. *Getting into Europe: Identification, prejudice and politics in English football culture*. Saarbrücken: VDM.

———. 2011. *The global football league: Transnational networks, social movements and sport in the new media age*. London: Palgrave Macmillan.

Mitchell, Kristine. 2015. Rethinking the 'Erasmus effect' on European identity. *Journal of Common Market Studies* 53 (2): 330–348. https://doi.org/10.1111/jcms.12152.

Mittag, Jürgen. 2018. Europäische Sportpolitik zwischen Wachstum und Differenzierung: Entwicklungslinien, Analyseperspektiven und Erklärungsansätze. In *Europäische Sportpolitik: Zugänge – Akteure – Problemfelder*, ed. Jürgen Mittag, 13–49. Baden-Baden: Nomos.

Niemann, Arne, and Alexander Brand. 2008. The impact of European integration on domestic sport: The case of German football. *Sport in Society* 11 (1): 90–106. https://doi.org/10.1080/17430430701717822.

———. 2018. Die Europäisierung des Fußballs: Von der Umsetzung politischer Vorgaben zur Gestaltung europäischer Realitäten. In *Europäische Sportpolitik: Zugänge – Akteure – Problemfelder*, ed. Jürgen Mittag, 167–180. Baden-Baden: Nomos.

———. 2020. The UEFA champions league: A political myth? *Soccer & Society* 21 (3): 329–343. https://doi.org/10.1080/14660970.2019.1653859.

Niemann, Arne, Borja García, and Wyn Grant. 2011. Introduction: The transformation of European football. In *Transformation of European football*, ed. Arne Niemann, Borja García, and Wyn Grant, pp. 1–19. Manchester: Manchester University Press.

Pawlowski, Tim, Christoph Breuer, and Arnd Hovemann. 2010. Top clubs' performance and the competitive situation in European domestic football competitions. *Journal of Sports Economics* 11 (2): 186–202. https://doi.org/10.1177/1527002510363100.

Pearson, Geoff. 2012. *An ethnography of English football fans: Cans, cops and carnivals*. Manchester: Manchester University Press.

Porat, Amir Ben. 2010. Football fandom: A bounded identification. *Soccer & Society* 11 (3): 277–290.

Pyta, Wolfram, and Nils Havemann, eds. 2015. *European football and collective memory*. London: Palgrave Macmillan.

Ranc, David. 2012. *Foreign players and football supporters: The Old Firm, Arsenal, Paris Saint-Germain*. Manchester/New York: Manchester University Press.

Recchi, Ettore, et al., eds. 2019. *Everyday Europe. Social transnationalism in an unsettled continent*. Bristol: Policy Press.

Redhead, Steve. 2003. *Post-fandom and the millennial blues: The transformation of soccer culture*. Abingdon: Taylor and Francis.

Risse, Thomas. 2010. *A community of Europeans?: Transnational identities and public spheres*. Ithaca/London: Cornell University Press.

Schmidt, Vivien A. 2002. Europeanization and the mechanics of economic policy adjustment. *Journal of European Public Policy* 9 (6): 894–912. https://doi.org/10.1080/13501760220000046418.

Schwell, Alexandra, Malgorzata Kowalska, and Nina Szogs, eds. 2016. *New ethnographies of football in Europe: People, passions, politics*. London, s.l.: Palgrave Macmillan.

Taylor, Ian. 1972. 'Football mad': A speculative sociology of football hooliganism. In *Sport: Readings from a sociological perspective*, ed. Eric Dunning, 352–377. Toronto: University of Toronto Press.
Trenz, Hans-Jörg. 2004. Media coverage on European governance. *European Journal of Communication* 19 (3): 291–319. https://doi.org/10.1177/0267323104045257.
Vreese, Claes H. de, and Rens Vliegenthart. 2012. Europe: A laboratory for comparative communication research. In *The handbook of global media research*, ed. Ingrid Volkmer, 470–484. Oxford: Wiley-Blackwell.

2

Europeanisation of Football

2.1 Introduction

Europeanisation has become a ubiquitous term in the lexicon of European integration studies and the wider social sciences. In recent years, it has also made inroads into the study of sport (cf. Sakka and Chatzigianni 2012; Gasparini 2020), and in particular football (cf. Armstrong et al. 2008; Mittag and Legrand 2010; Niemann et al. 2011a). However, nothing mandates the choice of this particular concept for grasping the transformation of the structures of football in the European context and any eventually ensuing changes in the consciousness and evaluations of those interested in the game. In what follows, we aim to briefly trace the emergence of the concept of "Europeanisation" in the literature on sport/football against the background of European integration since the 1990s. First, we outline other theoretical approaches that also attempted to tackle specific aspects and processes in that subject domain. We then seek to clarify our understanding of "Europeanisation", as it can be applied fruitfully to capture important aspects of change in the governance structures and dynamics of football over the last three decades. Finally, we indicate how an extended and broadened understanding of Europeanisation might be helpful to gauge shifting perceptions and understandings among the fans and followers of football within the gradually transforming space of European football.

2.2 Sport/Football in the Context of European Integration Since the 1990s: Theories and Concepts

A broad range of approaches has been used to conceptualise the role of sport, in particular football, vis-à-vis Europe and the European integration process.[1] Of the grand theories of European integration, perhaps the oldest and most widely referenced, neofunctionalism, has been invoked to explain certain aspects of the emergence and development of EU policy making in the area of sport. Neofunctionalism emphasises that integration tends to be a dynamic forward-moving process, due to functional interdependences requiring further supranationalisation in fields related to initial integrative steps. Any supranational institutions emerging from this process are assumed to strengthen and advance such integration, as they are likely to benefit from its further deepening (Haas 1958; Lindberg 1963; Niemann 2006). It has been argued that the EU became involved in the area of sport as a result of functional pressures from the internal market (Parrish 2003, 33). Rulings of the European Court of Justice suggested that sport-related activities are subject to EU law in so far as they constitute an economic activity within the meaning of the Treaty. The Bosman ruling of 1995 proved particularly influential in demonstrating the extent to which sports federations such as FIFA and UEFA, and the regulation of the commercial aspects of sport, fall under the scope of EU internal market law. The ruling also empowered the Commission to enforce compliance more rigorously.

Intergovernmentalism—neofunctionalism's rival in the early grand theoretical divide—emphasises Member States' power to control the

---

[1] This section draws on Brand et al. (2022). Special thanks to Arnout Geeraert who wrote the first draft of the corresponding part in that publication.

development of the European integration process (Hoffmann 1966; Moravcsik 1998), but has been applied less explicitly in this context. Nonetheless, a certain case may be made for intergovernmentalism in the area of sport/football. Member governments have hardly been drivers of the process, for example neither anticipating nor appreciating the ECJ's *Bosman*, nor the Commission's subsequent increased regulatory practice in sport cases (García 2007). It can be argued that member governments have shown reservations about further integration in the area of sport, if it was not aligned to perceived national interests. There were cases where the Commission was constrained in the application and enforcement of EU law on sports federations by member governments (Geeraert 2016; Geeraert and Drieskens 2015).

Multilevel governance approaches developed in the 1990s and early 2000s—particularly as a critique of intergovernmentalist theory—highlight the dispersion of decision-making across multiple territorial levels (Hooghe and Marks 2001; Marks et al. 1996). Such multilevel dynamics arguably also shaped policy choices in the realm of European sport governance. The drafting process of sports legislation has been described as "crowded and difficult" (García 2008, 112), influenced by multiple actors and institutions in a "myriad of policy-specific subsystems" (Parrish 2003, 202). Within this complex system, the EU assumes the function of a "metagovernor" by moulding and arbitrating interactions between different actors (Geeraert 2014).

In line with the shift in scholarly work on European integration from grand theorising towards more mid-range theories, many attempts to conceptualise sport/football in the context of European integration moved in a similar direction. Parrish (2003), for example, interpreted the development of an EU policy on sport (and specifically football) through the framework of advocacy coalitions. According to Parrish, two coalitions formed during the 1990s, which tried to influence legislation according to their own respective preferences. As he argued, a "Single Market advocacy coalition" favoured a regulatory approach and highlighted the commercial aspect of sports. The second coalition, the so-called sociocultural coalition, emphasised the social, cultural and educational functions of sport, and called for a distinction between the spheres of sport and the economy. According to this logic, sports should thus be partially exempt from Single Market rules. Subsequently, a nascent "football business coalition" (e.g. big clubs' and media representatives) contended with an opposing "sporting autonomy coalition" (mostly sports federations and governing bodies) for influence in the EU institutions, trying to protect their interests by either pushing for legislative measures or trying to curb the EU's interference in this area (Parrish 2011).

Other concepts applied to sport and football in Europe have been principal-agent (PA) analysis and that of "normative market power Europe" (Geeraert 2016; Geeraert and Drieskens 2017). The former emphasised that while football stakeholders (i.e. national football federations, fans, players and players' agents) and public authorities as principals have only a limited ability to direct and control FIFA and UEFA (the agents), they may rely on the European Court of Justice (ECJ) and the Commission (the supervisors) to exercise control on their behalf. Whereas stakeholders' influence is diffuse and limited, the EU has proved capable of significantly constraining the autonomy of football's main governing bodies (Geeraert 2016; Geeraert and Drieskens 2015). The EU exercises such a supervisory role mainly through two avenues: EU law and EU sports policy. In contrast, FIFA and UEFA are trying to avert such control by employing counter-strategies in the form of direct engagement with the Commission, or attempts to change the preferences of stakeholders, member governments and the European Parliament (ibid.).

Geeraert and Drieskens (2017) have also tried to further define the type of power the EU exerts in the area of sports. Focusing on the case of football, their analysis utilises an integrated approach combining norm-setting and market power dynamics into a concept of "normative market Europe" (ibid., 79). By combining normative and market dynamics, the EU is exerting considerable power in the sphere of sports governance, as exemplified in the Commission's impact on the restructuring of the football transfer system (García 2007, 210–2; Parrish 2003) and by its ability to agree with UEFA and other stakeholders on the promotion of minimum requirements for player contracts, primarily through social dialogue (Geeraert and Drieskens 2017, 86). The EU's market power could be successfully leveraged to convince FIFA to align its transfer regulations to EU standards because the clubs and leagues in the domain of the EU internal market have a significant share of the international transfer market (also cf. García and Meier 2017).

These conceptual advances notwithstanding, we nevertheless opt for the more fluid and multidimensional concept of "Europeanisation" in order to grasp the transformation of European football since the early 1990s. The advantage in doing so is threefold. First, "Europeanisation" allows us to integrate important insights into the interplay of actors and their respective governance capabilities, which have been put forth by the approaches sketched above. Second, Europeanisation also allows for shifting attention more thoroughly to the level of societal actors and transnational interactions, including ultimately very lifeworldly and seemingly apolitical ones. Third, while the very term Europeanisation denotes the procedural character of our object of study, at the same time it also indicates a certain direction of the dynamics under study. Instead of merely depicting sport/football in the context of European integration as the interplay of many forces, it argues that the net effect of all (re-enforcing, unrelated and even at times countervailing) dynamics at play might be a heading towards closer alignment with, and further normalisation of, Europe as a frame of reference.

2.2.1 The Concept of Europeanisation[2]

Scholars began to explore the impact of European integration at the national and sub-national levels in the mid-1990s. Since then, the term Europeanisation has been applied in most academic disciplines which are involved in the study of Europe, but it is used most prominently in the field of Political Science, especially in the literature concerning European Integration.

Europeanisation has been used in a number of different ways to describe a variety of phenomena and processes of change (Olsen 2002). Most frequently Europeanisation refers to domestic change, specifically the substance and instruments of policy, processes and politics as well as polity, driven or altered by European integration (Ladrech 1994, 69;

---

[2] This section draws on Brand and Niemann (2005) as well as Niemann et al. (2011b).

Radaelli 2000, 3). *Policies* are increasingly made at the European level, leading to substantial changes in the policy fabric (and content) of EU Member States (Caporaso and Jupille 2001; Graziano 2012; Rees et al. 2013). In terms of *politics*, European governance shapes domestic processes of political and societal interest representation and aggregation as well as policy style (Harcourt and Radaelli 1999; Heinkelmann-Wild et al. 2020; Ladrech 2014). On the level of *polity*, Europeanisation denotes the effect of EU integration and European-level governance on domestic (mainly political) structures and institutions (Beyers and Bursens 2013; Börzel 2001).

Top-Down and Bottom-Up Europeanisation
Fundamentally, Europeanisation is defined as the process by which governance and politics at the European level drives changes in the domestic arena. This works in both ways, that is, it should be understood as a two-way process operating both from the top-down and from the bottom-up. Top-down perspectives largely emphasise vertical developments where the European affects the domestic level, also referred to as "downloading" (Ladrech 1994; Schmidt 2002). Bottom-up (or "uploading") accounts concentrate on how national receivers of EU level pressure (Börzel 2002). This conceptualisation of Europeanisation as a two-way process stresses the interdependence between the European and domestic levels and their respective impact on Europeanisation (processes). Although this re-framing of Europeanisation does suffer somewhat in terms of reduced conceptual parsimony, in our view these drawbacks are outweighed by an increased explicatory power in respect to significant empirical phenomena. It has been shown, for instance, that Member States' reactions to Europeanisation processes affect European-level decision-making in turn. European/EU policies, institutions and processes cannot thus be taken as *causa sui*, but are, to some degree, shaped by competing domestic preferences that play out at the European/EU level (Börzel 2001, 2002; Dyson 2000).

However, modelling the process of Europeanisation simply as the interaction of politics on the European and the domestic level would not do justice to the complexity of the process. For example, Europeanisation may be driven or affected by transnational developments external or parallel to the EU; thus, the general term "Europeanisation" is broader than strict "EUisation". There are other transnational structures and institutions which play formal and informal roles in the process of Europeanisation. Although clearly an important actor, the EU remains only one player in the game, embedded in a wider network of transnational governance in Europe (cf. Wallace 2000, 371, 376). European institutions or associations at the societal level that are concerned with integration and cooperation in a broader sense, such as the Council of Europe (COE), the *Association Européenne des Conservatoires* (AEC) or— more importantly in this context—the Union of European Football Associations (UEFA), may also shape and drive Europeanisation.

While the chosen model of Europeanisation is comparatively broad, it is nevertheless important to clearly delimit the concept's boundaries. For example, "the emergence and development *at the European level* of distinct structures of governance" is taken to fall outside of our definition of Europeanisation (Risse et al. 2001, 3; authors' emphasis). Similarly, this conception of Europeanisation is not so broad as to encompass any general movement towards the "political unification of Europe" (Olsen 2002, 940). Hence, Europeanisation will not be used here as a synonym for established notions such as European integration or political communitarisation (Radaelli 2000, 3; Vink 2005).

By the same token, Europeanisation is not held to be synonymous with ever-growing "harmonisation" or ever-increasing "convergence". Such harmonisation and convergence may be the product of Europeanisation, but this outcome is neither inevitable nor uniform. Empirical findings suggest that the impact of Europeanisation on national policymaking may be contingent and heterogeneous, allowing for significant domestic diversities (cf. Caporaso and Jupille 2001; Héritier et al. 2001). In this regard we largely follow Radaelli's (2000, 5) distinction between the process (Europeanisation) and its consequences (e g potentially harmonisation and convergence).

The Societal/Transnational Dimension of Europeanisation
While top-down (downloading) and bottom-up (uploading) modes of Europeanisation have both received considerable scholarly attention, a

third mode, the societal/transnational dimension (which could also be seen as a form of "cross-loading"[3]), has been less thoroughly examined. This dimension can be distinguished from the downloading and uploading in two respects: (1) the *level and sphere* of change and (2) the type of *agency* driving or resisting change. Incorporating this societal dimension into the analysis accounts for the impact of adaptational pressure exerted by European regulation beyond the political sphere (cf. Bretherton and Mannin 2013; Howell 2014), to include its influence in various societal contexts, such as the realm of sports. Moreover, this additional dimension recognises that EU regulation may elicit reaction and resistance from societal actors, who may in turn create transnational spaces that impact European football governance.

Including this societal/transnational dimension in an expanded conceptualisation of Europeanisation broadens the analytical scope of the model, but comes at the cost of analytical parsimony (cf. Radaelli 2000). We argue that the ability to recognise particular under-researched dynamics of Europeanisation between and across the European and domestic levels outweighs the risk of overextending the analytical framework.

Examining this societal dimension of Europeanisation concentrates our analysis on a particular *sphere* of change. We focus on a subject (football and its fans), which has been deemed "non-political" by many (at least until very recently), but nonetheless constitutes a significant and consequential component of the "life worlds" of many Europeans. While the sphere of politics impacts citizens in ways that are often subjectively remote and abstract, for football fans the game and the processes that shape it are of more proximate and immediate relevance. Processes of Europeanisation that play out at this societal level thus have a more direct and personal effect on citizens' lifeworlds. The study of Europeanisation of lifeworlds through societal-level processes may thus particularly cast light on the broader question of emerging European identity (e.g. Mayer and Palmowski 2004; Risse 2004, 166–71; also see Chap. 4 on this).

---

[3] It can be seen as a form of "cross-loading" in so far as the term refers to horizontal adaptation processes. The term has so far mostly been used in the context of learning and adaptation processes amongst EU Member States that are taking place (Howell 2004; Strang 2007).

Although "transnational dimensions" of Europeanisation have not been ignored entirely in Europeanisation studies, the concept of "transnationalism" itself is less frequently explicitly defined, and rarely illustrated empirically. In earlier literature, the transnational nature of relationships or an ongoing transnationalisation within EU-Europe, was often simply asserted or assumed (Féron 2004; Menz 2003; Winn 2003). Only recently has such *bottom-up* and *across boundaries* Europeanisation received more systematic attention (cf. Büttner et al. 2022; Greiner et al. 2022, section 3; Kauppi 2013). Following the emerging literature on *social transnationalism* (Mau 2010), transboundary forms of activity and mobility on the individual level are accordingly held to affect perceptions and articulations of people across Europe considerably (cf. Kuhn 2011, 2015; Recchi 2015; cf. Chap. 4).

Taking football as a field of study allows the research to develop insights into genuinely "everyday life" activities of a diverse set of people across Europe. Defining transnational actors in a broad sense as societal actors who coordinate their actions across Europe, thereby creating transnational reactions to EU institutions and/or creating transnational institutions, our conceptualisation embraces societal actors like clubs and fans that have been given less consideration in the current literature. Hence, transnationalism within Europe in the field of football rests on transboundary networks of actors, whose interests and perceptions are either aggregated or amalgamated within these networks and institutions. While the specific Europeanisation processes described in this book were in fact preceded by the establishment of transnational government networks, for example transnational sports bodies such as UEFA (founded in 1954) and its global counterpart, the International Football Federation (FIFA, founded in 1909), since the 1990s transnational Europeanisation processes have induced a new quality of transnational agency.

The term "societal/transnational dimension" of Europeanisation is here taken to encompass both the sphere of change and the type of agency at play, while acknowledging that the two are essentially interrelated: football is presented as a societal sphere characterised by an increasing transnationalisation. Broadening the field of Europeanisation research to embrace this dimension further reveals the remarkable complexity of Europeanisation processes, while also integrating the consciously perceived Europeanised lifeworlds of citizens into the academic literature.

2.2.2 The Europeanisation of Football

Since the mid-1990s the governance structures of football have undergone a significant degree of Europeanisation. In line with the distinctions outlined above, at first glance one can broadly distinguish two different dynamics of Europeanisation in the realm of football (Niemann et al. 2011b). The first comprises the top-down pressure, that is downloading from the European level, such as rulings by the European Court of Justice (ECJ) or investigations and decisions by the European Commission. These pressures are matched by various attempts on the part of domestic actors (such as national governments, national football associations and select football clubs) to influence such measures, that is bottom-up Europeanisation or uploading. These reciprocal processes must be distinguished, upon closer examination, from societal/transnational (or "crossloading") Europeanisation dynamics fed by transnational processes, such as the formation of cross-border lobby networks (e.g. the former G-14, now the European Club Association, ECA) or the creation of a de facto pan-European football league, the Champions League (Graph 2.1).

Works that have analysed the Europeanisation of football have primarily focused on four developments that have influenced the game across

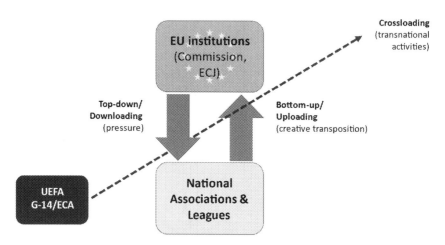

Graph 2.1 Structural Europeanisation dynamics and dimensions in football. (Based on Brand et al. 2013)

the continent since the mid-1990s: (1) the regulation of player markets after the Bosman ruling by the ECJ, (2) regulation of the sale of broadcasting rights, (3) increasing coordination of clubs on the European level and (4) the growing prominence of the Champions League (Brand and Niemann 2007, 2011; Brand et al. 2013; Niemann and Brand 2020).

The Regulation of Player Markets After the Bosman Ruling

Of these factors, the Bosman ruling and the subsequent lifting of caps on overseas players have exercised the most visible effect on the game in Europe. The ECJ's 1995 ruling in its essence consisted of two general findings: first, the traditional transfer system with transfer fees to be paid for out-of-contract players infringed upon the right of every European (worker) to move freely under Article 48 of the Treaty establishing the European Community (TEC), and thus had to be abolished; and second, "nationality restrictions" as a means to limit the number of foreign players that a football club could field were ruled illegal in so far as they discriminated against players from other countries within the European Union (Foster 2000, 42).

First, concentrating on the latter aspect, research findings suggest that the ruling was implemented without much resistance domestically, sometimes even beyond what was strictly required, as in Germany and Austria (Brand et al. 2013). Although the ruling sparked numerous domestic responses, most of these merely tried to mitigate its adverse repercussions. While the Bosman ruling truly brought about a "system transformation" in terms of the nationality regime, countries such as England, Austria and Switzerland already had relatively internationalised player markets by the mid-1990s. The Europeanisation pressures emanating from the Bosman ruling also had a substantial impact on new or non-EU Member States. Poland changed its nationality regime immediately upon accession in 2004, having already adapted its transfer regime in 2001—a transformation which was amplified through membership in UEFA and FIFA (Kędzior and Szczepanik 2011). Non EU member Switzerland implemented the nationality aspect of the Bosman ruling when the bilateral agreement between the EU and Switzerland on the free movement of persons came into effect in 2004, while the transfer regime had already been gradually changed from 1996, three years before the bilateral agreement was signed (Lehmkuhl and Siegrist 2011). In all countries for which data are available, the transformed nationality regime led to a substantial Europeanisation and further internationalisation of player markets (e.g. Brand et al. 2011; Brand and Niemann 2007; Croci et al. 2011).

In reaction to the opening of player markets legally forced by the Bosman ruling, regulations for so-called home-grown players have been introduced across Europe. Home-grown players are understood as those who, regardless of their nationality, have been trained by their clubs or any club in the national association in question for at least three years between the age of 15 and 21. UEFA requires clubs participating in European competitions to have at least eight home-grown players in their squad. In this way, while avoiding direct discrimination of players from other EU countries, clubs should be encouraged to invest in their own football academies, thus providing a pool of playing talent in every European country. In the light of the rapid increase in broadcasting revenues, the regulations on home-grown players are also believed to prevent big clubs from hoarding the best players, making it more difficult for them to dominate both national and European competitions. UEFA took an active role in lobbying various EU actors that respective regulations should be considered compatible with EU law, despite more sceptical academic legal analyses in view of the rights on freedom of movement for workers (Downward et al. 2014; Lynam 2006).

In adapting to the new post-Bosman reality, different competition organisers in Europe have come up with similar frameworks aligning with EU law. For example, Premier League clubs are not allowed to employ more than 17 players who have not been registered with any English or Welsh club for three entire seasons or 36 months before their 21st birthday (Gardiner and Welch 2016). In Germany, the UEFA regulation for home-grown-player is complemented by the requirement that each Bundesliga club has at least twelve German players under contract. The legal arrangements for the Belgium Pro League limit the number of squad members over the age of 21 to 25 players, including eight players trained in Belgium. Moreover, at least six home-grown players must be included in the game day squad (for more countries, see Dalziel et al. 2013). Interestingly, Belgium club Royal Antwerp has recently challenged this stricter version of the regulation for home-grown players. In

October 2021, the respondent judge in Belgium decided to refer this case to the Court of Justice of the European Union in Luxembourg to examine whether the UEFA-backed regulations for home-grown players are really compatible with EU law. This has already prompted speculation in the media about a potential "new Bosman case" that could also significantly change European and global football (Díaz and Winterburn 2021; Gabilondo 2021).

Secondly, transfer systems have also been substantially amended in European football as result of the Bosman ruling. The almost feudal rules that used to permit clubs to retain players against their will have been eliminated. However, the transformation is less radical than in the case of nationality regimes, for two reasons: first, there are some countries where national factors contributed to modifications well before *Bosman*, normally due to the belligerence of footballers' trade unions. England, France and Spain modified their transfer regulations in the 1970s and 1980s as a result of domestic factors. Second, the response of football bodies was slightly more confrontational and also politicised in some countries, with interventions from the national governments of Germany and the United Kingdom, thus countering Europeanisation pressures (García et al. 2011).

Regulating the Sale of Broadcasting Rights
Overall, broadcasting has been a key element in the larger-scale commercialisation of European football (Maguire 2020), which has drawn decisive intervention from EU institutions and Community law in the sector. The Commission's preoccupation with football has been driven by its need to monitor the broadcasting sector given its competences in competition policy (McGowan 2000; Weatherill 2003, 74). A key issue in this respect has been the system mediating the sale of broadcasting rights. An established commercial practice in European football has been the central marketing and joint sale of broadcasting rights on behalf of individual participants. This system offers only prospective buyers the opportunity to compete for a single package comprising a league's entire output. Purchasers are unable to conclude deals with individual clubs. Such collective selling is an equalising arrangement through which revenues are distributed more evenly than in a decentralised model. The main

argument in favour of this collective system is that it helps sustain vibrant (inter-club) competition.

From the perspective of EU law two questions were important here: first, whether preventing clubs from entering into individual agreements with broadcasters amounts to a restriction of competition and thus falls within the scope of Article 81 (1) TEC; and second, whether the collective sale of broadcasting rights is necessary to ensure the survival of the financially weaker participants in the league, in which case an exemption under Article 81 (3) from the application of Article 81 (1) TEC may be granted (Parrish 2002, 9). The Commission started procedures to investigate the selling of broadcasting rights for the UEFA Champions League (European Commission 2001), the English Premier League (European Commission 2002) and the German Bundesliga (European Commission 2005). Its concerns were that football bodies were selling their broadcasting rights to a single operator per market for long periods, hence contributing to the creation of de facto monopolies. The Commission also objected to the fact that few games were broadcast and that clubs were not allowed to market unsold commercial rights. It was not against central selling prima facie, but it regarded that principle with mistrust from a legal and competitive point of view. However, the Commission insisted early on that it did not aspire to become a general sports competition policy regulator. It thus gradually deviated further from an orthodox articulation of Articles 81–82 in its communications and has become increasingly eager to show respect for the social and cultural benefits of sports in recent years (Weatherill 2003). In addition, the lobbying efforts of select clubs and associations developed and intensified, resulting in effective coordination behind the scenes to resist wide-ranging decentralisation of this domain (Brand and Niemann 2011; Grant 2011).

Eventually, arrangements for the sale of broadcasting rights were modified, but not to the extent of a full liberalisation. The end result could thus be categorised as partial adjustment. A pattern has consequently emerged in European football where central marketing is accepted by competition watchdogs so long as broadcasting rights are divided into small packages of several games that can then be sold to different broadcasters. Such a structure was accepted by the Commission in the three cases mentioned above (Brand and Niemann 2011; Grant 2011; Hill

2011). It has been also implemented in other countries where there was no Commission investigation such as Austria (Brand et al. 2011), France (Ranc and Sonntag 2011) and Poland (Kędzior and Szczepanik 2011).

Interestingly, in both Italy and Spain, public authorities initiated a transition from individual selling of broadcasting rights to joint marketing schemes in order to address the massive imbalance between top teams and the rest of the league. In both cases, the system of central marketing has also been contingent on the condition that broadcasting rights are split up into different packages. In Italy, the corruption scandal in domestic football in the mid-2000s led to public campaigns against the influence of big clubs, prompting the Italian government to designate the league the exclusive licensor of audiovisual rights (Ferrari 2010). Similarly, in the light of the increase in financial and competitive disparity within Spanish football, the national government intervened on the commercialisation of broadcasting rights. Based on Royal Decree-Law 5/2015, the respective governing bodies (Liga Nacional de Fútbol Profesional [LNFP] in the case of La Liga, and the Royal Spanish Football Federation [RFEF] in the case of Copa del Rey) are now responsible for selling the audiovisual rights for Spanish domestic football. In both competitions, the central marketing is also conditional upon the broadcasting rights being split into separate packages, with operators limited to acquiring at most two lots in any one auction (Alcolea-Díaz and García-Santamaría 2019). As a result, we can observe an approximate levelling of broadcasting rights systems across Europe.

The Increasing Coordination of Clubs on the European Level
In parallel, the1990s saw the inception of a more intense transnational coordination between individual football clubs throughout Europe both as a consequence of emerging EU-level pressures and as an effort to anticipate them. As international football governing bodies such as UEFA had been built as umbrella organisations of national football associations, individual clubs remained sidelined for much of the twentieth century. As a counterweight, several "top clubs" from certain European countries united in what became known as the G14, thereby seeking to influence UEFA (and FIFA) by leveraging their individual power positions as "best-selling" clubs in European football (Mittag 2018).

The G-14's early decision to open an office in Brussels as early as 2001 reflected the growing awareness in football circles that the EU had become a force to be reckoned with in sport policy. The G-14 by then regarded the Commission as a potential ally (vis-à-vis the various associations) in reforming football in accordance with a 'business perspective" (Ducrey et al. 2003, 34). While the G-14 had not been recognised by either UEFA or FIFA as an official organisation, the Commission nonetheless allowed the G-14 to explain its position as employer of footballers in the talks between FIFA and the Commission about a new transfer regime in 2001. UEFA, not surprisingly, exhibited a somewhat distanced relationship to the G-14 throughout the years. Attempts to strengthen ties with European football clubs outside the G-14 already hinted at its aim of weakening this grouping of elite clubs.[4]

Looking at G-14's dissolution in 2008, three issues are worth pointing out. First, the internal coherence of the G-14 was far more precarious than all talk about largely overlapping interests of big European clubs might have initially suggested. As long as the G-14 could be used as a tool to influence UEFA (regarding the selling of broadcasting rights of the Champions League, for instance), it seemed to be a promising venue. When specific demands (for instance, the German demand for a salary cap as a means to establish a fair level of competition) were introduced, the G-14's consensus crumbled. Second, the morphing of the G-14 into the ECA indicated that the former lobby group had been at least partially successful in pressuring UEFA/FIFA, especially regarding the *Oulmers* case and the issue of compensation payments to clubs for the release of their players to international tournaments (Geey and Lima 2008; Pijetlovic 2015). But this came at a price. While UEFA/FIFA agreed to pay compensations, the compromise also required that the G-14 drop all its ongoing legal disputes against UEFA/FIFA. The deal ultimately resulted in the official dissolution of the G-14 and the establishment of the ECA, respectively. Thus, successful pressure for financial compensation (G-14's success) was accompanied by a successful solution of legal

---

[4] In 2002, UEFA established the Club Forum as an expert panel/advisory body with representatives from 102 European clubs as members. Similarly, the European Professional Football Leagues (EPFL), an association of 15 professional leagues founded in 1998, temporarily also became more vocal.

quarrels as well as the dissolution of one of UEFA's chief rivals (UEFA/FIFA's success). Third, the ECA is considerably more inclusive in its membership than was the comparatively elitist format of the former G-14, and consequently cannot be dismissed so readily by UEFA as was the unrecognised G-14 (Ennis 2007).

Despite featuring more than 230 ordinary and associated members to date, the institutional composition of the ECA is said to ensure that it effectively still acts in the particular interests of Europe's top clubs (Keller 2018). Firstly, membership in the ECA depends on the club's national association. Even though the best-placed clubs in the top divisions of each of UEFA's 55 member associations become ordinary members of the ECA, the number of eligible clubs per association is subject to the UEFA association coefficient ranking (Geeraert 2016; Pijetlovic 2015). According to the ECA Statutes, the top three associations receive five ordinary members, whereas each association below the 29th place in the UEFA five-year ranking gets only one equivalent spot. The intra-associational eligibility for full membership is then established according to the UEFA club coefficient ranking, securing the dominance of the top clubs from the big European leagues. Moreover, clubs that have won a UEFA competition at least five times can also be offered ordinary membership (European Club Association 2020).

Secondly, the staffing of the executive board and the nomination of ECA delegations to UEFA and FIFA committees are also based on the international success of the national associations. In this way, top executives of the big clubs remain overrepresented in lobbying of the clubs' interest in the European football sphere. Hence it can be argued that the G14 "has not ended de facto, it has just been deinstitutionalised, re-institutionalised, and legitimised in the form of the European Club Association" (Pijetlovic 2015, 79). A recent example of the power of the big teams within the ECA is the Champions League reform, which is to be implemented from the 2024/2025 season onwards. In addition to the prospect of more revenues due to the expansion of the competition, the European elite also profits from two wildcards, which will be awarded to the two associations with the best collective performance by their clubs in the previous season (UEFA 2022). This mechanism will increase the likelihood of big clubs qualifying, as even fifth place in the top domestic leagues could be enough to secure a Champions League starting place.

Nonetheless, the abortive European Super League (ESL) scheme showed that some top clubs of different European leagues continue to flirt with the idea of organising a competition themselves. Instead of participating in the Champions League organised by the UEFA based on the system of national associations, twelve clubs from England, Italy and Spain proposed a pan-European league of top clubs, prioritising those clubs' interests over those of national associations (Brannagan et al. 2021). Even though the ESL plan seems to have failed within days (cf. Welsh 2022; Meier et al. 2022), important from our point of view is that an increasingly complex web of transnational networks and relationships has been established throughout the realm of European football. The G14, the ECA and the ESL represent(ed) a qualitatively different type of transnationalism from those of UEFA or FIFA, since the latter are, above all, constituted through national associations. The *transnational* character of the club-based organisations and projects, in contrast, was based more on personal relationships between top club executives, who had frequent contact with each other and acted on the basis of their overlapping (transnational) interests. In other words, strictly "national" concerns tended to dissolve at least partially,[5] in contrast to UEFA where national interests seem to be more important. Through providing a *trans*-national platform for the debate and eventual articulation of common interests, the ECA has also partially altered the perspectives taken by its members, who increasingly shifted their outlooks towards the supranational arena (Brand and Niemann 2011).

The Growing Prominence of the Champions League

Finally, the evolution of the former European Club competitions—most notably the European Champions Cup—into a de facto European league system in the form of the UEFA Champions League is perhaps one of the most tangible signs of a Europeanisation in football. Once established in 1992—mainly through the pressure exerted by big European clubs and

---

[5] Interview with Christian Hockenjos, Managing Director at Borussia Dortmund, 2005; see also the Ducrey et al. (2003, 60) as well as Levermore and Millward (2007, 150–1).

media groups to expand European club-level competition in order to exploit its commercial potential—the Champions League itself became a source of Europeanisation. The Champions League has turned into an important focal point for the more (or most) competitive clubs across European football leagues. This development has been spurred by the substantial financial benefits of CL participation, the high media exposure of the Champions League, the (positive) development of the CL-brand and (largely as a result of the previous two factors) the prestige associated with CL participation.

However, the salience of European club competition is not uniform across different countries and leagues. Among the big national leagues the CL quickly became an important revenue stream and source of prestige, even in the financially most potent and perhaps sportingly most competitive domestic league, the English Premier League (Grant 2011). In other big leagues across Europe, the Champions League has become even more of a focal point. In Germany, for example, due to the comparatively less lucrative domestic TV marketing conditions, CL participation has been even more important for the top clubs than for their English, Spanish or Italian rivals in order to stay competitive on the European level (Brand and Niemann 2011). And in Italy the advent of the Champions League, and more attractive UEFA club competitions more generally, reportedly brought about an important new element of competitive interest to a league that had been perceived as in decline and notably suffering from waning spectator interest (Croci et al. 2011). Variations of this argument could be made to different degrees also for other leagues.

For clubs in the smaller leagues, even for the more competitive sides, the CL usually remains an "exception" or even a "distant dream", as studies on Austria, Sweden and Switzerland have indicated. When qualifying for the Champions League this amounts to "winning the jack-pot" (Andersson et al. 2011; Brand et al. 2011; Lehmkuhl and Siegrist 2011). With the establishment of the Europa League in 2009, this has changed to some extent, since appearance in the group stage of this competition— for which clubs still have to qualify—is more lucrative than for the old UEFA Cup group stage. Moreover, due to the rapid increase in UEFA payouts, mere participation in the qualifying rounds of European club competitions in countries such as Luxembourg or Montenegro has become important, allowing teams to dominate domestic competition financially and in sporting terms in the long term (Menary 2016). However, as several studies on Austria have suggested, for most of the more competitive clubs in smaller leagues even participation in the UEFA Cup/Europa League is still treated as a bonus rather than a normal undertaking to be relied upon in the regular calculations/budgets of these clubs (Brand et al. 2013, 2023).

As for the CL, the relatively consistent pattern of recurrent participation over time of largely the same "big clubs" throughout Europe (Pawlowski et al. 2010) can be regarded as near-equivalent to a pan-European "league mode" (Niemann and Brand 2020). Against this background, the Champions League has been dubbed an "engine that supposedly makes Europe hang together more closely", but also a "political myth" that may contribute to more Europeanised mindsets and the European idea in general (ibid., 329). It is in this spirit that the development of such a de facto European League and increasingly Europeanised players markets throughout the continent, which also bring fans and spectators into frequent contact with Europe domestically, may thus facilitate more "affective attachments" with a "European frame" (Sandvoss 2012, 94).

2.3 A Europeanisation of Football Fan Identities?

The Europeanisation dynamics outlined above are likely to have affected fans. Earlier studies (King 2000, 2003, 2004; Millward 2006, 2009) explored the idea of a growing "European consciousness" amongst football club fans who began to see themselves as more European (see Chap. 4). Mechanisms at work included the increased opportunity to travel across Europe due to the growing number of Champions League games and the greater coverage of European leagues on television; in that sense, the structural transformation and Europeanisation of the game also seemed to indicate strengthened European identifications through "societal" avenues (Levermore and Millward 2007, 118–9).

While our own research before the EUFOOT project was only able to provide some anecdotal evidence of changed mindsets due to the ongoing Europeanisation of football governance (Brand et al. 2013; Niemann and Brand 2018), the evident research gap concerning the potentially Europeanised identities of people regularly following the game as a leisure activity was addressed to some degree by the multi-year trans-European research project FREE (Football Research in an Enlarged Europe, 2012–15, c.f. FREE 2015). However, the everyday aspects of continuously practiced football fandom in its impacts on fans' perceptions, articulations, identifications and discourses remained a desideratum even after FREE's efforts had come to an end.

Two of the most promising linkage points between the interest in an ongoing Europeanisation of mindsets among fans as a consequence of following sport and conceptual advances in the fields of sociology and European integration studies have been "Banal Europeanism" and "subjective Europeanisation". "Banal Europeanism"—a term that was first coined by Cram (2001) to describe the potentially shifting focus of EU citizens towards the European level prompted by a normalisation of the EU in people's daily lives—adapted Billig's (1995) notion of "Banal Nationalism". In doing so, it highlighted the rather implicit and subconscious forms identifying with a political entity (a nation in Billig, a supranational institution in Cram). As these entities, their existence and presence, are reiterated through normal everyday practices and activities, they are not recognised and thematised as political creatures any longer; they come to form part of the everyday, quasi-natural fabric of life (see Chap. 4 on the EU's symbolism in this regard). As suggested by Weber (2021), football provides a fertile ground to analyse "banal" identifications with Europe in a lifeworld context. The Europeanisation of football governance and structures in this regard offers fans "direct links" to Europe: pan-European competitions characterised by recognisable signs and symbols, contested by teams made up of internationally mobile players recruited on a pan-European transfer market, overseen by similarly cosmopolitan managers and broadcast across the continent acculturate fans to regularised quotidian exposure to Europe and thus arguably normalise it through a mundane and repeated set of banal experiences.

In contrast, "subjective Europeanisation", as a concept, is inspired by Robertson's notion of "subjective globalisation" (Robertson 1992, 9) and shares his criticism of the neglect of ideational aspects of supposedly objective social change such as "objective globalisation" (Robertson 2009, 121). Subjective Europeanisation denotes gradual and subconscious shifts in perceptions and identifications. A rather similar dichotomy seems to emerge between the objective transformation of governance structures in the field of football pointed out above, and a potential gradual change of perspectives and mindsets among those people following the game.

In keeping with Steger and James (2011), who emphasised the interpretative quality of human beings' renderings of change at the macro level (e.g. globalisation), "subjective Europeanisation" also analyses subjective "imaginaries" and "modes of understanding" of an individual's surrounding lifeworld; for example, how fans position themselves vis-à-vis the significant domain, to which they dedicate a large portion of their leisure (and life) time. Subjective Europeanisation thus seeks to capture the effects of experience and exposure to a (changing) European (football) setting more subtly than through any search for articulations that speak the language of "political integration" or "pan-Europeanism" (as a political project).

While the concept of "Banal Europeanism" particularly highlights the repetitive and normalising process of everyday experiences, "subjective Europeanisation" emphasises the ideational nature of change, occurring through the (re-)interpretation of perceptions and frames towards a more European perspective. Both understandings of Europeanisation of identities share a focus on subconscious processes of identification, covering the shape of attitudes, emotional attachment and perceptions. We will depart from these concepts and further integrate them in an operationalised version of Europeanisation of identity among football fans (see Chaps. 4 and 5).

Our point of departure for studying fans and followers of football thus imbues them with societal and political significance. They are investigated in their capacity to act as carriers of "Europeanisation". In asking whether the transformation of the game has also had an impact on the perceptions and narrations of those who invested emotionally, time- and resource-wise in following football (a considerable share of the wider European populace!), we may take a slightly different path from the conventional social science approaches towards such fans. This necessitates a brief sketch of how football fans have so far been included as objects of study in analyses of broader societal trends (see Chap. 3).

References

Alcolea-Díaz, Gema, and Jose Vicente García-Santamaría. 2019. Football broadcasting rights in Spain in the digital age: Between pay television and streaming services. *Latina Revista de Comunicación* 74 (3): 418–433. https://doi.org/10.4185/RLCS.

Andersson, Torbjörn, Jyri Backman, and Bo Carlsson. 2011. Sweden: The development of club football on the periphery of Europe. In *The transformation of European football: Towards the Europeanisation of the national game*, ed. Arne Niemann et al., 187–203. Manchester: Manchester University Press.

Armstrong, Gary, et al. 2008. *Global and local football. Politics and Europeanization on the fringes of the EU*. London etc.: Routledge.

Beyers, Jan, and Peter Bursens. 2013. How Europe shapes the nature of the Belgian Federation: Differentiated EU impact triggers both co-operation and decentralization. *Regional and Federal Studies* 23 (3): 271–291. https://doi.org/10.1080/13597566.2013.773898.

Billig, Michael. 1995. *Banal nationalism*. Los Angeles etc.: SAGE.

Börzel, Tanja A. 2001. *Shaping states and regions. The domestic impact of Europe*. Cambridge: Cambridge University Press.

———. 2002. Member state responses to Europeanization. *Journal of Common Market Studies* 40 (2): 193–214. https://doi.org/10.1111/1468-5965.00351.

Brand, Alexander and Arne Niemann. 2005. *The societal/trans-national dimension of Europeanisation: The case of German football*, Queen's papers on Europeanisation, no. 2/2005, 1–40.

Brand, Alexander, and Arne Niemann. 2007. Europeanisation in the societal/trans-national realm: What European integration studies can get out of analysing football. *Journal of Contemporary European Research* 3 (3): 182–201.

———. 2011. Germany: Between modest adjustment and system transformation. In *The transformation of European football: Towards the Europeanisation of the national game*, ed. Arne Niemann et al., 59–79. Manchester: Manchester University Press.

Brand, Alexander, Arne Niemann, and Georg Spitaler. 2011. The Europeanisation of Austrian football: Historically determined and modern processes of Europeanisation. In *The transformation of European football: Towards the Europeanisation of the national game*, ed. Arne Niemann et al., 171–186. Manchester: Manchester University Press.

———. 2013. The two-track Europeanization of football: EU-level pressures, transnational dynamics and their repercussions within different national contexts. *International Journal of Sport Policy and Politics* 5 (1): 95–112. https://doi.org/10.1080/19406940.2012.665381.

Brand, Alexander, Arnout Geeraert, and Arne Niemann. 2022. European (dis-)integration theories, Brexit and sport. A double disconnect and tentative remedies. In *Sport and Brexit. Regulatory challenges and legacies*, ed. Jacob Kornbeck, 23–40. London etc.: Routledge.

Brand, Alexander, Arne Niemann, and Regina Weber. 2023. Pipe dream or closed shop? Experiencing the Champions League from the sidelines. *Soccer & Society* 24: 520. https://doi.org/10.1080/14660970.2023.2194515.

Brannagan, Paul Michael, et al. 2021. The 2021 European Super League Attempt: Motivation, outcome, and the future of football. *International Journal of Sport Policy and Politics* 14 (1): 169–176.

Bretherton, Charlotte, and Michael L. Mannin, eds. 2013. *The Europeanization of European politics*. Houndsmills: Palgrave.

Büttner, Sebastian, Monika Eigmüller, and Susann Worschech, eds. 2022. *Sociology of Europeanization*. Berlin: DeGruyter.

Caporaso, James, and Joseph Jupille. 2001. The Europeanization of gender equality policy and domestic structural change. In *Transforming Europe. Europeanization and domestic change*, ed. Maria Green Cowles et al., 21–43. Ithaca: Cornell University Press.

Cram, Laura. 2001. Imagining the union: A case of banal Europeanism? In *Interlocking dimensions of European integration*, ed. Helen Wallace, 233–246. Houndsmills: Palgrave Macmillan.

Croci, Osvaldo, Nicola Porro, and Pippo Russo. 2011. Italy: The least of the great leagues? In *The transformation of European football: Towards the Europeanisation of the national game*, ed. Arne Niemann et al., 115–133. Manchester: Manchester University Press.

Dalziel, Murray, et al. 2013. *Study on the assessment of UEFA's "home grown player rule."* https://ec.europa.eu/assets/eac/sport/library/studies/final-rpt-april2013-homegrownplayer.pdf. Accessed 22 Dec 2022.

Díaz, José Félix, and Chris Winterburn. 2021. The new Bosman case that could revolutionise world football. *Marca*, https://www.marca.com/en/football/international-football/2021/10/19/616ef7acca47412c4a8b458e.html. Accessed 22 Dec 2022.

Downward, Paul, Richard Parrish, Geoff Pearson, and Anna Semens. 2014. An assessment of the compatibility of UEFA's home grown player rule with article 45 TFEU. *European Law Review* 39 (4): 493–510. https://doi.org/10.1111/j.1468-0386.2008.00444.x.

Ducrey, Pierre, et al. 2003. *UEFA and football governance: A new model*. Final project work, Centre International d'Etude du Sport (CIES).

Dyson, Kenneth. 2000. EMU as Europeanization: Convergence, diversity and contingency. *Journal of Common Market Studies* 38 (4): 645–666. https://doi.org/10.1111/1468-5965.00258.

Ennis, Darren. 2007. Interview – Soccer – New club body could replace G-14. *ESPN*. https://www.espn.com/espn/print?id=3098962. Accessed 22 Dec 2022.

European Club Association. 2020. *ECA Statutes. September 2020 Edition*. https://www.ecaeurope.com/media/4856/eca-statutes-september-2020.pdf. Accessed 22 Dec 2022.

European Commission. 2001. Commission opens proceedings against UEFA's selling of Tv rights to UEFA Champions League. European Commission Press Release. IP/01/1043, 20 July 2001.

———. 2002. Commission opens proceedings into joint selling of media rights to the English Premier League. European Commission Press Release. IP/02/1951, 20 December 2002.

———. 2005. Details of broadcasting rights commitments by the German football league [Press Release MEMO/05/16], Brussels.

Féron, Élise. 2004. Anti-globalization movements and the European agenda: Between dependence and disconnection. *Innovation: The European Journal of Social Science Research* 17 (2): 119–127. https://doi.org/10.1080/1351161042000238625.

Ferrari, Luca. 2010. Rights to broadcast sporting events under Italian law. *The International Sports Law Journal* 9 (1–2): 65–74.

Foster, Ken. 2000. European law and football: Who's in charge? *Soccer & Society* 1 (1): 39–51. https://doi.org/10.1080/14660970008721247.

FREE. 2015. *Project final report. Report to the EU Commission, FP7-SSH-2011-2* (SSH.2011.5.2-1).

Gabilondo, Aritz. 2021. The Refaelov ruling: A law which could change football. *AS*. https://en.as.com/autor/aritz_gabilondo/a/. Accessed 22 Dec 2022.

García, Borja. 2007. UEFA and the European Union: From confrontation to co-operation? *Journal of Contemporary European Research* 3 (3): 202–223.

———. 2008. *The European Union and the governance of football: A game of levels and agendas*. PhD thesis, Loughborough University.

García, Borja, and Henk Erik Meier. 2017. Global sport power Europe? The efficacy of the European Union in global sport regulation. *Journal of Common Market Studies* 55 (4): 850–870.

García, Borja, Arne Niemann, and Wyn Grant. 2011. Conclusion: A Europeanised game? In *The transformation of European football: Towards the Europeanisation of the national game*, ed. Arne Niemann et al., 239–261. Manchester: Manchester University Press.

Gardiner, Simon, and Roger Welch. 2016. Nationality based playing quotas and the international transfer system post-Bosman. In *The legacy of Bosman: Revisiting the relationship between EU law and sport*, ed. Antoine Duval and Ben van Rompuy, 51–80. Cham: Springer.

Gasparini, William. 2020. The Europeanisation of sport. In *Sport, welfare and social policy in the European Union*, ed. Nicola Porro et al., 69–74. London: Routledge.

Geeraert, Arnout. 2014. New EU governance modes in professional sport: Enhancing throughput legitimacy. *Journal of Contemporary European Research* 10 (3): 302–321.

———. 2016. *The EU in international sports governance: A principal-agent perspective on EU control of FIFA and UEFA*. Houndsmills: Palgrave Macmillan.

Geeraert, Arnout, and Edith Drieskens. 2015. The EU controls FIFA and UEFA: A principal–agent perspective. *Journal of European Public Policy* 22 (10): 1448–1466. https://doi.org/10.1080/13501763.2015.1022206.

———. 2017. Normative market Europe: The EU as a force for good in international sports governance? *Journal of European Integration* 39 (1): 79–94. https://doi.org/10.1080/07036337.2016.1256395.

Geey, Daniel, and Ross Lima. 2008. The end of G14, and rise of the European Club Association. *Sport&EU Newsletter* 6 (December): 6–7.

Grant, Wyn. 2011. England: A liberal model under challenge? In *The transformation of European football: Towards the Europeanisation of the national game*, ed. Arne Niemann et al., 80–96. Manchester: Manchester University Press.

Graziano, Paolo. 2012. *Europeanization and domestic policy change: The case of Italy*. London: Routledge.

Greiner, Florian, Peter Pichler, and Jan Vermeiren, eds. 2022. *Reconsidering Europeanization. Ideas and practices of (dis-)integrating Europe since the nineteenth century*. Berlin: DeGruyter.

Haas, Ernst B. 1958. *The uniting of Europe: Political, social, and economic forces 1950–1957*. Stanford: Stanford University Press.

Harcourt, Alison J., and Claudio Radaelli. 1999. Limits to EU technocratic regulation? *European Journal of Political Research* 35 (1): 107–122. https://doi.org/10.1111/1475-6765.00443.

Heinkelmann-Wild, Tim, Lisa Kriegmair, and Berthold Rittberger. 2020. The EU multi-level system and the Europeanization of domestic blame games. *Politics and Governance* 8 (1): 85–94. https://doi.org/10.17645/pag.v8i1.2522.

Héritier, Adrienne, et al. 2001. *Differential Europe. New opportunities and restrictions for member-state policies*. Lanham: Rowman & Littlefield.

Hill, Jonathan. 2011. UEFA and the European Union: The green shoots of a new European public space. In *The transformation of European football: Towards the Europeanisation of the national game*, ed. Arne Niemann et al., 40–56. Manchester: Manchester University Press.

Hoffmann, Stanley. 1966. Obstinate or obsolete? The fate of the nation-state and the case of Western Europe tradition and change. *Daedalus* 95 (3): 862–915.

Hooghe, Liesbet, and Gary Marks. 2001. *Multi-level governance and European integration*. Lanham: Rowman & Littlefield.

Howell, Kerry E. 2004. *Developing conceptualisations of Europeanization: Synthesising methodological approaches*. Queen's papers on Europeanisation, no. 3.

———. 2014. *Europeanization, European integration and financial services*. Houndsmills: Palgrave.

Kauppi, Niilo, ed. 2013. *A political sociology of transnational Europe*. Colchester: ECPR Press.

Kędzior, Magdalena, and Melchior Szczepanik. 2011. Poland: New shape, old problems. In *The transformation of European football: Towards the Europeanisation of the national game*, ed. Arne Niemann et al., 204–219. Manchester: Manchester University Press.

Keller, Berndt. (2018). *Sectoral social dialogue in professional football: Social partners, outcomes and problems of implementation*. European Trade Union Institute, working paper 2018.04. https://www.etui.org/sites/default/files/18 WP 2018 04 Sectoral social dialogue football Keller Web version.pdf. Accessed 22 Dec 2022.

King, Anthony. 2000. Football fandom and post-national identity in the New Europe. *British Journal of Sociology* 51 (3): 419–442. https://doi.org/10.1111/j.1468-4446.2000.00419.x.
———. 2003. *The European ritual: Football in the New Europe*. London etc.: Routledge.
———. 2004. The new symbols of European football. *International Review for the Sociology of Sport* 39 (3): 323–336. https://doi.org/10.1177/1012690204045599.
Kuhn, Theresa. 2011. Individual transnationalism, globalisation and euroscepticism: An empirical test of Deutsch's transactionalist theory. *European Journal of Political Research* 50 (6): 811–837. https://doi.org/10.1111/j.1475-6765.2011.01987.x.
———. 2015. *Experiencing European integration: Transnational lives and European identity*. Oxford: Oxford University Press.
Ladrech, Robert. 1994. Europeanization of domestic politics and institutions: The case of France. *Journal of Common Market Studies* 32 (1): 69–88. https://doi.org/10.1111/j.1468-5965.1994.tb00485.x.
———. 2014. Europeanization of national politics: The centrality of politics parties. In *Handbook of European politics*, ed. José M. Magone, 620–633. London etc.: Routledge.
Lehmkuhl, Dirk, and Oliver Siegrist. 2011. Switzerland: Professionalisation and internationalisation, courtesy of the EU and UEFA. In *The transformation of European football: Towards the Europeanisation of the national game*, ed. Arne Niemann et al., 221–238. Manchester: Manchester University Press.
Levermore, Roger, and Peter Millward. 2007. Official policies and informal transversal networks: Creating "pan-European identifications" through sport? *The Sociological Review* 55 (1): 144–164. https://doi.org/10.1111/j.1467-954X.2007.00686.x.
Lindberg, Leon N. 1963. *The political dynamics of European economic integration*. Stanford: Stanford University Press.
Lynam, Ian. 2006. UEFA's homegrown player rule. *Sport and the Law Journal* 14 (2): 30–36.
Maguire, Kieran. 2020. *The price of football. Understanding football club finance*. Newcastle: Agenda Publishing.
Marks, Gary, Liesbet Hooghe, and Kermit Blank. 1996. European Integration from the 1980s: State-centric v. multi-level governance. *Journal of Common Market Studies* 34 (3): 341–378. https://doi.org/10.1111/j.1468-5965.1996.tb00577.x.

Mau, Steffen. 2010. *Social transnationalism: Lifeworlds beyond the nation-state*. London etc.: Routledge.
Mayer, Franz C., and Jan Palmowski. 2004. European identities and the EU – The ties that bind the peoples of Europe. *Journal of Common Market Studies* 42 (3): 573–598. https://doi.org/10.1111/j.0021-9886.2004.00519.x.
McGowan, Francis. 2000. Competition policy. The limits of the European regulatory state. In *Policy-making in the European Union*, ed. Helen Wallace and William Wallace, 4th ed., 115–147. Oxford: Oxford University Press.
Meier, Henk Erik, Borja García, Mara Konjer, and Malte Jetzke. 2022. The short life of the European Super League: A case study on institutional tensions in sport industries. *Managing Sport and Leisure*, online first. https://doi.org/10.1080/23750472.2022.2058071.
Menary, Steve. 2016. One rule for one: The impact of Champions League prize money and Financial Fair Play at the bottom of the European club game. *Soccer & Society* 17 (5): 666–679. https://doi.org/10.1080/1466097 0.2015.1103073.
Menz, Georg. 2003. Re-regulating the Single Market: National varieties of capitalism and their responses to Europeanization. *Journal of European Public Policy* 10 (4): 532–555. https://doi.org/10.1080/1350176032000101226.
Millward, Peter. 2006. 'We've all got the bug for euro-Aways': What fans say about European football Club competition. *International Review for the Sociology of Sport* 41 (3–4): 375–393. https://doi.org/10.1177/1012690207077706.
———. 2009. *Getting into Europe: Identification, prejudice and politics in English football culture*. Saarbrücken: VDM.
Mittag, Jürgen. 2018. Aufstieg und Auflösung der G14: Episode oder Paradebeispiel der Konfliktregulierung europäischer Sportpolitik? In *Europäische Sportpolitik: Zugänge, Akteure, Problemfelder*, ed. Jürgen Mittag, 195–215. Baden-Baden: Nomos.
Mittag, Jürgen, and Benjamin Legrand. 2010. Towards a Europeanization of football? Historical phases in the evolution of the UEFA European Football Championship. *Soccer & Society* 11 (6): 709–722.
Moravcsik, Andrew. 1998. *The choice for Europe: Social purpose and state power from Messina to Maastricht*. Ithaca: Cornell University Press.
Niemann, Arne. 2006. *Explaining decisions in the European Union*. Cambridge: Cambridge University Press.
Niemann, Arne, and Alexander Brand. 2018. Die Europäisierung des Fußballs: Von der Umsetzung politischer Vorgaben zur Gestaltung europäischer

Realitäten. In *Europäische Sportpolitik: Zugänge, Akteure, Problemfelder*, ed. Jürgen Mittag, 167–180. Baden-Baden: Nomos.

———. 2020. The UEFA Champions League: A political myth? *Soccer & Society* 21 (3): 329–343. https://doi.org/10.1080/14660970.2019.1653859.

Niemann, Arne, Borja García, and Wyn Grant, eds. 2011a. *The transformation of European football: Towards the Europeanisation of the national game*. Manchester: Manchester University Press.

———. 2011b. Introduction: The transformation of European football. In *The transformation of European football: Towards the Europeanisation of the national game*, ed. Arne Niemann et al., 1–21. Manchester: Manchester University Press.

Olsen, Johan P. 2002. The many faces of Europeanization. *Journal of Common Market Studies* 40 (5): 921–952. https://doi.org/10.1111/1468-5965.00403.

Parrish, Richard. 2002. Football's place in the single European market. *Soccer & Society* 3 (1): 1–21. https://doi.org/10.1080/714004867.

———. 2003. *Sports law and policy in the European Union*. Manchester: Manchester University Press.

———. 2011. Social dialogue in European professional football. *European Law Journal* 17 (2): 213–229.

Pawlowski, Tim, Christoph Breuer, and Arnd Hovemann. 2010. Top clubs' performance and the competitive situation in European domestic football competitions. *Journal of Sports Economics* 11 (2): 186–202. https://doi.org/10.1177/1527002510363100.

Pijetlovic, Katarina. 2015. *EU sports law and breakaway leagues in football*. Cham: Springer.

Radaelli, Claudio M. 2000. Whither Europeanization? Concept stretching and substantive change. *European Integration Online Papers (EIoP)* 4 (8). http://eiop.or.at/eiop/pdf/2000-008.pdf. Accessed 22 Dec 2022.

Ranc, David, and Albrecht Sonntag. 2011. France – A case of UEFA-isation? In *The transformation of European football: Towards the Europeanisation of the national game*, ed. Arne Niemann et al., 97–114. Manchester: Manchester University Press.

Recchi, Ettore. 2015. *Mobile Europe. The theory and practice of free movement in the EU*. Houndsmills: Palgrave Macmillan.

Rees, Nicholas, Brad Quinn, and Bernadette Connaughton. 2013. *Europeanisation and new patterns of governance in Ireland*. Manchester: Manchester University Press.

Risse, Thomas. 2004. Social constructivism and European integration. In *European integration theory*, ed. Thomas Diez and Antje Wiener, 159–176. Oxford: Oxford University Press.

Risse, Thomas, James A. Caporaso, and Maria Green Cowles. 2001. Europeanization and domestic change: Introduction. In *Transforming Europe: Europeanization and domestic change*, ed. Maria Green Cowles et al., 1–20. Ithaca: Cornell University Press.

Robertson, Roland. 1992. *Globalization: Social theory and global culture*. SAGE: Los Angeles etc.

———. 2009. Differentiational reductionism and the missing link in Albert's approach to globalization theory. *International Political Sociology* 3 (1): 119–122. https://doi.org/10.1111/j.1749-5687.2008.00066_5.x.

Sakka, Stavroula, and Efthalia Chatzigianni. 2012. Enhancing Europeanisation through European sport-related programmes: The case of Greece. *Choregia* 8 (8): 32–56.

Sandvoss, Cornell. 2012. Jeux sans frontières? Europeanisation and the erosion of national categories in European club football competition. *Politique Européenne* 36 (1): 76–101. https://doi.org/10.3917/poeu.036.0076.

Schmidt, Vivien A. 2002. Europeanization and the mechanics of economic policy adjustment. *Journal of European Public Policy* 9 (6): 894–912. https://doi.org/10.1080/1350176022000046418.

Steger, Manfred B., and Paul James. 2011. Three dimensions of subjective globalization. *ProtoSociology* 27: 53–70. https://doi.org/10.5840/protosociology2011274.

Strang, Bennet. 2007. *Winds of change: The Europeanization of national foreign policy*. Maastricht European Studies papers, no. 1.

UEFA. 2022. UEFA approves final format and access list for its club competitions as of the 2024/25 season. https://www.uefa.com/insideuefa/mediaservices/mediareleases/news/0275-151c779310c3-b92bbf0d24f9-1000%2D%2Duefa-approves-final-format-and-access-list-for-its-club-competi/. Accessed 22 Dec 2022.

Vink, Maarten. 2005. What is Europeanization? And other questions on a new research agenda. *European Political Science* 3 (1): 63–74.

Wallace, Helen. 2000. Europeanisation and globalisation: Complementary or contradictory trends? *New Political Economy* 5 (3): 369–382. https://doi.org/10.1080/713687780.

Weatherill, Stephen. 2003. 'Fair play please!': Recent developments in the application of EC law to sport. *Common Market Law Review* 40 (1): 51–93.

Weber, Regina. 2021. Banal Europeanism? Europeanisation of football and the enhabitation of a Europeanised football fandom. *Sport in Society* 24 (11): 1893–1909. https://doi.org/10.1080/17430437.2021.1893697.

Welsh, John. 2022. The European super league debacle: Why regulation of corporate football is essential. *Soccer & Society*, online first. https://doi.org/10.1080/14660970.2022.2054805.

Winn, Neil. 2003. The European Union's external face: The 'Europeanisation' of JHA and CFSP. *Perspectives on European Politics and Society* 4 (1): 147–166. https://doi.org/10.1080/15705850308438856.

3

Football Fandom Research

Tobias Heck, Alexander Brand, Arne Niemann, Regina Weber, and Vincent Reinke

3.1 Introduction

With the increasing popularity of European football over the course of the twentieth century—and its concomitant development into a mass media phenomenon—different academic disciplines have turned their attention to the sport as a legitimate and fascinating object of study. In this context, the principle object of this growing academic attention has not been those who distinguished themselves by their outstanding footballing skills, but rather by their emotional investment in the game: the fans.

This chapter is dedicated to the conceptual insights and innovations of football fandom research to date. To this end, different interpretations of the term 'football fandom' as well as wider dynamics which influence football fandom are discussed. This requires us to consider football fans not as a single, homogenous group, but rather to pay attention to different fan communities' composition and varying forms of communality. A redefinition and refinement of the term 'football fandom' as applied in this research context is essential, given the fuzziness and inconsistency with which notions of fandom have been applied in previous studies. Surveying the current state of football fandom research serves the purpose of identifying links to our endeavour and elucidating how this body of work connects to the wider issue of fan identification in the context of Europe. In an attempt to unravel different research intentions and academic approaches, the chapter continues with a thematic and temporal contextualisation of fan identification research, covering heterogeneous literature traditions in sociology, sport studies and sport management research. A particular emphasis is put here on the most significant typologies developed to categorise football fans. Delving into this strand of fandom research, different construction principles are explained (dichotomous/tiered/multidimensional) in order to subsequently differentiate various typologies and their thematic guideposts.

Examining such theory-based assumptions about, and classifications of, football fans also allows us to identify key research gaps that have not yet been thoroughly addressed. They provide starting points for our investigations. These gaps reveal that in particular the transnational qualities of football fandom have been explored only rarely, if at all, and that fan identifications within a *Europeanised* football system have so far received insufficient attention. A further crucial missing link in this regard is that the bulk of the existing literature starts from the premise of an active and conscious formation of identities around thematic clusters, while identification dynamics among and between football fans have often been sidelined, in particular those relating to everyday activities in a lifeworldly sphere shaping identities more subconsciously.

3.2 Considerations on the Notion of Fandom

As a research topic, 'fandom' denotes far more than the mere state of being a fan. For the principal subject of a wide range of different disciplinary approaches (first and foremost sociological and cultural studies), no consensus conceptual definition has been put forward. Principally, '[e]ach of these definitions of fandom has its own implied explanations, exclusions, consequences and counter-arguments' (Duffett 2013, p. 49). Going beyond the singular consideration of what constitutes being a fan, the term fandom implies 'a collective strategy, a communal effort to form interpretive communities' (Gray et al. 2007, p. 1). It is this communal aspect which can be found as a constantly recurring and constitutive factor in different definitions of fandom as the lowest common denominator.

Ha-Ilan (2018, p. 914) has suggested viewing football fandom first and foremost as 'a form of collective behaviour conducted within social networks'. Such collective performances highlight that there is both a social and a relational aspect to fandom. In many cases, different kinds of communal rituals occur, which are characterised, among other things, by jointly attending or observing events, in the case of football: specific matches. What sets football apart here is that, in addition to its high degree of communality and companionship, fandom in the football context is characterised by a high degree of emotional attachment to the respective team: during the game, 'fans share the roller-coaster of wins and defeats, the exhilaration of scoring goals, and the despair of conceding' (Cleland et al. 2018, p. 15). This emotional investment goes beyond the regular playing time and is thus of particular importance: according to Porat (2010, p. 277), 'supporting a football club is a life-long project that begins at an early age and ends with the life of the fan'. As a consequence, football fandom significantly shapes a fan's perception of reality and connection to the outside world, both on match day and in everyday life. Thus, investment within the realm of fandom goes beyond the sheer emotional level and expands to the material and temporal level. Stone (2007) understands that for most supporters, football is of paramount importance in people's everyday lives off the pitch. The significance of football for the everyday life is also central in the work of Brown et al. (2008, p. 308) who argue that 'being a supporter is a key part of their 'real' lives: a regular, structuring part of their existence that enables them to feel belonging in the relative disorder of contemporary social formations'. This approach towards football reveals the importance of a collective sense of belonging and thus identity formation, as an integral, of often not thoroughly reflected, component of football fandom.

As major factors influencing the development and eventual transformation of football fandom, professionalisation and marketisation challenge more traditional conceptions of fandom. Delving further into wider political, economic and social changes affecting the game, their influence on football fandom in terms of a diversification of types of football fans has already become obvious. In line with this, the ever proliferation of both off- and online football broadcasting is of particular note, as it increases the opportunities for potential followers to develop a commitment to a team without the necessity of attending matches in the stadium. Proximity and location are thus transcended as prerequisites for fandom. Broadening the spectrum of people who can be counted as football fans, Redhead's (2003, p. 31) notion of 'post-fan' only consequently proceeds from the assumption that a fan today 'does not have to leave the home or the bar to see the object of the gaze'. On the supposition that 'we are all "post-fans" now' due to the omnipresence of football in popular and media culture, Redhead acknowledges these structural developments as shaping factors of new forms of fandom. While the developments during the first two years of the Covid-19 pandemic have potentially contributed to such 'home fandom', such an account risks underestimating the persisting layer of more conventional fandom. Fillis and Mackay (2014) depart still further from traditional understandings, discarding the notions of fans and supporters and speaking instead of consumers. While their perspective undoubtedly captures (football) fandom as an economically exploitable set of dispositions and behaviour, it also seems to unduly limit the scope of fandom and arguably also downplays the non-commercial aspects of the emotional attachment at its heart.

The understanding of football fandom used here avoids narrowly following the above-mentioned definitional approaches. We include in our concept of a 'football fan' all those who articulate an interest in following a football team, be it occasionally or on a regular basis, passively watching or actively following a team or a club competition.[1] This approach enables us to look at football fandom as a field of activities in which several key criteria must be met. Following previous research approaches, communality and a collective sense of belonging is of central importance. In this regard, our conceptual understanding requires only that a basic emotional, monetary or temporal investment on behalf of a fan exists. Following from that, fans must be engaged with football in their everyday life. This engagement need not be of any particular intensity, but rather refers to a generalised commitment. It must not be confused with representing one's team to the outside world by, for instance, wearing mer-

---

[1] Hence, we restrict our approach to fans of football clubs and disregard fandom of national teams.

chandise (nor with being a member of an organised fan-group). It rather encapsulates the idea that being a fan can find various expressions in everyday life. Lower-threshold forms of this commitment are expressed, for example by following press and online coverage of a club or representing one's club in conversations with friends, whereas high-threshold forms may include, for example, the preparation and planning of choreographies on match days, organised fan travel to away games or engaging in fan representation boards. In this sense, our understanding of fandom comprises not only fanatic fans, organised ultras and supporters, but also, and equally, the so-called flâneurs, glory hunters, consumers, mere TV spectators and so forth (cf. Giulianotti 2002; cf. Heitmeyer and Peter 1988; cf. Redhead 2003).

This broad understanding allows us to include a broad spectrum of fans in our research. Within the strand of fan typology studies, for instance, differently operationalised ideas of fan intensity are applied. The divergence becomes clear by looking at the following example: applying a hot-cool vertical axis in his fan typology, Giulianotti (2002, p. 31) alludes to both intense and superficial 'kinds of identification and solidarity with the club'. This implies that even if the intensity of engagement is on a comparatively low level, it still makes up part of Giulianotti's (2002) conceptual understanding of a football fan and thus corresponds with our approach. In contrast, the operationalisation of Grau et al. (2016) only partially overlaps with ours. As their elaboration of different types of fans is 'based on statements describing an ideal stadium experience for home games' (Grau et al. 2016, p. 23), it neglects those fans who invest in, or commit to, following their club outside the stadium only. Conceptually, it thus places a high (and exclusive) threshold for being covered as fan in their typology at all.

Since the vast majority of studies on football fandom focus on sets of fans within a particular country, mostly tied to a club, a broader interpretation of fandom is required for our purposes. Given the heterogeneous nature of football supporters and the fact that fan scenes in different countries may differ considerably, comparative studies of different types of fans often run into difficulties. A case in point here is that, as Winands (2015, p. 27) points out, in the UK ultras, prevalent in many other European contexts, can hardly be found, which then poses difficulties for comparisons due to the immense discrepancies in fan constellations in different countries. This also holds true for different expressions of fandom and followership across countries or even leagues, as fan scenes deviate from each other. Depending on the socio-spatial conditions, the concept of fandom can hardly be analogically extended to other geographical areas.

In view of our research ambition, it is therefore necessary to avoid concentrating on overly specific and particular fan affiliations and forms of fandom, which rather serve to differentiate varying national or regional fan cultures and styles of expression from one another. Instead, our focus is on overarching concerns and football-related forms of identification. With such an approach, territorial distinctions can be transcended and productively overcome to study fandom in a cross-national context. For these reasons, we argue that fandom in transnational studies must be understood as a post-national construct with a loose and all-encompassing notion of 'being a fan', including both high- and low-threshold forms of engagement.

3.3 (Multi-)disciplinary Approaches to Football Fandom

Football fandom as a research topic has been treated from different perspectives and encompasses a wide array of approaches. We take a number of typological studies of football fandom as a starting point in order to show the breadth of attempts to order and classify different expressions of fandom. This enables us to shed light on the different disciplines as well as their accompanying scientific interests with regard to football fans. Since the early studies by Taylor (1972) and Clarke (1973) were put forward, scholars from diverse disciplinary backgrounds have looked into drawing up typologies of football fans. One particular distinction becomes visible between the research strands of sociology and sport studies on the one hand, and sport management studies on the other. Whereas early sociological research on football fandom by Clarke (1973), Critcher (1973) and Taylor (1972) attempted to link it to wider societal dynamics such as shifts in post-war society and the increasing commercialisation of social life, more recent studies in sport management have focused on the applicability of fan classifications for marketing endeavours (Bouchet et al. 2011; Samra and Wos 2014).[2]

Following a research approach similar to the early sociological studies, Heitmeyer and Peter (1988) introduced a typology particularly of younger football fans, which they differentiated into one group that followed a commercial experience-orientation and another which blended the fan experience with violent behaviour. In the latter case, the scholars pioneered a research domain interested in exploring behavioural and cultural dispositions towards criminal activities among football fans. Consequently, another dividing line in football fandom research runs between sociology/criminology on fan-related violence and cultural studies/sociology on more positive notions of fan activism (Winands 2015, p. 23). The first strand put major emphasis on exploring the phenomenon of hooliganism and categorised football fans in criminological and regulatory classifications at the same time. Literature on the phenomenon of hooliganism hence often took a more criminological approach by examining supporters who are isolating themselves from others, mostly being interested in fighting their peers from other sides. In contrast, the second strand explored various forms of wider political and societal activism among football fans and how their activities may form 'an area of political mobilization' (Cleland et al. 2018, p. 9), which is based on a collective sense of belonging (cf. Numerato 2016).

Towards the end of the twentieth century, a paradigm shift in sport and football fan research occurred to the extent that a research domain spearheaded by sociologists and sport studies scholars began to draw interest from academics in the field of sport management studies. Ironically, one point of origin for this broadening of the perspective might have been an increased interest by sociologists themselves, who registered the increasing impact of marketisation and (hyper-)commercialisation in the field of football (Giulianotti 2002; Stewart et al. 2003).

---

[2] In addition to marketing, such investigations also serve the purposes of market segmentation and the measurement of various levels of receptiveness of advertisement campaigns and sponsorship deals.

Sport management studies, in their effort to come up with fan typologies, seem to take such developments for granted and thus as fertile ground to develop more elaborate analyses of fan behaviour as *consumer* behaviour, which can in turn be used to fine-tune and adapt marketing activities. Two important concepts in this regard have been BIRGing (basking in reflected glory) and CORFing (cutting off reflected failure): while the former signifies reinforced association of a fan if his/her team is successful, the opposite occurs with the latter, in the form of dissociation in case of non-success. Wann and Branscombe (1990, p. 111) make use of these concepts by mapping patterns and intensities of social identification among different fans on them: as a result, a high level of fan identification mitigates the described effect, so that 'die-hard fans will persevere with their chosen team through almost anything, including years of defeat'. The social identification of fans with 'their' team is hence of central importance in Sport Management studies: it can, among other things, help identify the brand loyalty of supporters (Lock et al. 2014, p. 119). This shift in interest signifies how the more recent Management-oriented research approach is geared towards a better understanding of fandom for commercial interests (also cf. Samra and Wos 2014).

Taking the professionalisation of European football as a point of departure, King's (2000, 2003, 2004) ethnographic approach centred on the changing reality of football fans and how fandom had eventually morphed into a post-national phenomenon. His insights constitute a significant departure from looking at football fandom from a national perspective and, in doing so, pioneered a turn towards *European* football studies with a focus on fans. Building on this work, the trans-European football research project FREE, funded by the European Commission (2012–2015), also included a track, which was decidedly geared towards football fans 'beyond the realm of the nation-state' (FREE 2015, p. 3). Such transcending of the national frame of reference drew renewed interest from researchers in the fields of Political Science and Sociology. In this regard, García and Llopis-Goig (2021) address the question of how European fans respond to the complex new (governance) structures in modern football with the aim of arriving at a typology that can do justice to new forms of, and contexts to, fandom, with the latter having morphed into a significantly post-national and transnational phenomenon. In so doing, the authors introduced yet another new facet of research on football fans, which assigns evolving governance structures an influential role for fan identifications and, in turn, categorisations of different types of fandom.

It is in this sense that the ongoing progress of research on football fan typologies has brought forward paradigmatic shifts and resulted in a considerable breadth of approaches, enabling quite distinct research ambitions to coexist. However, it was not until recently that scholars turned towards fandom as a transnational phenomenon, and one on which a pan-European perspective could be developed.

3.3.1 Football Fan Typologies—Construction Principles

Typologies serve the purpose of making complex phenomena more intelligible by applying classifications and clusters. The central purpose of typologies is to point out ideal types and allow for systematic and meaningful distinction, thereby revealing key aspects, characteristics and factors associated with the classified phenomena. Accordingly, the underlying concern of typologies of football fans and fandom is to point out major variations among fans based on distinguishable behavioural patterns.

Broadly speaking, three different types of such typologies exist in football fan research: dichotomous, tiered and multidimensional. As this distinction makes clear, all three exhibit a specific construction principle: they either juxtapose two different types, construct different boxes (along a continuum or within a simple 2 × 2-matrix) or allow for a multidimensional classification on the basis of several determinants. In so doing, the respective approaches also display different degrees of conceptual depth. In our attempt to gauge the impact of the Europeanisation of football on fans, it appears useful to briefly discuss the main findings of such classification attempts for at least two reasons. First, it will allow us to identify anchor points for our own research results, elements of existing typologies, which are compatible with and useful for our investigation. Second, such an overview of the state of affairs after five decades of research may also help us spot missing elements and unaccounted forms of fan-related identification dynamics. Given our research focus, the following brief review is limited to fan typologies designed to include fans of professional European football clubs.

Dichotomous Typologies

Up until now, a large (and almost unmanageable) number of studies have dealt with football fan typologies as a research topic, distinguishing groups of fans based on a wide array of criteria. These include, but are not limited to, different values, intensities, behaviours or attitudes towards actors in the field (Fillis and Mackay 2014, p. 344; Samra and Wos 2014, p. 268; Stewart et al. 2003, p. 206ff.). The above-mentioned studies of Clarke (1973), Critcher (1973, p. 11ff.) and Taylor (1972, p. 364) can be considered the starting point of such classification attempts. Their approaches centre on a dichotomy between *traditional post-war male working-class supporters* and *genuine middle-class spectators*. Whereas the former are closely related to their local community clubs, the latter select their favoured team from a broad range of options, like consumers. To Taylor (1972, p. 364), the local connection of fans constitutes the differentiating criterion between the lower-class fans, who cheer for a club in their locality, and the middle-class fans, who pick their club elsewhere, while Clarke (1973, p. 11) differentiates between *genuine fans* and *others*.

By establishing this duality, both scholars put forth what has been dubbed 'the most basic classification of fans' (García and Llopis-Goig 2019, p. 2); lack of nuance notwithstanding, the impact of these early studies remains undisputed. In a somewhat similar fashion, Redhead (2003, p. 23f.) differentiates between *active/participatory* and *passive* supporters. The former type of football fan has evolved through the emergence of local supporter organisations, which are club-based but work independently, and football fanzines (nowadays more commonly online discussion forums). The latter fan type is a result of the increasing amount of consumer products in football and can be found in the seating area of stadiums or, thanks to increasing television coverage, at bars or on the couch at home.

A number of other authors who have adapted the dichotomous approach in their studies could be mentioned here (cf. Boyle and Haynes 2011; cf. Quick 2000). Despite their significance and influence on subsequent typology studies, dichotomous concepts force the behaviours, ambitions and views of fans into an either/or structure. This results in some argumentative strength, but at the expense of conceptual narrowness. In particular, it seems to have more limited explanatory power/significance, the larger and more locally and nationally diverse a fan community under study becomes. It is partially for this reason that dichotomous typologies are often seen today as the starting point only for the design of more multifaceted models of sport consumption (cf. Stewart et al. 2003, p. 208).

Tiered Typologies
Breaking with the pattern of dichotomous categorisations, Heitmeyer and Peter (1988) suggested a three-tiered fan typology instead. By introducing entertainment as a key influencing factor, they distinguished *consumption-oriented, football-centred* and *experience-oriented fans* (ibid., p. 32ff.) While consumption-oriented fans typically approach football in a more opportunistic fashion, for example when other leisure opportunities arise alongside watching or attending a match, football-centred fans attach highest personal priority to match attendance. The third category is that of experience-oriented fans and ideally depicts those fans who seemed to take football matches only as an occasion to engage in brawls and to incite turmoil. Here, the aspect of entertainment (of a sort) is the central motivation, with football and sport only providing a pretext. According to Heitmeyer and Peter (1988, p. 61), this motivation is ambiguous in the sense that this type of fan does value the sporting significance of the competition, but rather prioritises the violence away from the pitch. Hence, the attachment to their club and the involvement in football as a sporting event tend to be lower in comparison.

Another influential study based on a tiered categorisation of football fans is that of Giulianotti (2002), who proposes a four quadrant-taxonomy of (British) football fans against the backdrop of their overall increasingly market-driven orientations. Based on two dualistic opposites—hot-cool and traditional-consumer—the author deduces four ideal-typical fan types: *supporters, followers, fans* and *flâneurs*. Although the model proposed by Giulianotti (2002) is figured as a 2 × 2 matrix and thus represents a conceptual development beyond dichotomous approaches, it is still characterised by a rigid ordering of ideal-type categorisations. While supporters (traditional and hot) are characterised by a strong local attachment and frequent visits to 'their' stadium, followers (traditional and cold) lack a personal local network, so they receive updates about the respective clubs through (online) media. Moreover, followers have a range of favoured clubs and support them with varying levels of intensity depending on their competitiveness. Contrary to this, fans (consumer, hot) represent those who identify themselves through a non-reciprocal relation with the club's players while being market-oriented. Non-reciprocity, in Giulianotti's (2002, p. 37) understanding, here refers to engaging with players intensively, for example their transfer history and biographical details. The author completes his conception by introducing *flâneurs* (consumer, cool), who represent a new cosmopolitan football fan without being tied to a specific location and/or club. 'Walking' from one club to another is possible, because 'the football flâneur's natural habitat is increasingly the virtual arena' (Giulianotti 2002, p. 39). That also includes the increasing availability and ubiquity of broadcasting.

Building on the sociological notion of *flâneur*, Giulianotti (2002) treats this type of football fan as invasive, and depicts how the flâneur gradually supersedes the financially poorer supporter type when it comes to match attendance. Opposing Giulianotti's characterisation, Petersen-Wagner (2017) contends that flâneurs may aim at forming a mutual bond of loyalty with a football club. Hence, flâneurs should be perceived as traditionalist rather than consumerist, which is very close to Giulianotti's supporter fan type. Despite the study's influence on subsequent typologies, Giulianotti's (2002) approach has been criticised for juxtaposing two categories which are essentially two-dimensional, thus also fuelling debates and doubts on categorising his model as tiered in the first place (García and Llopis-Goig 2019, 3).

Multidimensional Typologies

More recently developed multidimensional approaches have sought to introduce an even more diversified and multi-layered set of factors/dimensions of classification to grapple with the complexities of fan attitudes and behaviours. In particular, this sort of study enables a 'more rounded' appreciation of fandom as it also includes 'geodemographic and psychographic dimensions' (Fillis and Mackay 2014, p. 340) as shaping factors (Stewart et al. 2003). In the context of football fandom, features related to the psychographic dimension typically involve consumption preferences, values or personal needs (such as emotional attachment) (Wann and Branscombe 1993; Fillis and Mackay 2014). Geodemographics, in turn, refer to characteristics of different group affiliations within a spatial framework (Gregory et al. 2009) and can lead to a more precise profiling of fans and fan communities.

On the basis of their findings through such a multi-layered fan structure, Grau et al. (2016, p. 28) argue that future research 'requires a subtly differentiated discussion of the phenomenon <football fans>'. This can be read as a call for more multidimensional approaches to typology studies as these can take account of more influences shaping various fan types. Following this call, García and Llopis-Goig (2019, p. 8) come up with a complex typology by considering attitudes towards the governance structures in modern football to detect five different types of fans in Europe. *Moderns*, *critics* and *clubs-militants*, who account for about two-thirds of football fans in Europe, distrust international governing bodies. In contrast, *globalists* are suspicious of national governing bodies, and *institutionalists* of club owners and presidents. Furthermore, the globalists and modernists differ from the institutionalists as well as the critics and especially the club-militants, since the former two fan types question whether their commitment in the club and fan community will (significantly) affect the respective club's management. Going beyond simple dichotomies, García and Llopis-Goig (2019) suggest that the growing differentiation and complexity of the governance structures of football—arguably one key structural development driving the Europeanisation of football (see Chap. 2)—requires a more nuanced and multifaceted approach towards football fans.

By producing slightly differing sets of classifications, it is obvious how typologies pay attention to select wider societal dynamics (or not) and may be shaped by geographical and temporal particularities. Not surprisingly then, fan typologies in football research have been subjected to a number of critiques. These include complaints of inflexibility, ignoring the most important, or exhibiting blatant normative undertones. Stewart et al. (2003, p. 207) join the critical ranks by stating that 'it is impossible to describe the archetypal sport consumer, because there are a multitude of interdependent values, attitudes, and behaviours to consider'. Arguably, even the most elaborate study design would not be able to account for all significant influencing factors to their full extent. More worrisome, some typologies might not easily match with the self-identifications of the respective football fans. In their study on the interdependence of local and global processes within football-related identities, Giulianotti and Robertson (2004, p. 556) discuss this with reference to the term consumer, often used in a derogatory fashion by fans and supporters: 'many fans reject their classification as "consumers" since, unlike purchasers of clothing or foodstuffs, they could never envisage "switching brands" by supporting other teams'. But does such repudiation of classification attempts necessarily mean that the typologies put forward lack utility and heuristic value?

3.3.2 Thematic Clusters of Fan Typologies

Fan typologies can be distinguished not only on the basis of construction principles; the characteristics used in the typologies of football fans can also be understood as different thematic clusters. This not only helps us to appreciate the diversity of perspectives and disciplinary inroads into football fans and their fandom, but also aids in identifying gaps in the existing research, which are to be filled through our attempts.

Class/Milieu
The first factor to be discussed for a more detailed topical classification of existing fan typology literature is the concept of class. Taking the sociopolitical circumstances of post-war Britain as a starting point for his research study, Clarke (1973) draws on this thematic cluster by tying his typological considerations to aspects of class. In so doing, he depicts the emergence of the so-called genuine *middle-class* spectators to be a consequence of sociopolitical developments in the UK. The presence of this type, in turn, leads to the continuous displacement of the traditional post-war masculine *working-class* supporters with close ties to their local community. By adopting this approach, Clarke (1973) not only follows

Marxist theory applied on a football fan context, but also places the aspect of displacement in the centre. The research by Taylor (1972) takes a similar point of departure, adding the notion of control. By introducing control, he alludes to the commercial mechanisms 'connected with the changing functions of football matches' (1972, p. 354), which account for the displacement of traditional and long-established fans. In this sense, he presents 'class' as the formative factor which constitutes particular social milieus. In addition, Taylor's (1972, p. 365) interpretation of the term 'control' is deeply linked with what he calls the 'Bourgeoisification' of football.[3] Such class-based approaches have not gone uncriticised, however (Stewart et al. 2003), mainly because of their neglect of additional factors influencing fan identifications such as structural developments of the game itself.

Commercialisation/Traditionalisation

Adopting Marxist terminology, Taylor (1972) refers to a progressive development that has transformed and continues to transform football into a commodity for the ruling class. At the level of fans, such commercialisation has led to contradictory responses: while at one end of the spectrum, fans cast themselves as custodians of traditional values and claim to fight 'modern' football, on the other end, fans have come to accept and embrace the modern lived fan experience more thoroughly (García and Llopis-Goig 2019). Two dynamics are hence at play, which seem to force fans of all stripes to position themselves in the field between commercialisation and traditionalisation.

As stated above, commercialisation of football was already recognised as a factor influencing fan structure in the very first typology efforts. However, it was only later that different authors dealt with commercialisation as a main criterion for fan typology studies. Among the first scholars who put attention to the continuum between commercialisation and traditionalisation is King (2000, p. 431), who established his dichotomous approach to fans of Manchester United, distinguishing the *new*

---

[3] With this term, Taylor (1972, p. 364) refers to a process 'which legitimises previously working-class activities for the middle class' and equates 'Bourgeoisification' with 'professionalization', without solely attributing this process to football, but considering it in a broader societal context.

fans from the *masculine fans* on the basis of their degree of commerciality. King (2000, p. 431) makes his differentiation explicit by referring to fans wearing a replica team shirt and explains how these fans 'are seen as emblematic of the commercialization of the club'. In addition, his studies ascertained that wearing a replica shirt is a sign of inauthenticity and is thus allotted symbolic importance. Closely related to conceptions of commercial/traditional are hence ideas of authenticity, with traditional values and anti-commercial attitudes often deemed more authentic. King's (2000) categorisation of the 'new' fan for the most part resembles Heitmeyer and Peter's (1988) *consumption-oriented* fan type. By returning to the concept of displacement, Pearson's (2012, p. 76) depiction of *non-genuine* fans also seems to align with King's basic idea: matching non-genuine fans with tourist fan stereotypes, Pearson argues that 'their presence at away matches is often resented as denying access to "proper" fans and "killing the atmosphere"'. Considering Heitmeyer and Peter (1988) and Giulianotti (2002) who highlight the increasing market orientation of fans ('hyper-commodification'), Grau et al. (2016) specify a typology of five groups with regard to fans' individual perception of an ideal stadium experience. Here, the *security-oriented passive* fan type combines the needs for security and non-aggressive behaviour (very similarly to Redhead's (2003) *passive* fan type) comes closest to a spectator that has been shaped by the forces of commercialisation. Similarly, commercialisation is seen as a background condition in the emergence of Giulianotti's (2002) *followers* and *flâneurs*. Finally, Redhead (2003, p. 1)—in considering football marketisation and privatisation dynamics—alludes to an intermingling of pop culture and fan culture as yet another indicator of the game's 'bourgeoisification'. It is hence more than plausible that the successive and commercially driven expansion of European football has not only resulted in structural changes (Cleland et al. 2018), but also had a more thorough, albeit nuanced, impact on identifications of fans; a point that will be investigated later in this book.

Violence-Orientation
The question of violence among football fans was already ascribed social-theoretic importance in the early studies of Taylor (1972), who touches on the issue of 'hooliganism' as a social problem. In his view, such forms

of fan violence resemble a form of resistance to the increasing control mechanisms that commercialise football. In the German context, this topic was further explored in Heitmeyer and Peter (1988). Starting from the idea of an increasing individualisation of young people, which is assumed to have contributed to the devaluation of normative identification patterns (ibid., p. 10), the authors put forward their thesis according to which 'the lost social integration' of young people is compensated by violence. As a result, Heitmeyer and Peter (1988) present *experience-oriented* fans as one of their three types, one in which the focus shifts from experiencing the game per se to the opportunity that the event affords for secondary experiences surrounding it, usually expressed in violent clashes which are often accorded greater importance than the football match itself. Such a typification is akin to the *active, confrontational conflict-seeker* introduced by Grau et al. (2016, p. 28), who is characterised by ascribing great importance to antagonising and clashing with opposing fans. At the same time, Grau et al. (2016) hold that this type only amounts for 4% of all respondents in their sample, while for Heitmeyer and Peter (1988), writing nearly two decades earlier, the similar type represented a much larger share.

Attitudes Towards Governance
As a final, more recently developed thematic cluster in fan typology studies, the degree of politicisation and the orientation towards football governance can be ascertained. As a central research finding of the Football Research in an Enlarged Europe (FREE) research project (2015, p. 3), European fans display 'limited trust in institutions and bodies of governance' leading to criticism regarding the increasing regulation of football. García and Llopis-Goig (2019), who were also part of FREE's research team, on the basis of this finding established a typology to account for the diversified attitudes towards different governing stakeholders on the local, national and European level. Displaying the highest ratio of mistrust and 'criticism towards every actor currently involved in the institutional governance of football in Europe' (FREE 2015, p. 12), *critics* make up the third largest subgroup among the fans studied across Europe as suggested by García and Llopis-Goig (2019). This type shares a few (not all!) characteristics with the traditional *post-war male working-class supporters*

identified by Taylor (1972), especially as regards their opposition towards mechanisms which lead to increasing control and support the ongoing commercialisation of football. At the same time, as García and Llopis-Goig (2019, p. 1) suggest, 'critics and globalists are heavy consumers of football games and merchandise'. Accordingly, and perhaps ironically, those who have the least confidence in professionalisation and commercialisation developments may be contributing to the further development and the very transformation of football away from past traditions and values. More importantly, though, the research by García and Llopis-Goig (2019) is among the few to date to explicitly acknowledge and incorporate *governance* as an influencing factor and reference point for fan identifications. This is also apparent in their recent study (García and Llopis-Goig 2021), in which they zoom in on fan involvement in governance structures. According to them, however, doubts remain as regards the efficacy of fans' activism (cf. also Kossakowski 2021) in the emergence of fans as shareholders in governing football. Nevertheless, their comparative approach hints at the post-national aspect, a subject which currently remains at the margins of fan studies, even though most observers agree on the existence of a thoroughly Europeanised football sphere (Table 3.1).

3.4 Instead of a Conclusion: Which Gaps Do Exist in Fan Typologies?

Two key aspects emerge from this brief review of the current state of football fan typology studies. First, it was shown how existing football fan research in Europe has produced classifications and taxonomies, which attempt to bring order to the complexity of fandom, and to foreground main drivers and clusters in such activities. Second, a number of research gaps, which tie in with our foray into the nexus of football fandom and Europeanised identifications, can be identified.

Already more than two decades ago, King (2000, p. 425) drew attention to the situation that the 'familiarity with Europe is significant because it could potentially play a part in the development of a supranational European identity'. In a similar spirit, Giulianotti and Robertson (2004,

Table 3.1 Football fan typology research overview

Author(s) (year)	Construction level	Classified fan types	Research context and thematic cluster
Taylor (1972)	Dichotomous	Lower-class fans Middle-class fans	Cultural research Class/milieu
Clarke (1973)	Dichotomous	'Genuine' middle-class spectators Working-class supporters	Cultural research Class/milieu
Heitmeyer and Peter (1988)	Tiered	Consumption-oriented fans Football-centred fans Experience-oriented fans	Cultural and criminological research Violence-oriented studies
King (2000)	Dichotomous	New fans Masculine fans	Research on commercial development Commercialisation/traditionalisation
Giulianotti (2002)	Tiered	Supporters Followers Fans Flâneurs	Sport management studies Commercialisation/traditionalisation
Redhead (2003)	Dichotomous	Active/participatory supporters Passive supporters	Research on commercial development Commercialisation/traditionalisation
Grau et al. (2016)	Multidimensional	Security-oriented passive Peaceful, supporting average Less aggressive supporters Active, emotional supporters Active, confrontational conflict-seekers	Cultural research Violence-oriented studies
Garcia and Llopis-Goig (2019)	Multidimensional	Moderns Critics Club-militants Institutionalists Globalists	Research on political and social activism Attitudes towards governance

p. 561) utilised the idea of 'glocalization', by means of which the authors attempted to dismantle the nexus of the local and the global in football fandom. This concept already suggested the potential of a post-national fan identity characterised by a dualism of local or regional and European spaces of reference (Porter 2008). Such a new 'European sense of belonging' (Levermore and Millward 2007, p. 159) in turn may provide discursive and spatial references for football fans in their everyday life that serve their local communities.

As the majority of the reviewed fan typologies reveal, however, the underlying frameworks and sets of factors have often been derived from nationally confined geographical contexts. In contrast, the considerations by King (2000) as well as those of Giulianotti and Robertson (2004) have remained surprisingly peripheral to the development of fan typologies. A clear exception to this rule have been the recent publications by García and Llopis-Goig (2019, 2021), who developed a well-crafted typology on the basis of studying football fans within a cross-country, comparative design *throughout Europe*. Their research findings clearly show that fandom has morphed into a post-national phenomenon, and not only in certain countries (say: the UK and the thoroughly internationalised English Premier League) or club milieus. What is more, García and Llopis-Goig (2021) maintain a strong and so far unusual focus on aspects of politics and governance as shapers and main frames of reference. The political dimension is explicitly addressed in their work rather than resembling a sort of background noise.

Many studies on football fans, and most of the typologies, also seem to focus on rather conscious, active and expressive forms of behaviour and identity work. An example of this is the approach of Cleland (2010), who focuses on tangible, explicit instances of collective fan action as embodiments of a shared sense of belonging, or of joint emotional attachment. However, as Stewart et al. (2003, p. 206) point out, zooming in on the explicit and active, on visible traits and given reasons risks missing the unconscious, not thoroughly reflected and subliminal cultural forces that might be powerful shapers of identification.

Finally, so far most typologies have failed to consider fans' attitudes towards Europe and their self-identification within a Europeanised football setting. Combining the latter two aspects, we start from the premise that unconscious impacts of regional identifications are of fundamental significance, especially in lifeworldly contexts such as football. The premise of our work is that the ongoing structural Europeanisation of football has an influence on fans' attitudes, that is fans are believed to have come to identify, wittingly or not, with positions on the transformations taking place in European football. They may have developed heterogeneous attitudes towards aspects such as the role of European competitions and European player markets, which can be regarded as indicators for European identifications through societal ways (Levermore and Millward 2007). Or they may navigate an increasingly Europeanised frame of reference, even without recognising it as such: they travel to away matches, populate internet discussion boards and so forth and thus inadvertently help strengthen the transversal dimensions of 'belonging within Europe' (Levermore and Millward 2007, p. 149). On this basis, we propose to turn our focus to supposedly mundane, subtle and unconscious changes in people's perceptions and imaginations which happen through and alongside everyday activities of football—a lifeworld that is exposed to (objective) Europeanising processes.

References

Bouchet, Patrick, Guillaume Bodet, Iouri Bernache-Assollant, and Faycel Kada. 2011. Segmenting sport spectators: Construction and preliminary validation of the Sporting Event Experience Search (SEES) scale. *Sport Management Review* 14 (1): 42–53. https://doi.org/10.1016/j.smr.2010.02.001.

Boyle, Raymond, and Richard Haynes. 2011. *Power play: Sport, the media and popular culture*. 2nd ed. Edinburgh: Edinburgh University Press.

Brown, Adam, Tim Crabbe, and Gavin Mellor. 2008. Introduction: Football and community – Practical and theoretical considerations. *Soccer & Society* 9 (3): 303–312. https://doi.org/10.1080/14660970802008934.

Clarke, John. 1973. *Football hooliganism and the skinheads*. Birmingham: University of Birmingham.

Cleland, Jamie. 2010. From passive to active: The changing relationship between supporters and football clubs. *Soccer & Society* 11 (5): 537–552. https://doi.org/10.1080/14660970.2010.497348.

Cleland, Jamie, Mark Doidge, Peter Millward, and Paul Widdop. 2018. *Collective action and football fandom: A relational sociological approach*, Palgrave studies in relational sociology. Cham: Springer. https://doi.org/10.1007/978-3-319-73141-4.

Critcher, Charles. 1973. *Football since the war: A study in social change and popular culture*. Birmingham: Centre for Contemporary Cultural Studies. Retrieved from https://www.birmingham.ac.uk/Documents/college-artslaw/history/cccs/stencilled-occasional-papers/9and25to37/SOP29.pdf.

Duffett, Mark. 2013. *Understanding fandom: An introduction to the study of media fan culture*. New York: Bloomsbury.

Fillis, Ian, and Craig Mackay. 2014. Moving beyond fan typologies: The impact of social integration on team loyalty in football. *Journal of Marketing Management* 30 (3–4): 334–363. https://doi.org/10.1080/0267257X.2013.813575.

FREE. (2015). *Football Research in an Enlarged Europe – Project final report*. Fp7 project, funding scheme FP7-SSH-2011-2.

García, Borja, and Ramón Llopis-Goig. 2019. Club-militants, institutionalists, critics, moderns and globalists: A quantitative governance-based typology of football supporters. *International Review for the Sociology of Sport* 9 (3). https://doi.org/10.1177/1012690219868661.

———. 2021. Supporters' attitudes towards European football governance: Structural dimensions and sociodemographic patterns. *Soccer & Society* 22 (4): 372–387. https://doi.org/10.1080/14660970.2020.1790356.

Giulianotti, Richard. 2002. Supporters, followers, fans, and flaneurs. *Journal of Sport and Social Issues* 26 (1): 25–46. https://doi.org/10.1177/0193723502261003.

Giulianotti, Richard, and Roland Robertson. 2004. The globalization of football: A study in the glocalization of the 'serious life'. *British Journal of Sociology* 55 (4): 545–568. https://doi.org/10.1111/j.1468-4446.2004.00037.x.

Grau, Andreas, Andreas Hovermann, Martin Winands, and Andreas Zick. 2016. Football fans in Germany: A latent class analysis typology. *The International Journal of Sport and Society* 7 (1): 19–31.

Gray, Jonathan, Cornel Sandvoss, and C. Lee Harrington. 2007. *Fandom: Identities and communities in a mediated world*. 2nd ed. New York: New York University Press.

Gregory, Derek, Ron Johnston, Geraldine Pratt, Michael Watts, and Sarah Whatmore. 2009. *The dictionary of human geography*. 5th ed. New York: John Wiley & Sons.

Ha-Ilan, Netta. 2018. The (re)constitution of football fandom: Hapoel Katamon Jerusalem and its supporters. *Sport in Society* 21 (6): 902–918. https://doi.org/10.1080/17430437.2017.1300391.

Heitmeyer, Wilhelm, and Jörg-Ingo Peter. 1988. *Jugendliche Fussballfans: Soziale und politische Orientierungen, Gesellungsformen, Gewalt*. Weinheim/München: Juventa-Verlag.

King, Anthony. 2000. Football fandom and post-national identity in the new Europe. *British Journal of Sociology* 51 (3): 419–442. https://doi.org/10.1111/j.1468-4446.2000.00419.x.

———. 2003. *The European ritual: Football in the new Europe*. London/New York: Routledge.

———. 2004. The new symbols of European football. *International Review for the Sociology of Sport* 39 (3): 323–336. https://doi.org/10.1177/1012690204045599.

Kossakowski, Radosław. 2021. *Hooligans, ultras, activists: Polish football fandom in sociological perspective*, Football Research in an Enlarged Europe. Cham: Springer International Publishing. https://doi.org/10.1007/978-3-030-56607-4.

Levermore, Roger, and Peter Millward. 2007. Official policies and informal transversal networks: Creating 'pan-European identifications' through sport? *The Sociological Review* 55 (1): 144–164. https://doi.org/10.1111/j.1467-954X.2007.00686.x.

Lock, Daniel, Daniel Funk, Jason P. Doyle, and Heath McDonald. 2014. Examining the longitudinal structure, stability, and dimensional interrelationships of team identification. *Journal of Sport Management* 28: 119–135. https://doi.org/10.1123/jsm.2012-0191.

Numerato, Dino. 2016. Behind the digital curtain: Ethnography, football fan activism and social change. *Qualitative Research* 16 (5): 575–591. https://doi.org/10.1177/1468794115611207.

Pearson, Geoff. 2012. *An ethnography of English football fans: Cans, cops and carnivals*. Manchester: Manchester University Press.

Petersen-Wagner, Renan. 2017. The football supporter in a cosmopolitan epoch. *Journal of Sport and Social Issues* 41 (2): 133–150. https://doi.org/10.1177/0193723517696967.

Porat, Amir Ben. 2010. Football fandom: A bounded identification. *Soccer & Society* 11 (3): 277–290. https://doi.org/10.1080/14660971003619594.

Porter, Chris. 2008. Manchester united, global capitalism and local resistance. *Belgeo* 2008 (2): 181–192. https://doi.org/10.4000/belgeo.10271

Quick, Shayne. 2000. Contemporary sport consumers: Some implications of linking fan typology with key spectator variables. *Sport Marketing Quarterly* 9 (3): 149–156.

Redhead, Steve. 2003. *Post-fandom and the millennial blues: The transformation of soccer culture*. Abingdon: Taylor and Francis.

Samra, Balwant, and Anna Wos. 2014. Consumer in sports: Fan typology analysis. *Journal of Intercultural Management* 6 (4–1): 263–288. https://doi.org/10.2478/joim-2014-0050.

Stewart, Bob, Aaron Smith, and Matthew Nicholson. 2003. Sport consumer typologies: A critical review. *Sport Marketing Quarterly* 12 (4): 206–216.

Stone, Chris. 2007. The role of football in everyday life. *Soccer & Society* 8 (2–3): 169–184. https://doi.org/10.1080/14660970701224319.

Taylor, Ian. 1972. 'Football mad': A speculative sociology of football hooliganism. In *Heritage. Sport: Readings from a sociological perspective*, ed. Eric Dunning, 352–377. Toronto: University of Toronto Press. https://doi.org/10.3138/9781442654044-027.

Wann, Daniel L., and Nyla R. Branscombe. 1990. Die-hard and fair-weather fans: Effects of identification on BIRGing and CORFing tendencies. *Journal of Sport and Social Issues* 14 (2): 103–117. https://doi.org/10.1177/019372359001400203.

———. 1993. Sport fans: Measuring degree of identification with their team. *International Journal of Sport Psychology* 24 (1): 1–17.

Winands, Martin. 2015. *Interaktionen von Fußballfans: Das Spiel am Rande des Spiels*. Springer eBook Collection. Wiesbaden: Springer Fachmedien Wiesbaden. https://doi.org/10.1007/978-3-658-09080-7.

4

Identity Research and the Europeanisation of Identity

4.1 Introduction

This chapter elaborates the current state of the art in identity research in the context of Europeanised identities and social identity more generally. It defines core approaches to research and measurement of Europeanisation in the realm of identities. Based on Brubaker and Cooper's (2000) understanding of identity as a tripartite structure consisting of identification, self-understanding and communality, it sets out to critically discuss the shortcomings of the established "Europeanisation of identities" literature. Particular importance is assigned to the impact of the leisure world/everyday life on identity dynamics.

Identity, social identity and collective identity have become ubiquitous terms not only in the social sciences and humanities but have increasingly been appropriated for purposes of collective and political mobilisation, too. This gives loose identity talk an evasive and ambiguous as well as a dangerous quality (for a good overview, cf. Schmitt Egner 2012, 28–40). As Kohli (2000, 114–5) has put it succinctly, identity has become "[…]one of those terms that have haunted the sociological imagination because they are so exceedingly vague or even vacuous but at the same time seem to capture such important dimensions of social life". It is in this sense that any new application and usage of such slippery, yet unavoidable terminology has to be transformed into clearly delineated concepts.

This is also necessitated by the ambition to truly guide and structure any investigative effort instead of merely confusing the reader and clouding conceptual fuzziness. As Eder (2009, 429) warns: "[c]ategorical ornamenting or fashionable category-dropping should be avoided", in particular when dealing with identity-related subject matters. Heeding this advice, the following chapter seeks to concisely elaborate the current state of the art in identity research in the context of Europeanised identities and social identity more generally. In particular, it sets out to define core approaches to research and measurement of Europeanisation in the realm of identities in the following manner.

First, we introduce general renderings of (Social) Identity Theory and its application to the realm of sports. This allows us to justify our choice of an identity concept aligned with the ideas of Brubaker and Cooper (2000), who suggested to substitute the all-too-vague identity talk with a tripartite structure consisting of identification, self-understanding and communality. Second, we aim at a critical discussion of the shortcomings of the established "Europeanisation of identities" literature. As this research domain is heavily populated by political scientists, the very understanding of "European(ised) identities" is usually narrowcast. Often, such identities are tied to *political* aspects in the stricter sense: for example, to political values and symbols, and to the efforts of sociopolitical elites to forge a closer allegiance of the wider population to the "European project" (or even the EU). Third, we highlight the need to move beyond a restricting focus on politics and elites as the main drivers of any Europeanisation of identities among the European populace. In contrast, we suggest taking a closer look at the impact of the leisure world/everyday life on identity dynamics, a pathway that has been proposed by recent sociological research.

4.2 Social Identity Theory and Identity Approaches in Sport

4.2.1 General (Social) Identity Theory

What exactly constitutes "identity" can easily be labelled the million-dollar question. For us, the most fundamental definition has been provided by Tajfel, in his ground-breaking attempt to define "social identities" as "[…]that part of the individual's self-concept which derives from his knowledge of his membership of a social group (or groups) together with the value and emotional significance attached to that membership" (Tajfel 1981, 255, cit. in: Hermann and Brewer 2004, 6). As identities are necessarily social—or relational (see below)—it seems to be of only limited value to engage in semantic hair-splitting as to whether there is a fundamental difference between the terms "identity" and "social identity", from our point of view. What Tajfel's definition achieves is to make clear that we can distinguish between the dimensions of identifying *as* (i.e. denoting that one perceives oneself as belonging to a certain group of people) and identifying *with* (an indication of emotional attachment to that group). Although it remains controversial to what extent Tajfel himself accorded importance to the second dimension, and to emotional antecedents as well as the affective aspects of identity in general (cf. Thoits and Virshup 1997, 119), these seem to constitute core ingredients of identity work. This is also demonstrated by the ample discussion that has been devoted to them ever since (cf. Garcia-Prieto and Scherer 2006; Spears 2011).

However, whereas Tajfel has developed a functionalist account of "social identities"—highlighting their role in mediating and channelling intergroup conflict (cf. Tajfel and Turner 2004, 283–6; see also: Jussim et al. 2001)—we suggest sticking to the initial stages of identity work, that is the so-called cognitive grouping (cf. Islam 2014, 1781). This means that the primary mechanism in forging new as well as transforming existing identities is constituted by repeated acts of categorisation through which the social reality of any group imagined as a community is created (cf. Thoits and Virshup 1997, 117). It is in this sense that an in-group based on ascribed or perceived commonality is formed, with out-groups perceived to be different, on one or more dimensions.

Taking such a perspective on "identity" necessarily means acknowledging that these are:

- *relational*, never unilateral (cf. Jenkins 2008, 42; Kohli 2000, 127)—that is, they emerge in response to others and outside objects of reference, whether at the individual or at the group level[1];
- *evolving and transforming*, as they are socially constructed, culturally variable and constantly redefined (cf. Thoits and Virshup 1997, 107)—in that sense, they represent a procedural category rather than a fixed entity;
- *imagined yet not imaginary*, as they have profound material consequences and tangibly shape social life to quite some extent (cf. Jenkins 2008, 11);
- *narrated* in the sense of being communicable and accessible primarily when communicated; one of the main spheres in which identities are made, remade, extended and transformed are consequently discursive performances and narrations (cf. Lawler 2014, 23–44, 122); and
- *multiple* not only across people but also within each person, as everyone can, in principle, be a member of, or perceive themselves as belonging to, different groups and communities (cf. Rosenberg 1997). Accordingly, the assumption that one identity necessarily comes at the expense of another, that is that identity work is necessarily either-or, does not hold true (even though not all imaginable identities can coexist without tensions).

In connection with the last point, several authors have gone to great lengths to describe the many different constellations in which several identities intersect within one person. According to Hermann and Brewer (2004, 8), multiple identities might come in a nested format, where identities are embedded into one another, for example under a spatial frame:

---

[1] Thoits and Virshup (1997, 106) have therefore argued that the term "social identity" has misleading qualities, as identities both at the individual and at the group level are social with regard to their origin and emergence. Consequently, they assert that one should better speak of "collective identities" or "we's".

4 Identity Research and the Europeanisation of Identity 91

a more local one embedded in a national one, with a transnational identity wrapped around them as a thin (or not so thin) outer shell. Identities, as Hermann and Brewer assert, might also be thought of as cross-cutting or overlapping. Citrin and Sides (2004) speak of layered identities, again hinting at the notion of a hierarchy between different levels of self-identification. Risse (2010, 25) adds the possibility that different identities might also blend into one another or come in an amalgamated form. For him, such a "marble cake" model of identity makes it very hard to separate the different components of one's identity from the mix.

Summarising the state of the art of social scientific identity research at the beginning of the twenty-first century, Brubaker and Cooper (2000) have nevertheless mounted a forceful critique of the very concept of "identity". In their often cited, often (critically) acclaimed account, they indeed seem to suggest getting rid of "identity", an agenda against which others have warned (cf. Duchesne 2008; Jenkins 2008).[2] Our understanding of the classical text, however, is that Brubaker and Cooper pledge for a clarification of concepts in order to make them more amenable to social science. Lamenting the "intellectual and political costs" of the social sciences' and humanities' "surrender to the word" (Brubaker and Cooper 2000, 1) does not lead them to change the analytic focus altogether. Hence, stating that the concept of "identity" has been used all too loosely, and with very different intentions (ibid., 7), is *not* the same as saying that its multiple renderings have no value. On the contrary, one could read their suggestion of an appropriate substitute for identity—the tripartite structure of *identification, self-understanding* and *communality/connectedness/groupness*—as an intervention which picks and chooses three core aspects and dynamics prevalent in most identity talk anyway.

Their first substitute term, "identification", is indeed conspicuously close to many accounts in the tradition of (Social) Identity Theory. Classified by Jenkins (2008, 13) as the "basic cognitive mechanism", or

---

[2] In no unclear language, Jenkins (2008, 14) states: "'Identity' is not only an item in sociology's established conceptual toolbox; it also features in a host of public discourses, from politics to marketing to self-help. If we want to talk to the world outside academia, denying ourselves one of its words of power is not a good communications policy." Convincing as the argument is, one only wonders if wholly abandoning the term in all communication was what Brubaker and Cooper had in mind.

"baseline sorting" upon which all identity work is based, it arguably marks no departure from previous conceptual attempts. However, as Brubaker and Cooper state, zooming in on identification as a set of activities has the advantage of inviting social scientists to specify the social actors who do the identifying (ibid., 14). Identification hence emphasises the act and the agents that are involved; it thus has the capacity to visualise the process and the relevant actors. In this, the distinction between self-identification and identification through others becomes apparent. Lamont and Molnár (2002, 170) point out that "individuals must be able to differentiate themselves from others by drawing on criteria of community and a sense of shared belonging within their subgroup. On the other hand, this internal identification process must be recognized by outsiders for an objectified collective identity to emerge." Identification is thus, in general, a bidirectional process of attribution and differentiation.

As Brubaker and Cooper (2000, 15) argue, we are constantly identified by different actors, wherever we go. Most of this identification is enacted through markers, which can be categorical (e.g. ethnicity, gender and religion), relational (e.g. belonging to a family) or institutional (e.g. passports or saved fingerprints) in nature. Seen from this angle, the very processes of identification are hugely dependent on contextual situations, with the analytic focus shifting to the identification done by external actors, or more external components of someone's identity in the format of ascribed markers of identification.

In contrast, Brubaker and Cooper's second identity-substitute—"self-understanding"—explicitly recognises the subjective nature of identity. It is also suggested that this notion captures any identity's distinctly tacit qualities by recognising that self-understandings may be formed in and through discourses, yet are ultimately not dependent on being articulated (ibid., 18). Self-understanding thus prioritises the aspect of identity that seeks to explain action or a person's behaviour in a non-instrumental fashion. It covers "[…] one's sense of who one is, of one's social location, and of how (given the first two) one is prepared to act" (ibid., 17).

Whereas identification describes *making* sense of the outside social world through contact with other actors and explicit articulations, self-understanding refers to the internal, at times even un- or subconscious nature of sense-making on one's own. This is arguably hinted at in their remark that self-understanding is "never purely cognitive" (ibid., 18). Whether conscious or not, however, it is still the individual on which the emphasis lies when it comes to analysing any self-understanding. The respective formations of such ideas about the self are undoubtedly co-shaped by a variety of social influences (e.g. school, family and friends), yet they ultimately vary from person to person and it is the subjective rendering that matters.

Finally, Brubaker and Cooper (2000, 19–21) suggest "commonality", "connectedness" and "groupness" as one particular set of aspects representing a conceptual alternative to identity. "Commonality" describes a group of common attributes (e.g. ethnicity, religion or gender). "Connectedness" captures the relations people have towards each other (e.g. family, friends and network), and is hence linked to the relational qualities of any identity. "Groupness" is a feeling (also cf. Weber 2018) which combines categorical "commonality" and relational "connectedness". It is described as "the sense of belonging to a distinctive, bounded, solidary group" (Brubaker and Cooper 2000, 20). This feeling is created, among other things, through time spent together in the group and joint experiences. Looking at "groupness" more closely, it becomes clear that "commonality" appears to be more foundational than mere "connectedness", as shared markers often precipitate the making of connections. However, it is both the perceived commonality and an ultimately realised connectedness that are key for the formation of groups and accompanying feelings of groupness (ibid., 21).

Brubaker and Cooper go to great lengths to distinguish between articulated identifications, on the one hand, and more subjective self-understandings—which are often implicit and at times subconscious—on the other. We nevertheless maintain that, for sheer practical reasons, their analytic toolkit should be amended. Harking back to the widely shared assumption that identities are narrated in character, we feel the need to reclaim "narratives" and narrations as a medium of analysis for all three identity substitutes Brubaker and Cooper put forth. Whereas they seem to reserve the concept of (public) narratives only for semantic contexts for processes of identification (cf. ibid., 16, 20, 21, 28), we also see narratives as the most promising analytic dimension for self-understanding(s) and groupness. Where else would a self-understanding become accessible than in the form of a (subjective) narration? Where else are perceptions of commonality expressed—and again accessible as objects of study—other than in narratives pertaining to, or developed in, a particular community? Are narrations not formative of the very discourses which, in turn, forge connectedness?

In this regard, Brubaker and Cooper's tripartite identity substitute can and should be extended by a definition such as the one put forth by Eder (2009, 427). He defines group identities as collectively held "self-understandings which are grounded in frames and narrative constructions delineating the boundaries between networks of actors". Eder himself, after having discussed the merits of Brubaker and Cooper, seems to develop his approach in the spirit of highlighting or adding "narratives" to the conceptual mix (ibid., 430). Similarly, Schmitt-Egner (2012, 45–6) has emphasised the narrated character of identity-related work, first and foremost at the level of collectives, yet at least implicitly also at the level of individual responses to such narrations. This seems most obvious with regard to the mix of different narratives at play at any given time—captured in the notion of a "narrative experiment" (ibid., 46–7)—from which both a group *and an individual* could pick and build their own stories as responses to the outside world and existing communities.[3]

4.2.2 Research Linking Identity and Sport

Equipped with such an understanding of identity as being constituted by identifications, self-understandings, forms of groupness and ultimately narrated in nature, it is surprising to see that many literatures on "sport and identity" hark back to this conceptual anchor. Whether such literatures have discussed athletes, the role of media and sports broadcasts or sport fans and followers in particular, cross-references and thematic links

---

[3] Eder (2009, 431) also remarks, if only in passing, that "[…] collective identities are linked primarily to individuals in concrete interaction situations". Narrative sharing hence occurs within groups, and narrative bonds are developed within such; yet the same can also occur at the individual level when seeking to accede to groups or to extend affections throughout communities.

4 Identity Research and the Europeanisation of Identity 95

seem to abound. Athletes in various domains of sport, for instance athletics (Black 2016), wrestling and American football (Brookes 2002), cricket and rugby (Bowes and Bairner 2018), have been found to be subject to outside identification and attribution (not seldom also "othering"). This is all the more true for athletes who have migrated or belong to an ethnic minority (cf. Gibbons 2015; Jansen 2018; Oonk 2021; Seiberth et al. 2017; Tamir and Bernstein 2014; Velema 2018). Sport broadcasting, in turn, and particularly the coverage of football tournaments, has been widely discussed as an instance of an ongoing negotiation and representation of national identities (cf. Boyle and Haynes 1996; Boyle and Montero 2005; Hagay and Meyers 2015; Kioussis 2018; Maguire et al. 1999; Poulton 2004), thereby feeding self-understandings and strengthening or undermining perceived commonalities.

Arguably the richest literature linking identity and sport—overwhelmingly football—exists in the form of research on fans. However, not all of the publications, including the classic ones, set out to specify their understanding of identity. For instance, one of the earliest monographs linking football to identity—while in fact bearing "social identity" in its title—does so largely without addressing identity theory or even describing a lead concept (cf. Giulianotti et al. 1994). Others have come to interpret (football) fan communities as often "symbolic" in nature (cf. Lamont and Molnár 2002, 182), thereby highlighting that connectedness need not include face-to-face contact, familiarity between all group members nor joint tournament or match-day experiences. This also ties in with more recent attempts at mapping Relational Sociology in the field of sport in order to show how networks between fans constitute communities across distances (cf. Cleland et al. 2018), which also may affect fans' patterns of identification and their self-understanding. Sport fans often engage in identity work through following sports as nationals cheering their national team (cf. Mutz 2013, 2018), a phenomenon that is by no means restricted to football (cf. Devlin et al. 2020; Llewellyn 2012). In doing so, they may discursively and cognitively and even subconsciously—stabilise their self-identifications (Kaelberer 2017; Meier et al. 2019) and hence their identities, while at the same time delineating themselves against others (Popp et al. 2016; Samuel-Azran et al. 2016; Tamir 2016). Such stabilisers for groupness can be ascertained not only at the level of national teams but also at that of clubs (cf. Bleakney and Darby 2018; Juventeny Berdún 2017).

A slightly different take on the nexus between sport fandom and identity can be found in the Sport Management and Sport Psychology literatures. Many of the investigations in this realm have focused on the idea that fan perceptions and aspirations are shaped by the sporting success of the respectively followed teams (Cialdini et al. 1976; Phua 2010; Wann and Branscombe 1990; Wann and Grieve 2005). It is also these strands of the debate that feature the most obvious engagement with Social Identity Theory along the lines of Tajfel (see above; cf. Lock et al. 2012; Lock and Heere 2017). In their effort to streamline the multitude of identity concepts employed by sport psychology, Lock and Heere (2017, 418) have recommended distinguishing between "team identification" (referring to aspirational group dynamics and mutual delineation in view of success/failure) and "fan identification" (individual-level perceptions of belonging, which are less subject to identity management and the expected benefits of sporting success). It does not seem too far-fetched to spot a parallel between their distinction and that of identification and self-understanding according to Brubaker and Cooper (2000).

While the Sports Studies literature hence might, in principle, prove more than amenable to our concept of identity, it suffers from one significant limitation. As our research project has been geared towards investigating the eventual *Europeanisation* of identities through sport and through following football as a fan or supporter, we cannot ignore the fact that the bulk of studies on the nexus between sport fandom and identity has so far focused on national (including localised) identities.

In part, this is easy to explain given that the basic format of most tournaments is either local or national in shape or, if internationally staged, centred on national delegations or athletes competing with a clearly discernible national marker. In that sense, it should not come as a surprise that the nation forms the predominant category of identity work in both sport *and its analysis*. This holds true even when theorising globalisation in its effects on the sporting world (cf. Giulianotti and Robertson 2009; Houlihan 2003); and also when contemplating that athletes are not only mobile at an ever-increasing pace but are also changing their citizenship *and nationality* more frequently (cf. Lanfranchi and Taylor 2001; Magee and Sugden 2002; Oonk 2022). Only recently, Storey (2021, 3; our emphasis) has therefore lamented that "[growing attention to the transnationalisation of sport] has tended to deflect attention *from the reality* that, in many respects, sport remains firmly rooted in place, induces place-based loyalties and takes place within geographically defined regulatory structures". But is this "the" reality, and the "only" reality? Are new terminologies such as the "transnational fan" (cf. Rowe 2015), "cosmopolitan fandom" (cf. Petersen-Wagner 2017)[4] or "conditional cosmopolitanism" among fans (cf. Skey 2015) not indicative of a possible shift, at least in the field of football and as regards fan identities and loyalties? Could sport in general, and football in particular, not be regarded as a vehicle for more fluid conceptions of groupness?

In what follows, we will hence broaden our perspective on identity concepts to include the vast literature on "European identity". If there are indeed "European(ised) identifications" emerging through following football, can these numerous works by political scientists and political sociologists contribute conceptually to our project?

4.2.3 The Europeanisation of Identities: Measures and Blind Spots

The field of European identity research has become almost overwhelming by now. At best, it could be considered heterodox and multifaceted. Already a decade ago, however, Kaina (2013, 184) criticised that research conducted under the rubric of European identity rather "provides inconsistent evidence, contradictory conclusions and controversial diagnoses". Yet, deploring the disorder does not automatically reduce it. More optimistically, Balks (2013) has argued that the field is home to many and diverse methodological approaches, and by now has also moved away from its early focus on elites. However, the latter point is more

---

[4] Admittedly, the list of researchers who have looked into such instances of "foreign fandom" in football is much longer, cf. among others Ludvigsen (2018); Millward (2011, 76–93); Nash (2000).

controversial (cf. Checkel and Katzenstein 2009, 3; Hermann and Brewer 2004, 21–2; Kaiser 2017; Wodak and Boukala 2015).[5]

What constitutes a "European identity" is also less consensual across various studies and conceptual frameworks than one could perhaps assume. More often than not, it is taken to denote the self-identification of people *as* Europeans (next to localised and national forms of identification). However, there is more disagreement on whether, as a reference object, the concept of European identity targets "Europe" in a wider understanding or rather "the EU" more narrowly conceived. It is thus not by chance that Dalton (2021, 3) criticises that what is still "[m]issing from the literature on European identities has been a better conceptualization and measurement of what it means to be 'European'. Is this a cultural identification to European history and traditions, an attachment to the European Community as a political institution, or a belief in the ideal of European integration?" In other words, what people across the continent might identify *with* is still subject to debate. In contrast, it is widely held that multiple identifications—for instance in relation to the region one is inhabiting, the respective nation-state and Europe—can coexist alongside each other (cf. Carey 2002; Díez Medrano and Gutiérrez 2001; Risse 2003, 488).

As a legacy of most European identity literature having emerged in the fields of Political Science, or in response to it, most conventional analyses have taken a rather restrictive, narrowcast view on where to discover relevant identity dynamics: how Europeans imagine, narrate and discursively construct "Europe" has predominantly been cast in strictly *political* terms (cf. Checkel and Katzenstein 2009; Risse 2010). Constituting the home turf of Political Science and Political Sociology, issues such as shared political norms, levels of appreciation for the EU's institutions, as well as attention paid to, and evaluations of, political action at the EU level have accordingly driven most forays into European identity.

---

[5] In an interesting twist, communication flows across Europe—which are assumed to shape identifications among Europeans—had largely "remained a project *by political elites* and, as far as discursive influence is concerned, *also to the benefit of political elites*" until very recently, as Koopmans (2010, 120) concluded on the basis of a thorough empirical analysis.

In other words, even when leaving the level of elite discourse and opening up towards wider publics within Europe (cf. Brigevich 2018; Maier and Risse 2003; Polonska-Kimunguyi and Kimunguyi 2011; Risse and Grabowsky 2008), the more traditional research angles and concerns tended to prevail. No doubt, most researchers did so for well-intentioned reasons, for instance when asking questions about people's knowledge on Europe in global politics, or the Union and its symbols, both with an eye to the function of a possibly emerging collective identity *for the political legitimacy* of European integration in general, or as a remedy for the "democracy deficit" (cf. Camia 2010; Duchesne 2008) seemingly built into the EU's emerging polity. Still, it cannot be ignored that taking such a particular stance on how to ascertain and measure the emergence of a European identity also brackets a lot from our view (see next sub-chapter).

In the literature on the Europeanisation of identities, three argumentative strands can be identified: the potential of shared values, normative understandings and political convictions to form the basis of a common European identity; the identity potential of the EU, including its symbols; and the contours of a European public sphere providing the necessary infrastructure for a collective identity to grow.

The first of the three aforementioned strands zooms in on shared ethical self-understandings (cf. Kantner 2006) across European societies, be they of a civic or cultural nature. According to Bruter (2003, 2004), a European identity may be anchored in more civic values such as shared adherence to, and appreciation of, the principles of democracy, the rule of law or more open and liberal orientations. In comparison, a more culturally defined European identity rests on the perception of cultural proximity and references to a shared cultural heritage. Although, as some have argued, the very cultural repertoire from which to draw in order to forge a unifying European identity is in fact limited due to often rivalling historical trajectories, clashing memories and the absence of one unifying language as a significant roadblock (cf. Mayer and Palmowski 2004), the reality of European integration knows quite a few instances of such culturalist self-identifications among Europeans. Kleiner and Bücker (2016, 203) assert that such references to shared and historicised values of democracy and liberalism in particular may allow for categorising oneself positively, in line with a general strive for constructing a positive social identity. Accordingly, some ideas and positions in discourse have increasingly been marked as "distinctly European", for example respect for human rights, the repudiation of the death penalty and a positive attitude towards welfarism, solidarity and social cohesion—all this with the effect of foregrounding and strengthening a particular identity, which is then claimed by many Europeans as "theirs" (cf. Cerutti 2003; Citrin and Sides 2004; Howarth and Torfing 2005).[6] In turn, such a value-based conception of identity is also assumed to work as a means of delineation and hence a vehicle for preventing outsiders from entering the community of Europeans (or the EU as an organisation). Inasmuch as the question of Turkey's accession to the EU became ever closer tied to a cultural project imbued with certain values throughout the first decade of the twenty-first century, the identification with a "union of values" worked against the enlargement of the EU (Aydin-Düzgit 2012, 138, 144) and reinforced groupness on the basis of cultural particularism (cf. Camia 2010, 111–12).

A second main theme in the Political Science-driven literature on European identity has been the "identity potential" of the EU, its institutions, its political accomplishments and the symbols it has generated to establish itself in the minds of people. Based on the idea that publics across Europe—and even more so, different strata of the respective populations within specific national contexts—identify to a different extent with the EU as a political project, it has attempted to elucidate the drivers for such identification and the reasons for variations in the resulting self-understandings. In this regard, Hermann and Brewer (2004, 3) have emphasised the ever-increasing presence of EU institutions in people's lives as an effect of the institution being drawn into a multitude of transnational problems and crises. In a similar vein, Mayer and Palmowski (2004, 592) have noted the political capital the EU amassed over the years in transforming hitherto international disputes into internal arguments, which were then resolved through mediation and the rule of law.

---

[6] Just for how many Europeans, and across which strata of society, this may be the case remains a subject of contestation among scholars, cf. Fligstein (2008).

Most notably and emblematic for many Political Science approaches, any identification with "Europe" under such a perspective is almost automatically operationalised as being tied to exposure towards *the EU*, be it information-wise or through direct experiences and encounters (cf. Bergbauer 2018).

The bulk of investigations into the EU's identity potential, however, has focused on the institution's symbols. As Heinrich (2016, 74) explains, the most basic mechanism here is that increased frequency of exposure to "banal stimuli"—such as signs, flags, slogans and anthems (cf. Pryke 2020)—may lead to a normalisation, the familiarity with such symbols and subsequently, perhaps, credibility and trust. Symbols thus constitute powerful channels and safeguards of purposively engineered identification; they first mobilise awareness and then generate sentiment (cf. Cram and Patrikios 2016). Not by chance have many authors pointed towards the intended identity dimensions of the EU (cf. Gillespie and Laffan 2006, 142–44) as well as several "identity technologies" enacted through it (cf. Kaina 2016, 254; Karolewski 2010, 47). The introduction of a common currency hence not only had a monetary and an economic dimension, but also one related to identity. Visa, passports and border controls not only serve as devices of security management, they also allow for "enhanc[ing] and freez[ing] the salience of certain collective identities through political practices of categorization" (ibid.). The flag, an anthem, several European Days dedicated to select issues, landmark buildings and flagship programmes—the EU has employed considerable resources in order to generate symbols that resonate with national publics (cf. Cram and Patrikios 2016, 64), albeit with mixed success (cf. Kaelble 2009, 206). Experimental studies on the effect of such symbols on positive identifications have highlighted that their impact is hugely mediated by context factors such as the prevalence of crises and threats, hence making it far from straightforward (Cram and Patrikios 2016, 66).

Thirdly, questions of European identity have been discussed with an eye to the emergence of a European(-wide) public sphere. This, again, came in largely two variants. On the one hand, scholars put the formation of a European identity centre stage and sought to assess it via dynamics observable in public spheres, both nationally and supranationally (cf. Risse 2010). On the other hand, some studies clearly elevated normative concerns about the privileging of certain actors in an increasingly Europeanised sphere, and the analytic interest in demonstrating their very existence, above the consideration of any identity effects emanating from it (cf. Boomgaarden et al. 2010; Koopmans and Statham 2010a; Trenz 2004).

In his review of key literatures on the European public sphere a decade ago, Nitoiu (2013, 26) highlights as one overarching theme the disputed character of the very possibility of creating such a truly transnational, unified discursive space comprising the bulk of "communication fluxes and actors from all strata of society". It seemed, and still seems, more reasonable to assume a process of an increasing frequency of outside perspectives and extra-domestic concerns (cf. Fraser 2014, 133) permeating into formerly more closed national public spheres, including—and in particular—across Europe. In this sense, the difference between "transnational" and "transnationalised" is not only of marginal semantic nature (cf. Couldry 2014, 52): whereas the former denotes a more or less fully integrated type of entity, the latter refers to a long-standing process which may have attained a new intensity and velocity within the last two decades.

In line with this idea, Risse (2010, 5, 116–18) argued that an ongoing Europeanisation of public spheres can be observed whenever European issues—the bulk of which related to the EU, some of them also covering topics spilling over borders from a neighbouring country—are debated as common concerns, using similar frames of reference across various national publics. Converging thematic intensities, for example measured by the ratio of national-to-EU reporting, and the convergence of frames and topics are hence key in assessing the contours of such an increasingly Europeanised public sphere. Such a sphere is then assumed to constitute a site where communities of communication are being (re-)constructed, with the implication of the gradual emergence of a collective identity. In a very similar fashion, Koopmans and Statham (2010b, 37–38) report on the convergence of news agendas, frames and criteria of relevance in news reporting across Europe, yet they refrain from concluding too much on any identity effect. According to their interpretation, "Europe" might have become an increasingly visible and salient reference point in the mass media coverage of politics, but with rather differentiated effects on different actors: traditional (political) elites seem to have been strengthened and only marginal effects on empowering civil society could be ascertained. Much in line with the earlier insight of a segmented public sphere in Europe (Díez Medrano 2009), such differentiation poses conceptual difficulties for an inclusive and wide-ranging European identity. More recent research has consequently attempted to analyse complementary modes of building up "communities of relevance" from the grassroots level in order to fill the gap of the all too patchwork-like public sphere in Europe (cf. Zappetini 2019). Undoubtedly, such civil society activism could potentially lead to more cosmopolitan identifications throughout Europe. However, it remains rather marginal, at least if restricted to political issues.

While by and large compatible and even mostly aligned with the identity conception sketched out at the beginning of this chapter, most established approaches towards European identity clash with our ambition. Reducing the Europeanisation of identities to questions of the right and legitimate polity and underlying values constituting a community, responses to the symbolism of the EU as well as the eventual merger of national public debates and news agendas on more strictly political issues are highly likely to push football—the field we want to study—aside, and with it the main preoccupations and the not necessarily conscious political self-understandings of the people and communities that populate the field (fans, followers, spectators). While most authors in the tradition of Political Science-driven research on European identity have not been silent about their ambitions—illuminating the levels of identification with a work-in-progress, democratic European polity (cf. Duchesne 2008) or the marshalling of such a European identity as a resource for forging cohesion in times of multiple crises (cf. Verhaegen 2018)—these ambitions sit uneasily with the type of identity work that football fans seem to engage in (even if only in a subliminal fashion).

4.2.4 The Europeanisation of Identities Through Leisure Time Activities and Lifeworldly Experiences

Europeanisation in Everyday Contexts

Already fifteen years ago, Wodak (2007, 70–71) remarked that "what is experienced as European" results from multiple activities, some of which are "consciously planned in the sense of political, economic or cultural interventions" whereas others are more hidden and in the background. While subsequently referring to the everyday experiences of migrants and people-to-people internet communication across Europe in this context, she pointed out what was missing from many forays into European identity at that time and it still is exotic compared to traditional approaches today: an analytic interest in more mundane activities and their contribution to more subconscious identity effects—those below the level of reflexive action geared towards political objects (institutions, values, symbols, news). Only within the last one and a half decades, sociologists of different stripes, with a few political scientists siding with them, have opened up a whole new field of research under rubrics such as "social transnationalism" (e.g. Mau 2010), "Experiencing European integration" (e.g. Kuhn 2015) and "Everyday Europe" (e.g. Recchi et al. 2019). What they have in common is a turn towards more lifeworldly contexts such as travel, tourism and cross-border mobility, learning, studying and engaging in leisure-time activities related, inter alia, to culture, entertainment and sport, cooking and culinary choices, shopping and so forth.

The delay with which this turn was taken is somewhat surprising given the amount of time, attention, emotions and other resources ordinary European citizens invest in such domains, at least in comparison to more openly political activities. Path-breaking in this regard were the studies conducted in the context of the EUCROSS research project ("Crossing Borders—Making Europe", 2011–2014); almost ironically, their effort to move beyond identity effects in relation to politics and the EU was funded under the latter's 7th Framework Programme (cf. EUCROSS 2014; Favell et al. 2011; Hanquinet and Savage 2011). Harking back to earlier enquiries into the multidimensional nature of Europeanisation (cf. Delhey 2005), EUCROSS put the link between transnational mobility and transactions across European boundaries and eventually resulting patterns of attitudinal and/or identity change centre stage. In a similar fashion, Mau (and colleagues) had aimed at testing whether increased transnationality across Europe is accompanied by higher levels of identification with Europe. He found a strong correlation; however, as he himself stressed, causality could well run both ways: attitudinal change could constitute the result of increased transnationality, while a higher propensity to move across borders in the European context may, in turn, also have stemmed from an already Europeanised mindset (ibid., 118–19).

While the first generation of such studies often seemed to operate with rather generic identity concepts—Mau (2010), for instance, used labels such as "German", "European" or "both" as measures of identification—a second generation of studies has attempted to unpack the multifacetedness of self-identifications and self-understandings more thoroughly. Although restricting themselves more often than not to (quantitative) survey research and to a focus on migration and mobility as predominant shapers of any Europeanisation of identity, they have significantly extended the scope of research and shown how rich and encompassing identity research through the lens of lifeworldly and seemingly "mundane" social activities can be. Moreover, while assessing the articulation of commonality in, as well as the formation of communities through, leisure-time activities, more subliminal and unconscious forms of identity work enter the analytic fray.

For instance, Friedman and Thiel, in their edited collection linking European identity with culture (2012), set out not only to explore feelings of "transnational belonging" in Europe but also to trace from where these have emerged. Placing particular emphasis on the "cultures of the everyday" (ibid., 2; also: Gaggio 2012, 162–63) and the role of agency and intentionality in them, they arrive at the conclusion that more conscious identity engineering (such as when navigating ethnic and religious diversity due to increased migration into people's neighbourhoods) goes hand in hand with much less reflected activities, which are nevertheless identity-building (most notably when travelling, taking culinary choices or seeking joy and diversion in entertainment).

In summarising the results of the EUCROSS research project, Recchi et al. (2019) develop a thorough cartography of social transnationalism in Europe, comprising various activities and resulting structures and dynamics, most notably in the fields of mobility and migration. Building on a large quantitative survey among nationals, intra-EU movers and third-country nationals residing in six European countries, the research team was able to highlight which particular cross-border practices are more likely to shape some form of identification with the EU, and to what extent the effect was discernible among particular sub-populations. However, it is also instructive to note that among the many chapters in the book, only one zooms in more specifically on questions of "identifications" and a cosmopolitan widening of mindsets of frequent movers (Poetzschke and Braun 2019, 115–36).

Even more tellingly, Favell and Recchi (2019, 6) conclude that the social transnationalism they studied—mobility experiences and actions—frequently did not translate into identifications or attachments in a straightforward fashion, and occasionally not at all. As they assert, a disconnection between transgressing boundaries and experiencing Europe on a mass scale on the one hand, and the initiation of closer emotional bonds, or expressions of more intimate attachment (to Europe, or the EU), on the other seems to exist quite palpably. Important as the distinction between physical and virtual mobilities (cf. Salamonska and Recchi 2019) appeared to be at first glance, it could not explain the discrepancy between different intensities of identification change resulting from various forms of social transnationalism. More predictive proved to be the amount of emotional entanglement. Physical mobility can trigger very different responses on the identity scale—"[s]pending a weekend on the Costa Brava or occasionally chatting with a glamourous Instagram contact abroad is likely to have less impact than relocation to another country" (Favell and Recchi 2019, 12)—whereas virtual connectedness is far from being secondary in forging imaginations and building de-nationalised communities (ibid., 25).

Further studies have highlighted the potential of "lived experiences" through cultural events, installations and rituals—such as the European Capitals of Culture—to contribute to more Europeanised self-understandings among locals and visitors (cf. Sassatelli 2009). Particular prominence in this regard has been given to student mobility across Europe and the participants of Erasmus exchanges. Interestingly, the respective studies tend to reach very different conclusions. Mitchell (2015) is rather an outlier in describing, on average, huge and positive effects of Erasmus student exchanges: participants of such exchanges displayed enhanced levels of identification both as Europeans and with Europe. Cognitive mobilisation was hence triggered through being mobile, and particularly so when students mingled with host country nationals and other Europeans alongside their fellow nationals. The singular exception to this were the incomings to, and the outgoings from, the UK—a result which corroborated the findings of earlier studies (cf. Sigalas 2010). Even more stunningly, the incomings' identifications as Europeans seemed to deteriorate during their stay in the UK, leading Sigalas to hypothesise that the embedded, highly Eurosceptic context might have conditioned their experience in unexpected ways (ibid., 260).

Kuhn (2012), on the other hand, noted a ceiling effect, according to which patterns of identification towards Europe were only marginally transformed due to the already comparatively high identification levels of the group on the move before going on Erasmus. It is in this sense that top-down programmes of planned Europeanisation and European identity-engineering "fail" since they may cater to an already Europeanised elite, while the larger population—the real target audience lacking a more Europeanised horizon—remains unaffected. What is more, if an already high level of European identification works as *selector* for participation in such schemes, they ultimately cannot contribute a lot to overcoming the divide between "transnational Europhiles" and "local Eurosceptics" (Kuhn 2015, 144–58; similarly in: van Mol 2018).

From a more analytical point of view, then, "transnationalism from above" (Mau 2010) and the corresponding exchange programmes may not provide the most fruitful testing ground for Europeanisation effects at the level of identities. In contrast, non-elite fields of activity where transnationalism happens rather unconsciously, by default and in a bottom-up manner—"transnationalism from below"—seem more promising. This is also hinted at by more recent attempts to engage with "narrations of Europe from below" (Scalise 2015), instances of "cultural consumption" such as musical tastes and culinary choices (Hanquinet and Savage 2019), or even videogaming in a virtual, thoroughly Europeanised community of gamers (Sindelar 2022).

Even though there are indicators that suggest the capacity of such seemingly mundane practices to break up nationally siloed perspectives and narratives, not all forms of lifeworldly connectedness across boundaries inspire deep and authentic identity change. Díez Medrano (2020), in his unconventional study of the effects of cross-boundary marriages on bi-national couples and identification patterns in their proximate social context, has found that references to a shared European identity are rather strategically deployed. As an example, they serve the purpose of deflecting tensions between members of both families in instances in which cross-cultural differences and divergent habits seem to lead to disputes. In a similar vein, van Mol et al. (2015) demonstrated that, on the surface, bi-national couples in Europe appear to show a higher propensity to identify "as Europeans". However, such self-categorisation more often than not has a superficial quality and almost never translates into higher levels of solidarity with fellow Europeans in times of crisis.

Football Fandom as a Domain of Lifeworldly Identity Change: First Approaches

Still, the turn towards "Everyday Europe" seems especially promising in light of our research objectives and the first pilot studies into football fandom as a post-national and increasingly Europeanised phenomenon. Some of the by now already classical studies by King (2000, 2003, 2004), Millward (2006, 2007, 2009) and Levermore and Millward (2007) take a very similar point of departure.

King had, for instance, explored ideas of a growing "European consciousness" amongst a group of locally based Manchester United F.C. (Football Club) fans in the late 1990s based on ethnographic research. In doing so, he argued that these fans were beginning to see themselves as more European, and that two main mechanisms were propelling this change. These are, first, the increased opportunities to travel across Europe brought about by the greater number of Champions League games which made supporters progressively identify as "European" in a cultural sense (King 2000, 424–26). Beyond that, King (2000, 423) suggested that the increased coverage of all European leagues on British television made supporters more aware of other European national leagues, cities and countries and that this familiarity was also contributing to a growing European consciousness.

Millward had listened to the voices of Liverpool F.C. and Oldham Athletic F.C. supporters in order to investigate whether these were identifying with an idea of Europe. He found that Liverpool F.C. fans had developed a loose identification with football-related notions of Europe in response to their team competing at the European level and their experiences in following it across Europe (Millward 2006, 2009, 106–71). Meanwhile, Oldham Athletic A.F.C. supporters, in following a team that remained in the English lower divisions, exhibited only local and national patterns of identification (ibid.). Levermore and Millward (2007, 159) set up a framework to explore where a newly found "European sense of belonging" among fans was coming from.

Such and similar accounts also inspired the trans-European research project "Football Research in an Enlarged Europe" (FREE), which also included a track on identity-related research among football fans. This track focused on two specific aspects: first, a foray into feminisation and identities (from an anthropological perspective), and second, an interest in the relationship between football and feelings of Europeanness against the background of the eventual emergence of a European public sphere of football (with shared memories and communication channels as well as agendas to link fans across societies). Not by chance did the publication output of FREE (2015) build important bridges to fan research: in a more historical vein, into collective memories of a European football past (Pyta and Havemann 2015); in ethnographical terms, into fan experiences and expressions in select places throughout Europe (Schwell et al. 2016); and in a more sociological understanding, into fan activism as a particular type of social engagement on behalf of football fans as a distinctively shaped sub-population of the European citizenry (García and Zheng 2017).

4.3 Concluding Remarks

Among the multitude of identity concepts, definitions of and distinctions between terms such as "social identity" and "collective identity", the ones which emphasise elements such as identification (as, and with), subjective self-understandings and groupness based on communality and connectedness appear to be the most fertile. While introduced by Brubaker and Cooper (2000) in an apparent attempt to get rid of "identity", these rather resemble the fundamental building blocks of a concept of identity that is amenable to social science. In particular, as will be shown in the next chapter, this tripartite concept can be translated into meaningful analytic categories—such as communities of belonging (COB) and frames of reference (FOR)—and then further operationalised. While one could in principle also link it to investigations of "European identity", the more established existing research in the tradition of Political Science has unfortunately narrowly cast its object of study as primarily directed at political aspects, and observable in political attitudes and positioning. However, the identity work of football fans—particularly the work in response to the Europeanisation of the governance structures of the game (see Chap. 2)—cannot and should not be mapped onto the narrow concerns of the traditional agenda of those interested in political institutions, values, symbols and news. It is hence necessary to link up to more recent efforts to shed light on the Europeanisation of identities through mundane, lifeworldly activities and within everyday contexts.

References

Aydin-Düzgit, Senem. 2012. *Constructions of European identity*. Houndsmills: Palgrave.
Balks, Anne-Dörte. 2013. Studying European identity. *European Political Science* 12: 254–258.
Bergbauer, Stephanie. 2018. *Explaining European identity formation*. Cham: Springer.

Black, Jack. 2016. 'As British as fish and chips': British newspaper representations of Mo Farah during the 2012 London Olympic games. *Media, Culture & Society* 38 (7): 979–996.

Bleakney, Judith, and Paul Darby. 2018. The pride of east Belfast: Glentoran Football Club and the (re)production of Ulster unionist identities in Northern Ireland. *International Review for the Sociology of Sport* 53 (8): 975–996.

Boomgaarden, Hajo G., Rens Vliegenthart, Claes H. de Vreese, and Andreas R.T. Schuck. 2010. News on the move: Exogenous events and news coverage of the European Union. *Journal of European Public Policy* 17 (4): 506–526.

Bowes, Ali, and Alan Bairner. 2018. England's proxy warriors? Women, war and sport. *International Review for the Sociology of Sport* 53 (4): 393–410.

Boyle, Raymond, and Richard Haynes. 1996. 'The grand old game': Football, media and identity in Scotland. *Media, Culture & Society* 18 (4): 549–564.

Boyle, Raymond, and Cláudia Montero. 2005. 'A small country with a big ambition.' Representations of Portugal and England in Euro 2004 British and Portuguese newspaper coverage. *European Journal of Communication* 20 (2): 223–244.

Brigevich, Anna. 2018. Regional identity and support for integration: An EU-wide comparison of parochialists, inclusive regionalist, and pseudo-exclusivists. *European Union Politics* 19 (4): 639–662.

Brookes, Rod. 2002. *Representing sport*. London: Arnold.

Brubaker, Rogers, and Frederick Cooper. 2000. Beyond 'identity'. *Theory and Society* 29 (1): 1–47.

Bruter, Michael. 2003. Winning hearts and minds for Europe: The impact of news and symbols on civic and cultural European identity. *Comparative Political Studies* 36 (10): 1148–1179.

———. 2004. On what citizens mean by feeling 'European': Perceptions of news, symbols and borderlessness. *Journal of Ethnic and Migration Studies* 30 (1): 21–39.

Camia, Valeria. 2010. Normative discussions on European identity: A puzzle for social science? *Perspectives on European Politics and Society* 11 (1): 109–118.

Carey, Sean. 2002. Undivided loyalties. Is national identity an obstacle to European integration? *European Union Politics* 3 (4): 387–413.

Cerutti, Furio. 2003. A political identity of the Europeans? *Thesis Eleven* 72 (1): 26–45.

Checkel, Jeffrey, and Peter Katzenstein, eds. 2009. *European identity*. Cambridge: Cambridge University Press.

Cialdini, Robert B., Richard Borden, and Lloyd Sloan. 1976. Basking in reflected glory: Three (football) field studies. *Journal of Personality and Social Psychology* 34 (3): 366–375.

Citrin, Jack, and John Sides. 2004. More than nationals: How identity choice matters in the new Europe. In *Transnational identities*, ed. Richard K. Herrmann, Thomas Risse, and Marilynn Brewer, 161–186. Lanham: Rowman & Littlefield.

Cleland, Jamie, Mark Doidge, Peter Millward, and Paul Widdop. 2018. *Collective action and football fandom. A relational sociological approach.* Basingstoke: Palgrave.

Couldry, Nick. 2014. What and where is the transnationalized public sphere? In *Transnationalizing the public sphere*, ed. Nancy Fraser et al., 42–59. Oxford: Polity.

Cram, Laura, and Stratos Patrikios. 2016. European Union symbols under threat: Identity considerations. In *European identity revisited*, ed. Viktor Kaina, Ireneusz P. Karolewski, and Sebastian Kuhn, 61–70. London etc.: Routledge.

Dalton, Russell. 2021. National/European identities and political alignments. *European Union Politics* 22 (2): 340–350.

Delhey, Jan. 2005. Das Abenteuer der Europäisierung. *Soziologie* 34 (1): 7–27.

Devlin, Michael B., et al. 2020. 'My country is better than yours': Delineating differences between six countries' national identity, fan identity, and media consumption during the 2018 Olympic games. *Sociology of Sport Journal* 37 (3): 254–263.

Díez Medrano, Juan. 2009. The public sphere and the European Union's political identity. In *European identity*, ed. Jeffrey Checkel and Peter Katzenstein, 81–110. Cambridge: Cambridge University Press.

———. 2020. *Europe in love. Binational couples and cosmopolitan society.* London etc.: Routledge.

Díez Medrano, Juan, and Paula Gutiérrez. 2001. Nested identities: National and European identity in Spain. *Ethnic and Racial Studies* 24 (5): 753–778.

Duchesne, Sophie. 2008. Waiting for a European identity… reflections on the process of identification with Europe. *Perspectives on European Politics and Society* 9 (4): 397–410.

Eder, Klaus. 2009. A theory of collective identity: Making sense of the debate on a 'European identity'. *European Journal of Social Theory* 12 (4): 427–447.

EUCROSS. 2014. The Europeanisation of everyday life: Cross-border practices and transnational identifications among EU and third-country citizens: Final report. http://www.eucross.eu/eucross/images/docs/eucross_d9_17_final_report.pdf. Accessed 31 Mar 2020.

Favell, Adrian, and Ettore Recchi. 2019. Social transnationalism in an unsettled continent. In *Everyday Europe*, ed. Ettore Recchi et al., 1–33. Bristol: Policy Press.

Favell, Adrian, et al. 2011. The Europeanisation of everyday life: Cross-border practices and transnational identifications among EU and third-country citizens: State of the art report. EUCROSS working paper no. 1. http://www.eucross.eu/eucross/images/docs/eucross_d2_2_state_of_the_art.pdf. Accessed 5 June 2019.

Fligstein, Neil. 2008. *Euroclash: The EU, European identity, and the future of Europe*. Oxford: Oxford University Press.

Fraser, Nancy. 2014. Transnationalizing the public sphere. In *Transnationalizing the public sphere*, ed. Nancy Fraser et al., 8–42. Oxford: Polity.

FREE. 2015. Project final report: Football research in an enlarged Europe. Report to the EU Commission, FP7-SSH-2011-2.

Friedman, Rebecca, and Markus Thiel. 2012. *European identity & culture*. London etc.: Routledge.

Gaggio, Dario. 2012. Tourism, transnationalism, and the construction of everyday life in Europe. In *European identity and culture*, ed. Rebecca Friedman and Markus Thiel, 157–174. Aldershot: Ashgate.

García, Borja, and Jinming Zheng, eds. 2017. *Football and supporter activism in Europe*. Houndsmills: Palgrave.

Garcia-Prieto, Patricia, and Klaus R. Scherer. 2006. *Connecting social identity theory and cognitive appraisal theory of emotions*. London etc.: Psychology Press.

Gibbons, Tom. 2015. Fan debates on English national identity surrounding the Almunia case. *Soccer & Society* 16 (2–3): 344–359.

Gillespie, Paul, and Brigid Laffan. 2006. European identity: Theory and empirics. In *Palgrave advances in European Union studies*, ed. Michelle Cini and Angela K. Bourne, 131–150. Basingstoke/New York: Palgrave.

Giulianotti, Richard, and Roland Robertson. 2009. *Globalization and football*. London etc.: SAGE.

Giulianotti, Richard, et al., eds. 1994. *Football, violence, and social identity*. London/New York: Routledge.

Hagay, Haim, and Oren Meyers. 2015. Everybody's team? The national narrative in the Hebrew press covering Israeli national soccer team matches. *Media, Culture & Society* 37 (4): 530–546.

Hanquinet, Laurie, and Mike Savage. 2011. The Europeanisation of everyday life: Cross-border practices and transnational identifications among EU and third-country citizens: Operationalisation of European identity, cosmopolitanism and cross-border practices. EUCROSS working paper no. 2. http://www.eucross.eu/eucross/images/docs/eucross_d3_1_operationalisation_document.pdf. Accessed 31 Mar 2020.

———. 2019. Cultural boundaries and transnational consumption patterns. In *Everyday Europe*, ed. Ettore Recchi et al., 87–114. Bristol: Policy Press.

Heinrich, Philipp. 2016. Experimental exposure to the EU energy label: Trust and implicit identification with the EU. In *European identity revisited*, ed. Viktor Kaina, Ireneusz P. Karolewski, and Sebastian Kuhn, 71–83. London etc.: Routledge.

Hermann, Richard, and Marilynn Brewer. 2004. Identities and institutions: Becoming European in the EU. In *Transnational identities*, ed. Richard K. Herrmann, Thomas Risse, and Marilynn Brewer, 1–24. Lanham: Rowman & Littlefield.

Houlihan, Barrie. 2003. Sport and globalisation. In *Sport and society: A student introduction*, ed. Barrie Houlihan, 345–363. London etc.: SAGE.

Howarth, David, and Jacob Torfing, eds. 2005. *Discourse theory in European politics: Identity, policy and governance*. Houndsmills: Palgrave Macmillan.

Islam, Gazi. 2014. Social identity theory. In *Encyclopaedia of critical psychology*, ed. Thomas Teo, 1781–1783. Berlin etc.: Springer Reference.

Jansen, Joost. 2018. Nationality swapping in the Olympic Games 1978–2017: A supervised machine learning approach to analysing discourses of citizenship and nationhood. *International Review for the Sociology of Sport* 54 (8): 971–988.

Jenkins, Richard. 2008. *Social identity*. 3rd ed. Milton Park/New York: Routledge.

Jussim, Lee, Richard D. Ashmore, and David Wilder. 2001. Introduction: Social identity and intergroup conflict. In *Social identity, intergroup conflict and conflict resolution*, ed. David Wilder, Lee Jussim, and Richard D. Ashmore, 3–14. Oxford: Oxford University Press.

Juventeny Berdún, Silvia. 2017. Much 'more than a club': Football Club Barcelona's contribution to the rise of a national consciousness in Catalonia (2003–2014). *Soccer & Society* 20 (1): 103–122.

Kaelberer, Matthias. 2017. From Bern to Rio: Soccer and national identity discourses in Germany. *International Journal of Politics, Culture, and Society* 30: 275–294.

Kaina, Viktor. 2013. How to reduce disorder in European identity research. *European Political Science* 12 (2): 184–196.
———. 2016. 'In search of the unknown': An essay on the need of non-knowledge in European identity research. In *European identity revisited*, ed. Viktor Kaina, Ireneusz P. Karolewski, and Sebastian Kuhn, 246–258. London etc.: Routledge.
Kaiser, Wolfgang. 2017. One narrative or several? Politics, cultural elites, and citizens in constructing a 'New Narrative for Europe'. *National Identities* 19 (2): 215–230.
Kantner, Cathleen. 2006. Collective identity as shared ethical self-understanding: The case of the emerging European identity. *European Journal of Social Theory* 9 (4): 501–523.
Karolewski, Ireneusz P. 2010. *Citizenship and collective identity in Europe*. London/New York: Routledge.
King, Anthony. 2000. Football fandom and post-national identity in the new Europe. *British Journal of Sociology* 51 (3): 419–442.
———. 2003. *The European ritual: Football in the new Europe*. London/New York: Routledge.
———. 2004. The new symbols of European football. *International Review for the Sociology of Sport* 39 (3): 323–336.
Kioussis, George N. 2018. Remember the Teutons: English coverage of Germany at the 2010 World Cup. *Soccer & Society* 19 (2): 288–300.
Kleiner, Tuuli-Marja, and Nicola Bücker. 2016. Commonality and EU identification: The perception of value sharing as a foundation of European identity. In *European identity revisited*, ed. Viktor Kaina, Ireneusz P. Karolewski, and Sebastian Kuhn, 199–217. London etc.: Routledge.
Kohli, Martin. 2000. The battlegrounds of European identity. *European Societies* 2 (2): 113–137.
Koopmans, Ruud. 2010. Winners and losers, supporters and opponents in Europeanized public debates. In *The making of a European public sphere*, ed. Ruud Koopmans and Paul Statham, 97–121. Cambridge: Cambridge University Press.
Koopmans, Ruud, and Paul Statham, eds. 2010a. *The making of a European public sphere – Media discourse and political contention*. Cambridge: Cambridge University Press.
———. 2010b. Theoretical framework, research design, and methods. In *The making of a European public sphere*, ed. Ruud Koopmans and Paul Statham, 34–59. Cambridge: Cambridge University Press.

Kuhn, Theresa. 2012. Why educational exchange programmes miss their mark: Cross-border mobility, education and European identity. *Journal of Common Market Studies* 50 (6): 994–1010.

———. 2015. *Experiencing European integration: Transnational lives and European identity*. Oxford: Oxford University Press.

Lamont, Michèle, and Virág Molnár. 2002. The study of boundaries in the social sciences. *Annual Review of Sociology* 28 (1): 167–195.

Lanfranchi, Pierre, and Matthew Taylor. 2001. *Moving with the ball*. Oxford/New York: Berg.

Lawler, Steph. 2014. *Identity. Sociological perspectives*. 2nd ed. Cambridge: Polity.

Levermore, Roger, and Peter Millward. 2007. Official policies and informal transversal networks: Creating 'pan-European identifications' through sport? *The Sociological Review* 55 (1): 144–164. https://doi.org/10.1111/j.1467-954X.2007.00686.x.

Llewellyn, Matt P. 2012. *Rule Britannia: Nationalism, identity and the modern Olympic games*. London/New York: Routledge.

Lock, Daniel, and Bob Heere. 2017. Identity crisis: A theoretical analysis of 'team identification' research. *European Sport Management Quarterly* 17 (4): 413–435.

Lock, Daniel, Tracy Taylor, Daniel Funk, and Simon Darcy. 2012. Exploring the development of team identification. *Journal of Sport Management* 26: 283–294.

Ludvigsen, Jan Andre Lee. 2018. Transnational fan reactions to transnational trends: Norwegian Liverpool supporters, 'authenticity' and 'filthy-rich' club owners. *Soccer & Society* 20 (6): 872–890.

Magee, Jonathan, and John Sugden. 2002. 'The world at their feet': Professional football and international labour migration. *Journal of Sport and Social Issues* 26 (4): 421–437.

Maguire, Joseph, Emma Poulton, and Catherine Possamai. 1999. The war of words? Identity politics in Anglo-German press coverage of EURO 96. *European Journal of Communication* 14 (1): 61–89.

Maier, Matthias L., and Thomas Risse. 2003. Europeanization, collective identities and public discourses: IDNET final report. https://www.polsoz.fu-berlin.de/polwiss/forschung/international/atasp/Publikationen/4_artikel_papiere/25/index.html. Accessed 31 Mar 2020.

Mau, Steffen. 2010. *Social transnationalism: Lifeworlds beyond the nation-state*. London: Routledge.

Mayer, Franz C., and Jan Palmowski. 2004. European identities and the EU – The ties that bind the peoples of Europe. *Journal of Common Market Studies* 42 (3): 573–598.

Meier, Henk E., et al. 2019. Fan identification and national identity. *Sport in Society* 22 (3): 476–498.

Millward, Peter. 2006. 'We've all got the bug for Euro-aways': What fans say about European football club competition. *International Review for the Sociology of Sport* 41 (3–4): 375–393.

———. 2007. True cosmopolitanism or notional acceptance of non-national players in English football: Or, why 'bloody foreigners' get blamed when 'things go wrong'. *Sport in Society* 10 (4): 601–622.

———. 2009. *Getting into Europe. Identification, prejudice and politics in English football culture*. Saarbrücken: VDM.

———. 2011. *The global football league: Transnational networks, social movements and sport in the new media age*. Houndsmills: Palgrave.

Mitchell, Kristine. 2015. Rethinking the 'Erasmus effect' on European identity. *Journal of Common Market Studies* 53 (2): 330–348.

Mutz, Michael. 2013. Patrioten für drei Wochen. Nationale Identifikation und die Fußballeuropameisterschaft 2012. *Berliner Journal für Soziologie* 22 (4): 517–538.

———. 2018. Football-related patriotism in Germany and the 2016 UEFA EURO. *German Journal of Exercise and Sport Research* 48 (2): 287–292.

Nash, Rex. 2000. Globalised football fandom: Scandinavian Liverpool FC supporters. *Football Studies* 3 (2): 5–23.

Nitoiu, Cristian. 2013. The European public sphere: Myth, reality or aspiration? *Political Studies Review* 11 (1): 26–38.

Oonk, Gijsbert. 2021. Who may represent the country? Football, citizenship, migration, and national identity at the FIFA World Cup. *The International Journal of the History of Sport* 37 (11): 1–20.

———. 2022. Sport and nationality: Towards thick and thin forms of citizenship. *National Identities* 24 (3): 197–215.

Petersen Wagner, Renan. 2017. The football supporter in a cosmopolitan epoch. *Journal of Sport and Social Issues* 41 (2): 133–150.

Phua, Joe. 2010. Sports fans and media use: Influence on sports fan identification and collective self-esteem. *International Journal of Sport Communication* 3: 190–206.

Poetzschke, Steffen, and Michael Braun. 2019. Social transnationalism and supranational identifications. In *Everyday Europe*, ed. Ettore Recchi et al., 115–136. Bristol: Policy Press.

Polonska-Kimunguyi, Eva, and Patrick Kimunguyi. 2011. The making of the Europeans: Media in the construction of pan-national identity. *International Communication Gazette* 73 (6): 507–523.

Popp, Bastian, Claas Germelmann, and Benjamin Jung. 2016. We love to hate them! Social media-based anti-brand communities in professional football. *International Journal of Sports Marketing and Sponsorship* 17 (4): 349–367.

Poulton, Emma. 2004. Mediated patriot games. The construction and representation of national identities in the British television production of Euro '96. *International Review for the Sociology of Sport* 39 (4): 437–445.

Pryke, Sam. 2020. National and European identity. *National Identities* 22 (1): 91–105.

Pyta, Wolfram, and Nils Havemann, eds. 2015. *European football and collective memory*. Houndsmills: Palgrave.

Recchi, Ettore, et al., eds. 2019. *Everyday Europe. Social transnationalism in an unsettled continent*. Bristol: Policy Press.

Risse, Thomas. 2003. The Euro between national and European identity. *Journal of European Public Policy* 10 (4): 487–505.

———. 2010. *A community of Europeans? Transnational identities and public spheres*. Ithaca: Cornell University Press.

Risse, Thomas, and Jana K. Grabowsky. 2008. European identity formation in the public sphere and in foreign policy. RECON online working paper no. 4. https://www.polsoz.fu-berlin.de/polwiss/forschung/international/atasp/Publikationen/4_artikel_papiere/2009_paper_TR_european_identity_formation/RECON_wp_0804.pdf. Accessed 31 Mar 2020.

Rosenberg, Seymour. 1997. Multiplicity of selves. In *Self and identity. Fundamental issues*, ed. Richard D. Ashmore and Lee Jussim, 23–45. New York/Oxford: Oxford University Press.

Rowe, David. 2015. The mediated nation and the transnational football fan. *Soccer & Society* 16 (5–6): 693–709.

Salamonska, Justyna, and Ettore Recchi. 2019. The social structure of transnational practices. In *Everyday Europe*, ed. Ettore Recchi et al., 61–86. Bristol: Policy Press.

Samuel-Azran, Tal, et al. 2016. Jewish-Israeli attitudes towards the Iranian football team during the 2014 World Cup tournament. *Media, War & Conflict* 9 (3): 252–271.

Scalise, Gemma. 2015. The narrative constructions of European identity. Meanings of 'Europe from below'. *European Societies* 17 (4): 593–614.

Schmitt-Egner, Peter. 2012. *Europäische Identität: Ein konzeptioneller Leitfaden zu ihrer Erforschung und Nutzung*. Baden-Baden: Nomos.

Schwell, Alexandra, et al., eds. 2016. *New ethnographies of football in Europe. People, passions, politics*. Houndsmills: Palgrave.

Seiberth, Klaus, Ansgar Thiel, and Ramón Spaaij. 2017. Ethnic identity and the choice to play for a national team: A study of junior elite football players with a migrant background. *Journal of Ethnic and Migration Studies* 45 (5): 787–803.

Sigalas, Emmanuel. 2010. Cross-border mobility and European identity: The effectiveness of intergroup contact during the ERASMUS year abroad. *European Union Politics* 11 (2): 241–265.

Sindelar, Jakub. 2022. Playing through to Europe? Depiction and reception of the First World War in the Videogame Valiant Hearts. *Journal of Contemporary European Studies*: 1–14. https://doi.org/10.1080/14782804.2022.2097206.

Skey, Michael. 2015. 'What nationality he is doesn't matter a damn!' International football, mediated identities and conditional cosmopolitanism. *National Identities* 17 (3): 271–287.

Spears, Russell. 2011. Group identities: The social identity perspective. In *Handbook of identity theory and research*, ed. Seth J. Schwartz et al., 201–244. Heidelberg: Springer.

Storey, David. 2021. *Football, place, and national identity. Transferring allegiance*. Lanham: Rowman & Littlefield.

Tajfel, Henri, and John C. Turner. 2004. The social identity theory of intergroup behavior. In *Political psychology*, ed. John T. Jost and Jim Sidanius, 276–293. London/New York: Routledge.

Tamir, Ilan. 2016. Generation 3.0: Popularity of the national German team among Israeli soccer fans. *International Review for the Sociology of Sport* 53 (3): 371–386.

Tamir, Ilan, and Alina Bernstein. 2014. Do they even know the national anthem? Minorities in service of the flag – Israeli Arabs in the national football team. *Soccer & Society* 16 (5–6): 745–764.

Thoits, Peggy A., and Lauren K. Virshup. 1997. Me's and we's: Forms and functions of social identities. In *Self and identity. Fundamental issues*, ed. Richard D. Ashmore and Lee Jussim, 106–133. New York/Oxford: Oxford University Press.

Trenz, Hans-Jörg. 2004. Media coverage on European governance. *European Journal of Communication* 19 (3): 291–319.
van Mol, Christof. 2018. Becoming Europeans: The relationship between student exchanges in higher education, European citizenship and a sense of European identity. *Innovations* 31 (4): 449–463.
van Mol, Christof, et al. 2015. Falling in love with(in) Europe: European binational love relationships, European identification and transnational solidarity. *European Union Politics* 16 (4): 469–489.
Velema, Thijs A. 2018. A game of snakes and ladders: Player migratory trajectories in the global football labor market. *International Review for the Sociology of Sport* 53 (6): 706–725.
Verhaegen, Soethin. 2018. What to expect from European identity? Explaining support for solidarity in times of crisis. *Comparative European Politics* 16 (5): 871–904.
Wann, Daniel, and Nyla Branscombe. 1990. Die-hard and fair-weather fans: Effects of identification on BIRGing and CORFing tendencies. *Journal of Sport and Social Issues* 14 (2): 103–117.
Wann, Daniel, and Frederick Grieve. 2005. Biased evaluations of in-group and out-group spectator behavior at sporting events: The importance of team identification and threats to social identity. *The Journal of Social Psychology* 145 (5): 531–546.
Weber, Daniel. 2018. *Bedeutung und Wirkung gruppenbezogener Identifikation*. Heidelberg: Springer VS.
Wodak, Ruth. 2007. 'Doing Europe': The discursive construction of European identities. In *Discursive constructions of identity in European politics*, ed. Richard C.M. Mole, 70–94. Houndsmills: Palgrave.
Wodak, Ruth, and Salomi Boukala. 2015. European identities and the revival of nationalism in the European Union. *Journal of Language and Politics* 14 (1): 87–109.
Zappetini, Franco. 2019. *European identities in discourse*. London: Bloomsbury.

5

Analytical Framework and Research Approach

5.1 Introduction

This chapter develops the conceptual framework for our analysis, introducing the two concepts of *communities of belonging* (COB) and *frames of reference* (FOR) as core dimensions for our understanding of the Europeanisation of football fan identity. On the basis of this conceptual framework, the rationale for case selection is detailed and each of the clubs briefly described in terms of the main criteria relevant for the research question. Finally, the methodological approach of the study, consisting of three sequential steps (qualitative analysis of online message board discussion, online survey data analysis and semi-structured in-depth interviews), is briefly described.

5.2 Analytical Framework and Operationalisation of Football Fan Identity

The aim of our analysis is to explore how attitudes and perceptions may be unconsciously shaped through exposure to football and participation in fandom, and how such latent influence may be seen reflected in supporters' articulations in an evolving fan discourse. This sort of "identity work" falls outside the scope of traditional studies of political integration, and is perhaps a more subtle form of Europeanisation than that described by (political) "pan-Europeanism". Our interest is thus focused on the question of where and how such forms of "subjective Europeanisation" might be detected.

In constructing our conceptualisation of "identity" we follow the reasoning of Brubaker and Cooper (2000) who argued that the term "identity" itself might be usefully replaced with more robust concepts such as "identifications", "self-understandings" and "commonality, connectedness and groupness" (cf. Chap. 4). Recognising the fundamentally narrative character of such identity markers, as emphasised by Eder (2009), the conceptual framework employed here to capture this subjective Europeanisation among football fans and spectators comprises two principle analytic dimensions: "communities of belonging" (COB) and "frames of reference" (FOR).

COB describes forms of identification deriving from group affiliation, dealing with questions of inclusion and exclusion, group delineation vis-à-vis other groups and perceptions of "foreignness". FOR meanwhile refers to spatial or scalar dimensions of identity work. In the particular case of football fans this includes the comparative importance accorded to different levels of competition (domestic vs. European) and the factors driving the (re)orientation of fan priorities, along with the normalisation of cross-border trips for away matches or "going Europe" (Millward 2006) as a regularised part of fandom, and the consequent acculturating experiences that accompany European travel.

5.2.1 Communities of Belonging

Under the rubric of "communities of belonging" (COB), the framework incorporates in-group and out-group recognition, related dynamics of inclusion and exclusion, perceptions of community and discord and the role of narrative-building in the process of identification. This analytical dimension allows us to explore the means by which ideas of "sameness" (Brubaker and Cooper 2000, 7) within social groups and networks are perceived and articulated by their members, and conversely how boundaries are set to exclude outsiders. This broad understanding of COB thus differs from the narrower use (only referring to *strong* bonds of commonality and mutual support) preferred by Verdasco (2018), and from Alm and Martinsson's (2016) particular application of the concept in their analysis of emotional and affective aspects of community-building among political activists. We employ COB here in a somewhat looser fashion, to encompass three questions which can be subjected to empirical assessment: first, how in-group/out-group distinctions are formed and grounded in any given social group; second, the role of both discursive and non-verbal interaction in group construction; third, who or what constitutes the "other". To this end, we seek to analyse the patterns and underlying dynamics of inclusion and exclusion displayed in the articulations of football fans, the discursive construction of fan coalitions and networks, and the incorporation of on-field and off-field events into common narratives which serve both to foster group coherence and delineate boundaries to the exclusion of other fans or fan communities.

Inclusion/Exclusion

At its core, any form of group identification is essentially predicated on the inclusion of members and exclusion of others. This section accordingly seeks to elucidate the means and criteria through which fans define the boundaries of their communities and explore the processes of inclusion and exclusion employed to define these identifications. What distinguishes an in-group from an out-group? To what extent are such definitions and distinctions shared or challenged among fans? It is crucial to remember here that processes of discursive exclusion and "othering" need not be limited to rival fans, players or officials, but may equally be applied to the supporters, players and employees of a fan's own club.

In the context of the Europeanisation of governance structures and labour markets in football, an analysis of fan reactions to the Europeanisation of player markets provides a natural starting point. Have these transformations produced a subjective acclimation to European players, coaches or rivals for instance, resulting in the normalisation of "Europeanness", or are they still ascribed a quality of "foreignness", and if so to what degree is this contested?

Relations Between Fans—Coalitions and Networks

A second facet of the concept of communities of belonging is the construction of networks and relationships among fans of different teams, transcending both domestic rivalries and international borders. Despite a naturally oppositional animus between fans of different clubs, commonality of interest nonetheless fosters the development of contacts, relations and networks that may bridge both domestic and international rivalries. In the case of individual fans this is perhaps self-evident, but networks such as Fans Against Racism in Europe (FARE) and Fan Supporters Europe (FSE, merged with Supporters Direct Europe, as of 2022) are examples of formal transnational coalition-building involving rival fan-groups across Europe.

The goal of this analysis is to examine the factors conditioning the emergence of such cross-national fan-group coalitions, and the extent to which their construction and perception is shaped by national borders. Do supporters perceive foreign fans and fan-groups as "natural" rivals or potential allies in furthering common interests, and to what extent can this be seen reflected in positive or negative references or articulations regarding fans of foreign clubs, or foreign supporters of fans' own club? The analysis seeks to parse the interactions, references and mutual characterisation between fans across borders with the aim of casting light on the nature of the trans-club and transnational communities of which supporters see themselves as a part.

Encoding of Events in Narratives
The final aspect of COB considered here is that of collective memory, and how events are incorporated into the narratives constructed by fan communities. Prior research into such narrative-construction (Bishop and Jaworski 2003; Meier et al. 2019; Pyta and Havemann 2015; Young 2007) has dealt with such events as particularly memorable matches between certain clubs, as well as high-salience tournaments such as World Cups. It is hypothesised that such processes also play a role in the subliminal identity formation in the context of communities of belonging.

Taking as a point of departure the idea that narrative framing of events drives both community-building and discord, we consider the views expressed and contested in fan-discourse regarding given events (e.g. prominent matches, competitions, championships) to elucidate the manner and means by which they are encoded into collective memories. How are particular events incorporated into narratives? Are such narratives built primarily around European or domestic competition? Our analysis concentrates on the events around which collective memories are constructed, how they are perceived and incorporated into narratives and how these processes play into community-building.

5.2.2 Frames of Reference

Processes of group formation and delineation constitute only one aspect of "subjective Europeanisation", however. A complete analysis also requires the incorporation of supporters' perception and discussion of spatial (or scalar) reference frames. Compared to prior treatment of questions encompassed by the COB-label as outlined above, scholarly attention paid to "frames of reference" in this context has been rather less stringent or systematic, albeit not entirely absent. Eder, for example, explores the existence and nature of reference objects for a collective European identity (Eder 2009, 435–38), while Mau investigates the role of an individual's perceived affiliation with a particular level (of action) for subjective identity-formation (Mau 2010, 116, 119). Yet employing the term "frames of reference" itself implies the coexistence of multiple distinct frames—local, regional, national, continental, global—and the need for greater analytic clarity in regards to the distinctions and interplay between them (cf. Deacon and Schwartz 2007, 292; Pries 2005, 174).

Taking a somewhat different approach, we use "frames of reference" as a container category, allowing us to analyse the distinct social arenas and the attendant subjective perceptions of football supporters. To this end, we consider references to scalar or spatial differentiations such as home/away, national/international and domestic/European to shed light on the distinctions and categorisations perceived and imagined by fans. Thus "frames of reference" here includes spaces for attention, action and articulation such as following football events, travel activities, tourist activities in the context of away games, or network building. Our prime focus is on the normalisation or prioritisation of "going Europe"—that is cross-border attention and action—though the FOR dimension of the analysis also incorporates fans' perspectives on national competitions, European competitions and the relative importance accorded to them.

National Competitions

The first facet of FOR is fan perspectives on domestic club competition. The national competitions (here the top-tier league and cup competition) have traditionally been regarded as the principal focus of fan attention and attachment. Domestic fixtures comprise the majority of most clubs' schedules and consequently formed the core of media and fan narratives. We seek to illuminate how fans perceive these competitions in terms of relevance and purpose (e.g. whether they are seen as the pre-eminent focus of ambition or as a route to fulfil further European aspirations). By considering fan sentiments discerned in the discourse together with investment of attention and resources through match-day activity, we hope to reach a greater understanding of how fans frame and define domestic competitions and rivalries.

European Competitions

European club competitions constitute the second aspect of FOR. In the past national domestic competition has been the norm, and European competition thus categorised as "extraordinary". But the emergence of the Champions League, and now the Europa and Europa Conference

Leagues as a de facto tiered European club league structure, could shift perceptions of European competition towards the domain of the regular (indeed even the abortive and much-derided plans for a breakaway elite European Super League are to a degree reflective of this trend).

This analysis seeks to assess the extent to which supporters perceive European competition as either normal or extraordinary, with specific regard to both their own club and, more generally, the considerations underpinning the importance supporters ascribe to European competition. Do fans see European competition as the principle forum for elite club competition, or do they see their clubs as representing their local national league on the European stage? In short, the goal is to understand how fans conceive of both the "what" and "what-for" of European competition.

Context of National and European Competitions

The final aspect of FOR considered here is fan perception of the interplay between national and European competition, focusing on the distribution of attention accorded to the different levels of competition by supporters, and how fans frame the competitions as an arena for rivalries. What shapes the development of perceived rivalry between supporters of different clubs? Are such sentiments reserved primarily for domestic or regional rivals, or is there evidence of cross-border club rivalries? A related question considers fan attention accorded to, and propensity to travel for, different sorts of fixtures. How common is cross-border travel to attend European matches compared to domestic fixtures, and how do fans understand such travel? Are such trips in effect a kind of pretextual tourism, or is the motivation primarily the match experience? These questions are considered with regard to the relation between the two levels of competition: domestic and European.

Table 5.1 summarises the analytical grid used to make the subliminal "identity work" among football fans empirically accessible. The categories are chosen to reveal whether, and to what extent, a *subjective* Europeanisation among football fans—more Europeanised mindsets among regular people driven by lifeworldly leisure activities in an increasingly Europeanised field (football)—can be said to exist.

Table 5.1 Analytical framework with the two dimensions' communities of belonging and frames of reference

Dimension	Category	Aspects
Communities of belonging (COB)	Inclusion and exclusion	In-group and out-group phenomena, targeting fans, players and other actors
	Relations among fans	Coalitions and network with fans across clubs and borders
	Encoding of events in narratives	Narrations related to event creating community and discord
Frames of reference (FOR)	National competitions	Relevance and perception of national competitions
	European competitions	Relevance and role of European competitions (representation vs. appropriate level of play)
	Context of competitions	Rivalries, travel and match attention

5.3 Eight Fan Scenes Across Europe: Case Selection and Description

Our analysis is based on data from eight football clubs from four leagues, covering Austria, France, Germany and the UK (England). We seek to discern the extent to which identities of football fans across Europe are "Europeanised", and what factors influence the Europeanisation of supporters' identities. The eight cases were selected to differ in key conditioning factors, covering three nested contexts of football spectatorship: country, league and club. On the country level, the wider public attitude towards Europe and the European Union in the respective embedding national context may influence the identities of fans. The domestic leagues differ in terms of the internationalisation of their teams, as measured in terms of the players' citizenships. The selected clubs finally differ in how often they play in European club competitions. Table 5.2 provides an overview of the cases and the key selecting factors.

Table 5.2 Overview of selected cases and data on selection criteria. Club and league data from transfermarkt.de. Internationalisation and Europeanisation of player market are calculated as the 5-year-average 2013/14–2017/18. Participation in European club competition (any stage, any competition) during the seasons 2008/09–2017/18

Club	Public attitude towards Europe (country context)	League 2018/19	Europeanisation of player market (league context)[a]			Participation in European club competitions (club context)
				League: Share of EU nationals (as against share of non-native players in total)	Club: Share of EU nationals (as against share of non-native players in total)	
Olympique Marseille	Rather Europhile	Ligue 1 (L1)	Low-medium	12% (45%)	8% (43%)	High (8/10)
FC Toulouse	Rather Europhile				7% (53%)	Low (2/10)
FC Bayern München	Rather Europhile	German Bundesliga (GBL)	Medium-high	20% (46%)	33% (49%)	High (10/10)
Hannover 96					20% (49%)	Low (2/10)
Sturm Graz	Rather Eurosceptic	Austrian Bundesliga (ABL)	Low-medium	15.5% (27%)	14% (26%)	High (7/10)
Wacker Innsbruck					11.5% (14%)	Low (0/10)
Manchester United	Rather Eurosceptic	Premier League (EPL)	High	26.5% (63%)	42.5% (60%)	High (9/10)
Newcastle United					41% (69%)	Low (1/10)

[a]Including EEA, Switzerland

5.3.1 Case Selection Logic

Our case selection along the three key conditioning factors that were assumed to be drivers of (different degrees of) Europeanisation among football fans warrants more detailed description. These factors have been selected according to the following logic:

1. *The degree of Europhilia (vs. Euroscepticism) within the respective publics in general (country context)* is to control for the wider social context within which football fans are embedded. It can be held that citizens, including football fans, are influenced by the prevailing wider societal and political discourse, which informs their attitudes to perceived in-groups/out-groups and their preferred identification patterns. "Europe"—also in terms of football—is hence likely to resonate differently in the context of Eurosceptic publics than in more Europhile publics.
2. *The degree of Europeanisation/internationalisation of player markets (league context)* was chosen in accordance with the idea that more Europeanised player markets likely contribute to a normalisation effect among fans due to the followers' and spectators' greater "exposure" to (and potential identification with) non-domestic *European* players. It could then be theorised that if fans' teams are increasingly composed of foreign-born (here, in particular, European) players, and as their favourite players are gradually more foreign Europeans, this might be assumed to enhance alternative bases of self-identification (e.g. on the basis of performance and play-style) rather than common national ancestry.
3. *The level of participation in top European club competitions (club context)* finally shaped our case selection on the basis of the idea that the level of exposure to, and the depth and frequency of, interaction with European club competition—through their clubs' participation therein—is likely to impact, for example, how attractive such competitions are considered. Again, a process of normalisation is expected among supporters whose clubs routinely perform at the European level, making European-level competition less of an exotic event for them; in that sense, the fans' frames of reference are assumed to be likely more Europeanised.

Public Attitude Towards Europe

The "Europeanness" of the public opinion in the respective countries is assumed to have a rather generic conditioning influence on how fans' attitudes towards Europe in football are shaped. We distinguish between comparatively Europhile and Eurosceptic countries. This is understood as the general public attitude towards Europe and the country's historical disposition towards the European level (here mainly the European Union as political union of the continent). On the country level, the cases represent two countries with a relatively pro-European attitude (Germany and France) and two countries with substantial reservations regarding European integration (United Kingdom and Austria). In that sense, our selection also allows the analysis of "hard cases" (Seawright and Gerring 2008), as both the UK and Austria can be seen as "belated", vacillating and critical Europeans.

The four chosen countries have a diverse history of integration into Europe (Risse 2010, 63–86). While Germany and France were among the founding members of the European Communities following the Second World War, the United Kingdom and Austria joined later and remained sceptical participants in the European project, albeit for different reasons. In the British case, Europe has served as an antithesis to "Englishness", not only in the Eurosceptic tabloid media but also among the elites, leading finally to the Brexit decision in 2016 (Goodwin and Heath 2016; Hobolt 2016; Mölder 2018). The time frame of our study covers the period immediately after the referendum, in the context of various public discourses about how and when the United Kingdom should leave the European Union.

Austria has a different but likewise ambivalent relationship with the European Union. The delicate situation of the Austrian Republic between East and West during the Cold War made them refrain from the European communities until the 1990s (Agius 2018; Bischof et al. 2002). Even after the accession of the formerly neutral country, public scepticism of the European integration persisted with the Euro critical Austrian Freedom Party performing well in national and regional elections, and even participating in governing coalitions at times (Aichholzer et al. 2014; Gavenda and Umit 2016). Open aversion to Europe culminated in 2016 with a controversial presidential election campaign between a (finally successful) Europe-friendly Green Party candidate and a candidate from the populist right openly campaigning against the European Union. As in the United Kingdom, Europe was a prevalent topic of public discussion during the time of our study, and the public controversies led to a polarisation of opinions towards the EU. In the Austrian case, this has sparked countervailing support for the EU in the country, though the still-popular radical right—embodied by the Austrian Freedom party—retains a clear anti-European position (Schmidt 2021).

Germany and France are not only founding members of the European communities, their membership in the European Union also remains largely uncontested. In Germany, membership in European communities and commitment to European integration are foundational to its political elite and in public opinion alike. Only a decade ago has a political party (with electoral successes), Alternative for Germany, been established with a decisively anti-European programme, one that remained marginal in the public discourse (Böttger and Tekin 2021) before and during the time of our study. France also has a long pro-European history, which has been somewhat tarnished by the success of the radical right (the former Front National, now renamed to Rassemblement National) that is rather critical of the EU and European integration (Lorimer 2021).

Opinion poll data largely supports our classification of the German and French publics as relatively Europhile and the Austrian and UK publics as comparatively Eurosceptic. European Social Survey data from 2016—that is the year that our qualitative discourse analysis of fan forums begins—suggests that on the question whether European unification had already gone too far (score = 0) or should go further (score = 10), that German public is the most Europhile (mean score 5.8), followed by the French (mean score 5.0) and then the Austrian (mean score 4.2) and UK public (mean score also 4.2).[1] In addition, data from Eurobarometer (GESIS 2016) suggests that 71% (58%) of German, 61% (53%) of French, 57% (41%) of Austrian and 56% (46%) of British citizens polled felt very attached or fairly attached to "Europe" (and the European

---

[1] See European Social Survey (2016). These results are by and large echoed by the European Social Survey (2018); here the mean scores were Germany, 6.2; France, 5.3; Austria, 4.8; and the UK, 4.6.

Union, respectively). Similar tendencies can be found in Eurobarometer (GESIS 2017a).[2]

Despite the ongoing political developments and shifting public opinion on Europe and the European Union in the four countries, we maintain that it makes sense to classify the four selected publics in the above manner and thus draw a distinction between two historically Eurosceptic and two Europhile societal contexts.

Degree of Europeanisation of Player Markets

The Europeanisation (or even internationalisation) of player markets is regulated by the national football associations. While nationality played a major role in team composition in the twentieth-century football, the "Bosman case" changed the rules of the games for good: The European Court of Justice (ECJ) ruled in 1995 on player regulations in European club football, abrogating a system of transfer fees to be paid for out-of-contract players on the basis that it infringed upon the right to freedom of movement under Article 48 of the Treaty of Rome. It also abolished nationality restrictions that limited the number of foreign players from the EU and affiliated territories in a team. Both practices were ruled illegal as they discriminated against EU nationals. Based on these court rulings, national associations established new regulations for the composition of teams that differ significantly across countries (Duval and van Rompuy 2016; Niemann et al. 2011b). The leagues covered in this study show a wide spectrum of new regulations, from very liberal (Germany) to comparatively restrictive rules that are just within the margins of EU law (Austria). As a result, current squads of top-level football clubs look very different than three decades ago, but the extent of Europeanisation and internationalisation across teams and leagues differs strongly (Velema 2021; Velema et al. 2020).

Our case selection covers two leagues that have comparatively less Europeanised leagues. Following *Bosman*, the Austrian Bundesliga has implemented relatively strong rules that encourage the contracting of

---

[2] Other opinion poll data indicates a somewhat smaller gap between French and Austrian publics in terms of their level of support for Europe and the European Union (cf. e.g. GESIS 2017b).

Austrian players through financial revenues for clubs who select Austrian players. Consequently, the share of non-Austrian players is comparatively low (Brand et al. 2011). The case of the French Ligue 1 is different: It also has a relatively low number of non-French players, but in this case *Bosman* had not caused any regulatory change, as there were few existing restrictions on non-French players (Ranc and Sonntag 2011). These statistics might be taken with caution, however, as Ligue 1 has featured many players from former French colonies in Africa who often have dual citizenship and carry a French passport. The share of foreign players in France from other EU countries is hence rather low (ibid.). Thus both the French and Austrian leagues provide contexts for this study with a comparatively low level of Europeanisation in domestic club squads. While Ligue 1 has had a share of 45% of non-native players—27% of whom were EU/EEA nationals—the Austrian Bundesliga has had a share of 27% non-native players—58% of whom were EU/EEA nationals—between 2013 and 2018 (cf. Table 5.2). Both leagues have, on average, featured a share of 10–15.5% "EU foreigners" among their players in the five years preceding our study.

The other two leagues have implemented rules where nationality is not directly considered, but so-called home-grown players are supported, irrespective of their nationality. In the German case, the number of foreign players is not restricted. The league responded to *Bosman* with a remarkably liberal regulatory regime, without any restriction for non-EU-nationals. Regulations relating to youth and amateur teams were only implemented after this liberalisation led to a perceived shortage of domestic talent. The English Football League (EFL) has implemented a "Home Grown Player" rule requiring at least eight players who have played for English teams for at least three years before their 21st birthday, but the nationality of these players is not relevant.[3] Consequently, the

---

[3] The EFL manages the English top leagues below the English Premier League, cf. https://www.efl.com/-more/governance/efl-rules%2D%2Dregulations/efl-regulations/section-6%2D%2D-players/ [last access: Apr 14, 2023]. The rules differ for cup matches and across the leagues. The EPL has expressed similar limitations during the past years. Due to the Brexit situation, this issue has changed considerably. Contracting of overseas (including EU) players is now much more difficult, cf. https://www.efl.com/news/2020/december/joint-fa-pl-and-efl-statement-on-access-to-talent/ [last access Apr 14, 2023]. These changes were not yet in practice during our empirical investigation.

German Bundesliga and the English Premier League have large numbers of non-national players, with a high share of foreign players coming from European countries (Niemann et al. 2011a; Poli et al. 2019). While the German Bundesliga had an average share of 46% of non-native players—43% of whom were Europeans—the English Premier League had a share of 63% non-native players—42% of whom were Europeans—during the five-year period of 2013–2018. Both leagues hence averaged between 20% and 26.5% of "EU foreigners" among all players, with individual clubs fielding substantially higher shares of non-native EU/EEA nationals.

Participation in European Competitions
Participation in European competitions is regulated by the European football organisation UEFA. Based on their club's performances in previous European competitions, the national football associations are ranked and awarded a certain number of spots in the competitions, which they fill based on the performances of the club in national competitions.[4] The European competitions are tiered, the Champions League being the highest level, the Europa League the second, with the Europa Conference League—introduced in the season 2021/22—as third level. The Champions League is further differentiated into a qualification stage and a main competition stage.

The *English Premier League* (EPL) is often seen as the most international football league in the world (see above, cf. also Millward 2011). The Football Association, the English football association that operates the EPL, is ranked among the top three of European leagues throughout the past decades.[5] The German *Bundesliga* (GBL) also ranked among the top four since 2007. Consequently, seven clubs from each league participate in European competitions each year, giving a certain prevalence to

---

[4] For more information on the ranking, see the UEFA website. The particular calculation of the coefficient changes regularly, but the basic concept is a calculation of performance of all clubs from a certain league through the past five years, cf. https://www.uefa.com/nationalassociations/uefarankings/country/ [last access: August 25, 2022].
[5] https://www.uefa.com/nationalassociations/uefarankings/country/#/yr/2022 [last access: August 25, 2022].

coverage of these competitions in their national media. The French Ligue 1 has ranked a little lower through the past 15 years, but was still rated among the top 6. The *Austrian Bundesliga* (ABL) is less prominently represented and usually ranked among the top 15. According to the distribution of spots, Ligue 1 and ABL had five or six spots for European competitions over the years in question and thus also provided their fans a reasonable amount of European competition. Table 5.2 also specifies how often the eight selected clubs appeared in European club competition. As the table shows, one top-tier club with frequent European-level exposure was chosen from each league and contrasted with one "relegation battler", for which European appearances are either extraordinary or more of a distant dream.

5.3.2 Short Description of the Eight Club Cases

The eight clubs are briefly described in the following section to situate them broadly in the context of football Europeanisation, especially regarding their location within European football and the position in their national leagues, as well as detailing the national composition of their first team's squad.

Olympique Marseille
The French Ligue 1 club *Olympique de Marseille* (OM) is located in the southern French port city Marseille. It is the only French club that has ever won the UEFA Champions League (CL), in 1993. During its heyday in the early 1990s OM was a frequent participant at the European level. It was relegated twice to the second league in 1994 and 2001 due to corruption cases, fixed matches and subsequent legal investigations. Nevertheless, it has a reputation as the most widely followed club in France (Auclair 2015). Except for two years, the club has been a top club in the Ligue 1. While it had been successful at the national level, European success has been limited in recent years. Participation in European competition was frequent, but the club often exited at very early stages of the competitions. An exception was its success in the Europa League in

2017/18, where the club lost only in the final against Atletico Madrid.[6] Its share of foreign players is a bit below the average of the French Ligue 1. Nearly half of their players from abroad also have a French passport. Only few foreign players come from a European country, as most of them carry a passport from African and Maghreb countries.[7]

FC Toulouse
The French *Toulouse Football Club* is located in the city of Toulouse. Founded in 1970, it locates its roots in a former club with the same name founded in the 1930s.[8] Over its history it has played in the first, second and third French leagues, but between 2003 and 2020 it sustained an uninterrupted run in Ligue 1. One of its greatest successes was its first and only participation in the CL qualification stages in 2007, following a very successful national season 2006/07. It is usually to be found in the lower reaches of the Ligue 1 table, with only a small chance of qualifying for European competition.[9] (During the final stages of our study in 2020, the club was relegated to Ligue 2.) The first team's share of foreign players is a bit higher than that of the average French club (cf. Table 5.2). Between 2013 and 2018, 53% of its players were foreign-born, with one-third of them having a French passport as well. Much like in the case of OM, the number of non-French players with a European passport has been rather low.[6]

FC Bayern München
FC Bayern München is the most successful German football club. It is located in Munich, Bavaria. It is a members-based sport club with 290,000 members and the self-proclaimed biggest sport club in the world.[10] It has played in the Bundesliga since 1965; it has won the national championship more than 30 times, and participates regularly in

---

[6] Cf. https://www.om.fr/fr/ere/13502/13502-le-renouveau-mccourt [last access: October 15, 2022].
[7] This refers to the 5-year average 2013/14–2017/18; all data from http://transfermarkt.de. See also Table 5.2.
[8] Cf. https://www.toulousefc.com/fr/histoire [last access: October 15, 2022]
[9] Cf. https://www.ligue1.fr/clubs/historique?id=toulouse-fc [last access: October 15, 2022].
[10] Cf. https://fcbayern.com/de/club/mitglied-werden [last access: October 15, 2022].

European competitions, in which it has likewise won several trophies. The club has a strong fan base, which is considered to be international and local at the same time: the website lists more than 4000 fan clubs from around the world, including almost all European countries.[11] At the same time, it has a vivid and active local fan base organised in the fan organisation "Club Nr. 12".[12] Regarding the composition of its squad, the club diverges a bit from the average pattern among German Bundesliga teams in terms of its high degree of Europeanisation. Around half of its first team players are foreigners, and more than two-thirds of them come from other European countries.[6]

Hannover 96

The club *Hannover 96* (H96) is located in the capital of Lower Saxony, Hanover. The club has played in the German Bundesliga for most of its history, but in recent years it spent a few seasons in the second league. (As of 2023, it yet has to return to the first league.) H96 was usually positioned in the middle to lower ranks of the Bundesliga with one exception—the club qualified for the Europa League for two seasons in a row from 2010 to 2012.[13] The composition of its first team is fairly representative of the German Bundesliga—the share of players with a non-German passport is 50%, and less than half of them come from another European country.

Sturm Graz

The Austrian Bundesliga club *SK Sturm Graz* is located in Graz, Styria. The club has played in the first Austrian league since 1965 and has regularly participated in European competitions (at least on the level of qualification matches) throughout (Behr 2008). It can be considered a typical club for the Austrian Bundesliga in its share of foreign players. On

---

[11] Cf. https://fanclub.fcbayern.com/fanclubs/index.jsp?lang=de#/fanclub-suche [last access: October 15, 2022].
[12] Cf. https://www.clubnr12.org [last access: October 15, 2022]
[13] Cf. https://www.hannover96.de/ueber-96/historie/erfolge/europa-league.html [last access: October 15, 2022].

average, throughout the years 2013–2018, the squad featured a share of 26% non-Austrian players, with 55% of them from European (EU-28 and EEA) countries. As certain financial benefits as a club are contingent on minutes played by Austrian nationals in the league (cf. Chap. 2), the numbers for Sturm Graz present an uneven picture. While it fielded Austrian players 83% of the time during the first half of the 2016/17 season (rank 4 in the league), it ranked only second to last in the first half of the 2019/20 season, with a mere 60% of fielding time devoted to Austrian players.[14]

Wacker Innsbruck
The second Austrian club, *FC Wacker Innsbruck*, is located in Innsbruck, Tyrol. It has a turbulent history that covers successful times in European club football as well as, most recently, the forced relegation to the fourth highest division, the Tirol-Liga, because of massive financial problems and, ultimately, insolvency. Technically the current club was founded in 2002, but many consider it the successor of FC Wacker Innsbruck, founded in 1913.[15] It has played in the Austrian Bundesliga between 2004/05 and 2018/19, with a four-year stint at the second league in-between. Its European appearances date back to the 1970s, which makes the club the only one in our sample with no current exposure to European-level football. The club's share of Austrian player-minutes during the Bundesliga season 2018/19 was 71%, the fourth lowest share in the domestic league.[16] However, this must be interpreted against the, on average, rather low number of foreign-born players in its ranks in the five years before (cf. Table 5.2).

---

[14] Cf. http://oefbl.at ("Zuschauer, Österreicher-Topf & Spielfeldreporting—Organisatorischer Rückblick auf die Herbstsaison 2019"); https://www.bundesliga.at/de/redaktion/news/17-18/tbl/halbzeitbilanz-der-tipico-bundesliga/ [last access: October 17, 2018].
[15] Cf. https://www.fc-wacker-innsbruck.at/verein-2/geschichte.html [last access: September 18, 2022]
[16] Cf. https://www.oefbl.at/oefbl/aussendungen/mediainfo/2018/zuschauer-oe-topf-tbl18-19/ [last access: September 18, 2022].

Manchester United

The Premier League club *Manchester United* is based in Manchester, England. It is one of the biggest European football clubs, having successfully competed both at the national and European levels for several decades. It has won more trophies than any other English football team and has been identified as the most valuable football club in the world in two consecutive years in 2017 and 2018 (Armstrong 2018). It had a share of 60% non-English[17] players (2013–18). European players dominate here. Their share is much higher than in the EPL in general. The fan base also reaches far beyond England—the club has supporters all over the world (cf. Millward 2011, 76–115; Pearson 2012, 74–9). Though the club is characterised as "global", the dominance of Europe stands out. Almost half of the official supporter clubs outside the United Kingdom are located in European countries. This indicates that European fans shape a relevant part of the club's global image.

Newcastle United

The Premier League club *Newcastle United (NUFC)* is based in Newcastle, England. It has a long history in Premier League football, missing only three seasons in the top flight since the launch of the EPL at the end of the twentieth century and 2022. During the period of this study, the club played one season in the second league and all other seasons in the Premier League. While its most successful times have been passed,[18] it still draws upon a large fan community, especially in the area around Newcastle (Clarke 2006). The club has a strong regional imprint, but also supporters' clubs all around the world (Jones 2007). In view of its squad composition 2013–18, NUFC is very Europeanised. In this five-year period, 69% of its players had a non-UK citizenship, almost two-thirds of them coming from another European country.

---

[17] As the nationality in football is considered on the level of the football associations and not on the country level, players in the United Kingdom can be classified as being English (rather than British). This matters for eligibility to play in the respective national team and is well known among fans.

[18] Having said that, at the time this manuscript is going to the press (Spring 2023), the club is seriously competing for a Champions League ticket for the 2023–24 season.

5.4 A Three-Step Approach to Study Europe on Fans' Minds

We approach our research object by using a multi-method approach. The triangulation of data obtained through discourse analysis, survey research and in-depth interviews in combination with a comparative analysis (three sets of four paired comparisons, cf. Chap. 6; on the method cf. Tarrow 2010) seeks to answer our main research question: To what extent are identities of football fans across Europe "Europeanised"?

Here, our definition of "fandom" includes all those who articulate an interest in following a football team, be it occasionally or on a regular basis, passively watching or actively supporting a team (TV spectators, casual stadium visitors, organised supporters, self-styled ultras etc.). In that sense, we do not distinguish a priori between different intensities of following the sport, different degrees of attachment, different attitudes or milieu-based behaviours as many of the classifications so far have done (cf. Chap. 3). Nor do we pre-select according to various degrees of awareness of, or expectations towards, governance actors or stakeholders as more recent studies have done. Instead, we strive for an inclusive, all-encompassing understanding of "football fandom" to capture any Europeanising effects across all strata of those who are emotionally (and otherwise) invested in the game.

Our research strategy presents a mixed-method approach, combining different methods to assess the same phenomenon from various angles. Three methodological tools will be employed in the analysis of our research question: (1) a qualitative discourse analysis, (2) an online survey and (3) semi-structured/narrative interviews. Finally, structured paired comparisons will be carried out, in particular on the fan discourse and the interview material, in order to dig deeper into the role of the influencing factors on our context levels (club, league and country). Figure 5.1 illustrates the research strategy and the main aims of each step.

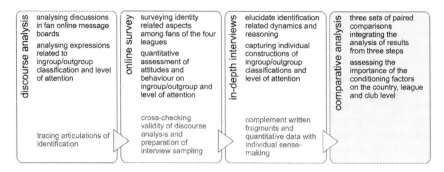

Fig. 5.1 Sequence of methodological steps in the mixed-methods research design

5.4.1 Qualitative Analysis of Online Message Boards Discussions

As a first step, our study presents an analysis of discussions in online message boards that relate to identity aspects and Europeanisation. We applied qualitative content analysis (using Atlas.ti software) to texts produced by fans in club-related forums that are publicly available on the internet (readable without registration). Such and other fan-made online publications heighten the discursive dimension of fandom by providing spaces where any fan can debate issues. Football supporters make extensive use of online communication for discussions of issues relevant to the club as well as for planning of travel, ticketing and other aspects of fandom, as previous research has established (Mcmanus 2015; Pearson, R. 2010; Pearson, G., 2012). Moreover, club-related forums are independent of the club and other gatekeepers such as editors or journalists. Usually, every registered user can contribute. This makes those forums a particularly *open* space for discussions.

The nature of publicly available forums (purely private forums are not the subject of this study) is that everyone can read the messages and follow the discussion without registration. Registration does not require any credentials, and hence the use of fake names is widespread (Cleland 2014, 417). On a positive note, the resulting "anonymity" lowers the threshold for expressing sentiments, especially those that contradict common social norms. However, the same anonymity of the participants and the lack of reliable information about the characteristics of the supporters—such as gender, age and location—make it impossible to claim representativeness. This has been previously elaborated in similar analyses (Cleland 2014; Millward 2006).

A major advantage of analysing message board discussions is the opportunity to access fan discussions without intervening in the field, making it a particularly useful approach for observing subtle aspects of identification. Other researchers have successfully chosen intervening methods to analyse such message boards, that is by starting one's own thread as a researcher to study football fans' attitudes and expressions of racism (Cleland 2014). Our aim was to prevent any bias caused by a researcher's intervention (Millward 2008, 307). While an open intervention allows participants to express an account of their honest feelings or opinions anonymously, our approach allows us to access more covert or even subconscious expressions of attitudes and self-understandings. To minimise any potential harm to the discussants (cf. Cleland et al. 2020, 46–8) who usually did not knowingly contribute to research purposes, the names of the users are not revealed. Quotations are kept to a minimum to restrict the opportunities to identify individual posters using search engines.

As a final step before starting the collection and analysis of our data, we identified one online fan forum (usually the largest) for each club.[19] We selected two league seasons—2016/17 and 2017/18—and sampled those threads which alluded to discussions about rivals, competitions and players/transfers and performance. As a check, we performed a term search on "Europe", "European", "[*name of respective country*]", but also football-related terms such as "UEFA", "[*name of respective league*]", "Champions League" and "Europa League"; this confirmed that these keywords and phrases were mostly found in threads (grouped messages under a joint headline) covering two topics: discussions about rivals and competitions, and transfer discussions. In total, our material covered 85 threads across the selected forums, with 74,422 individual posts.

---

[19] In one case (Wacker Innsbruck), two forums were selected, as there were two equally large ones, which—compared to the other clubs—were relatively small.

5.4.2 Online Survey Among Football Fans in the Four Leagues

Our analysis here is based on data from an online survey covering football fans from all clubs playing in the first leagues of Austria (Bundesliga), England (Premier League), France (Ligue 1) and Germany (Bundesliga) during the season 2018/19. It was conducted between March and July 2019. In total, 2950 fans completed the survey.

The survey addressed anyone who considered him-/herself to be a fan of a professional football club playing in one of the four leagues during the time of the survey. Our sample for this survey stage was thus broader, as we did not select particular clubs from the first leagues but rather targeted fans from all teams in all four relevant leagues/country contexts under study. It was disseminated through social media, via email, to all relevant clubs and shared numerous times by different actors, fan groups or clubs through social media. Though it cannot claim representativeness of the fans of each club, it provides a starting point for analysing the opinions of fans on important aspects of the game. The return overview (Table 5.3) shows the distribution of responses across the four leagues and the mean return per club.

How far the advertising posts for the survey were shared on social media by others and which clubs supported the research via distributing the call for participation were beyond the control of the researchers. As a result, the distribution of fans differs according to leagues and club types. The table shows that participation in the survey is unequal across the four leagues, with most responses coming from supporters of teams in the German Bundesliga. The distribution of fans across clubs within the leagues is rather biased towards clubs that frequently participate in European competition. Across the leagues, there are twice as many respondents who follow

Table 5.3 Survey responses, per league and total as well as mean return per club

League	N	Share	Club mean	Share of women
Bundesliga (AT)	256	9%	21.3	4%
Bundesliga (DE)	1562	53%	86.8	13%
Ligue 1	505	17%	25.2	7%
Premier League	627	21%	31.4	5%
Total	2950	100%	42.1	10%

a team that frequently plays in the European competitions (at least 8 appearances throughout the past 10 years). This likely has an influence on the interpretation of the results, as we can expect the respondents to be exposed to European competitions to an above average extent.

5.4.3 In-depth Interviews

The final methodological step consisted of conducting in-depth interviews with committed football fans from the six clubs in Austria, Germany and England: Wacker Innsbruck, Sturm Graz, FC Bayern Munich, Hannover 96, Newcastle United and Manchester United. The aim of this last step was to get a better understanding of individual logics and perspectives on Europeanisation of football and how it shapes fan experiences at the very individual level.[20]

The participants for the interviews were recruited through social media, during test matches, and using snowball sampling techniques. Especially for the latter, fan clubs were approached using the information available on club's websites and on the internet, on fan websites and online message boards. The final interview partners were selected to cover a maximal range of age and fandom intensity (frequency of visiting matches and involvement in fan activities). In total 63 interviews were conducted; depending on the preferred language of our interviewees, they were conducted in English or German. All interviews were based on a semi-structured questionnaire around the issues of rivalries, national and European competition as well as player transfers and attitudes towards other fans and players. The semi-structured approach allowed to focus on these pre-selected issues while there was enough room for individual narrations and specific topics that arose during the interview.[21]

The data was then transcribed and analysed using qualitative content analysis (Gläser and Laudel 2009; Schreier 2012) based on the analytical framework with the two pillars: "communities of belonging" and "frames of reference". The obtained data was therefore coded according to the

---

[20] Interviews with supporters of the two French clubs could not be included due to circumstances at the time of the interviews, along with restrictions imposed by Covid and the elusive nature of French supporters (see Chap. 9).
[21] A table with a full list of pseudonymised interviews is provided in Chap. 8.

framework and later summarised to extract the key content for each interview in each dimension. In a second step, the propositions were unified for each club to identify club-specific results for each of the dimensions. Based on these club-level results, paired comparisons again were possible and performed across the three assumed influencing factors.

5.5 Conclusion: Reflections on the Benefits of the Mixed Methods Approach

Our idea was that the different methods should complement each other and lead to a high degree of cross-fertilisation. First, weaknesses of a single method are mitigated. For example, discourse analysis balances the reliance on research subjects' self-reflections (and the potential biases resulting from this), which come with survey and interview research. Instead, through discourse analysis we aimed to trace perceptions and views in action rather than fans' self-reflections concerning their views. The survey was to compensate a potential major weakness of both discourse analysis and interviewing in that is it less prone to "confirmation bias" (Oswald and Groesjaen 2012). It also balances "evasive answer bias" that may be a problem in interviewing (Warner 1965). Semi-structured interviews provided the opportunity to, first, check (and follow-up) directly with supporters and to enquire certain aspects that remained vague from the analysis of discourse and survey data. Second, they allowed us to go into more detail and uncover specific (causal) mechanisms, which the other methods fail to do.

Second, our mixed methods approach should strengthen the validity of findings: discourse analysis, the online survey and interviews all seek inferences on the question concerning the degree to which (certain) football fans' identities are Europeanised. By assembling data on the same questions, these methods cross-check the findings of any single method and thus increase the validity of findings. While discourse analysis traced aspects relevant to communities of belonging and frames of reference in supporters' un-prodded articulations, the other two methods specifically prodded subjects in a one-way (survey) or interactive (interviews) fashion.

Third, by using these different methods, the overall number of observations per aspect could be increased (and thus also the generalisability of our findings). In particular, the online survey allowed us to enlarge the size of the targeted population and data points attained through discourse analysis and interviews. Although there are restrictions in terms of the extent to which results obtained from non-probability sampling can be generalised, the online survey should still allow us to extend the scope of our findings by increasing our data points. Finally, adding comparative analysis to the canon of methodologies allowed us to extend our inquiry to the question of which factors in particular do condition Europeanised identities.

References

Agius, Christine. 2018. Reinventing neutrality — the case of Austria, Finland and Sweden and the European Union. In *Europe: Rethinking the boundaries*, ed. Philomena Murray and Leslie Holmes, 155–173. London etc.: Routledge.

Aichholzer, Julian, Sylvia Kritzinger, Markus Wagner, and Eva Zeglovits. 2014. How has radical right support transformed established political conflicts? The case of Austria. *West European Politics* 37 (1): 113–137. https://doi.org/10.1080/01402382.2013.814956.

Alm, Erika, and Lena Martinsson. 2016. The rainbow flag as friction: Transnational, imagined communities of belonging among Pakistani LGBTQ activists. *Culture Unbound* 8 (3): 218–239. https://doi.org/10.3384/cu.2000.1525.1683218.

Armstrong, Marc. 2018. Manchester United remain Europe's most valuable football club. *Euronews*, May 23, 2018. https://www.euronews.com/2018/05/23/manchester-united-remain-europe-s-most-valuable-football-club

Auclair, Philippe. 2015. Only in Marseille: Where ultras rule and temptation is never far away. *The Guardian*, January 6, 2015. https://www.theguardian.com/football/blog/2015/jan/06/marseille-ultras-rule-temptation-never-far-away

Behr, Martin. 2008. *Wir sind Sturm! 100 Jahre Grazer Fußballgeschichte*. Graz: SK Puntigamer Graz.

Bischof, Günter, Anton Pelinka, and Michael Gehler. 2002. *Austria in the European Union*. New Brunswick: Transaction Publishers.

Bishop, Hywel, and Adam Jaworski. 2003. We beat 'em': Nationalism and the hegemony of homogeneity in the British press reportage of Germany versus England during Euro 2000. *Discourse & Society* 14 (3): 243–271. https://doi.org/10.1177/09579265030143001.

Böttger, Katrin, and Funda Tekin. 2021. Germany: Eurosceptics and the Illusion of an Alternative. In *Euroscepticism and the future of Europe: Views from the capitals*, ed. Michael Kaeding, Johannes Pollak, and Paul Schmidt, 51–53. Cham: Springer International Publishing. https://doi.org/10.1007/978-3-030-41272-2_13.

Brand, Alexander, Arne Niemann, and Georg Spitaler. 2011. The Europeanisation of Austrian Football: Historically Determined and Modern Processes. In *The transformation of European football: A case of Europeanisation?* ed. Borja Garcia, Wyn Grant, and Arne Niemann, pp. 171–186. Manchester: Manchester University Press.

Brand, Alexander, Arne Niemann, and Georg Spitaler. 2013. The two-track Europeanization of football. *International Journal of Sport Policy and Politics* 5 (1): 95–112. https://doi.org/10.1080/19406940.2012.665381.

Brubaker, Rogers, and Frederick Cooper. 2000. Beyond 'identity'. *Theory and Society* 29 (1): 1–47. https://doi.org/10.1023/A:1007068714468.

Clarke, Ged. 2006. *Newcastle United: Fifty years of hurt: A bittersweet story of near triumph and disaster*. Edinburgh: Mainstream.

Cleland, Jamie. 2014. Racism, football fans, and online message boards. *Journal of Sport and Social Issues* 38 (5): 415–431. https://doi.org/10.1177/0193723513499922.

Cleland, Jamie, Kevin Dixon, and Daniel Kilvington. 2020. *Online research and methods in sport studies*. London: Routledge.

Deacon, Bernhard, and Sharron Schwartz. 2007. Cornish identities and migration: A multi-scalar approach. *Global Networks* 7 (3): 289–306. https://doi.org/10.1111/j.1471-0374.2007.00170.x.

Duval, Antoine, and Ben van Rompuy, eds. 2016. *The legacy of Bosman*. The Hague: T.M.C. Asser Press.

Eder, Klaus. 2009. A theory of collective identity: Making sense of the debate on a 'European identity'. *European Journal of Social Theory* 12 (4): 427–447. https://doi.org/10.1177/1368431009345050.

European Social Survey. 2016. ESS round 8 – 2016. Welfare attitudes, Attitudes to climate change. Data file edition 2.2. Norwegian Centre for Research Data – Data Archive and distributor of ESS data for ESS ERIC. https://doi.org/10.21338/NSD-ESS8-2016.

———. 2018. ESS round 9 – 2018. Timing of life, Justice and fairness. Data file edition 3.1. Norwegian Centre for Research Data – Data Archive and distributor of ESS data for ESS ERIC. https://doi.org/10.21338/NSD-ESS9-2018.

Gavenda, Mario, and Resul Umit. 2016. The 2016 Austrian presidential election. *Regional & Federal Studies* 26 (3): 419–432. https://doi.org/10.1080/13597566.2016.1206528.

GESIS. 2016. Eurobarometer 86.2. November 2016. https://www.gesis.org/en/eurobarometer-data-service/survey-series/standard-special-eb/study-overview/eurobarometer-862-za6788-november-2016. Accessed 19 Dec 2022.

———. 2017a. Eurobarometer 87.3. May 2017. https://www.gesis.org/en/eurobarometer-data-service/survey-series/standard-special-eb/study-overview/eurobarometer-873-za6863-may-2017. Accessed 19 Dec 2022.

———. 2017b. Eurobarometer 88.3. November 2017. https://www.gesis.org/en/eurobarometer-data-service/survey-series/standard-special-eb/study-overview/eurobarometer-883-za6928-november-2017. Accessed 19 Dec 2022.

Gläser, Jochen, and Grit Laudel. 2009. *Experteninterviews und Qualitative Inhaltsanalyse als Instrumente Rekonstruierender Untersuchungen.* Wiesbaden: VS Verlag für Sozialwissenschaften.

Goodwin, Matthew J., and Oliver Heath. 2016. The 2016 referendum, Brexit and the left behind. *The Political Quarterly* 87 (3): 323–332. https://doi.org/10.1111/1467-923X.12285.

Hobolt, Sara B. 2016. The Brexit vote: A divided nation, a divided continent. *Journal of European Public Policy* 23 (9): 1259–1277. https://doi.org/10.1080/13501763.2016.1225785.

Jones, Matt. 2007. Newcastle United supporters club. *The Football Network*, April 17, 2007. https://www.thefootballnetwork.net/main/s70/st87767.htm. Accessed 18 Sept 2022.

Lorimer, Marta. 2021. What do they talk about when they talk about Europe? Euro-ambivalence in far right ideology. *Ethnic and Racial Studies* 44 (11): 2016–2033. https://doi.org/10.1080/01419870.2020.1807035.

Mau, Steffen. 2010. *Social transnationalism: Lifeworlds beyond the nation-state.* London: Routledge.

McManus, John. 2015. Driven to distraction: Turkish diaspora football supporters, new media and the politics of place-making. *Sociological Research Online* 20 (2): 159–172. https://doi.org/10.5153/sro.3588.

Meier, Henk Erik, Till Utesch, Charlotte Raue, Christina Uhlenbrock, Nabila Chababi, and Bernd Strauss. 2019. Fan identification and national identity. *Sport in Society* 22 (3): 476–498. https://doi.org/10.1080/17430437.2018.1504771.

Millward, Peter. 2006. 'We've all got the bug for Euro-aways': What fans say about European football club competition. *International Review for the Sociology of Sport* 41 (3–4): 375–393. https://doi.org/10.1177/1012690207077706.
———. 2008. The rebirth of the football fanzine. *Journal of Sport and Social Issues* 32 (3): 299–310. https://doi.org/10.1177/0193723508319718.
———. 2011. *The global football league: Transnational networks, social movements and sport in the new media age.* Houndsmills: Palgrave.
Mölder, Holger. 2018. British approach to the European Union: From Tony Blair to David Cameron. In *Brexit: History, reasoning and perspectives*, ed. David Ramiro Troitiño, Tanel Kerikmäe, and Archil Chochia, 153–173. Cham: Springer International Publishing. https://doi.org/10.1007/978-3-319-73414-9_9.
Niemann, Arne, Alexander Brand, and Georg Spitaler. 2011a. The Europeanisation of football: Germany and Austria compared. In *The making and mediatization of modern sport in Europe: States, media and markets 1950–2010*, ed. C. Young, D. Holt, and Alan Tomlinson, 187–204. London: Routledge.
Niemann, Arne, Borja García, and Wyn Grant, eds. 2011b. *The transformation of European football: Towards the Europeanisation of the national game.* Manchester: Manchester University Press.
Oswald, Margit E., and Stefan Groesjean. 2012. Confirmation bias. In *Cognitive illusions. A handbook on fallacies and biases in thinking, judgement and memory*, ed. Rüdiger F. Pohl, 91–108. London: Psychology Press. https://doi.org/10.4324/9780203720615-10.
Pearson, Roberta. 2010. Fandom in the digital era. *Popular Communication* 8 (1): 84–95. https://doi.org/10.1080/15405700903502346.
Pearson, Geoff. 2012. *An ethnography of English football fans: Cans, cops and carnivals.* Manchester: Manchester University Press.
Poli, Raffaele, Loïc Ravenel, and Roger Besson. 2019. Mapping the origin of English Premier League players (2009–2019). *CIES Football Observatory Monthly Report*, No. 43. http://www.football-observatory.com/IMG/sites/mr/mr43/en/. Accessed 19 Dec 2022.
Pries, Ludger. 2005. Configurations of geographic and societal spaces: A sociological proposal between 'methodological nationalism' and the 'spaces of flows'. *Global Networks* 5 (2): 167–190. https://doi.org/10.1111/j.1471-0374.2005.00113.x.
Pyta, Wolfram, and Nils Havemann, eds. 2015. *European football and collective memory. Football research in an Enlarged Europe.* London: Palgrave.

Ranc, David, and Albrecht Sonntag. 2011. France: A case of UEFA-isation? In *The transformation of European football*, ed. Arne Niemann, Borja García, and Wyn Grant, 97–114. Manchester: Manchester University Press.

Risse, Thomas. 2010. *A community of Europeans? Transnational identities and public spheres*. Ithaca: Cornell University Press.

Schmidt, Paul. 2021. Austria: Taking a walk on the wild side. In *Euroscepticism and the future of Europe: Views from the capitals*, ed. Michael Kaeding, Johannes Pollak, and Paul Schmidt, 5–8. Cham: Springer International Publishing. https://doi.org/10.1007/978-3-030-41272-2_2.

Schreier, Margrit. 2012. *Qualitative content analysis in practice*. Los Angeles etc.: SAGE.

Seawright, Jason, and John Gerring. 2008. Case selection techniques in case study research: A menu of qualitative and quantitative options. *Political Research Quarterly* 61 (2): 294–308. https://doi.org/10.1177/1065912907313077.

Tarrow, Sidney. 2010. The strategy of paired comparison: Toward a theory of practice. *Comparative Political Studies* 43 (2): 230–259. https://doi.org/10.1177/0010414009350044.

Velema, Thijs A. 2021. Globalization and player recruitment: How teams from European top leagues broker migration flows of footballers in the global transfer network. *International Review for the Sociology of Sport* 56 (4): 493–513. https://doi.org/10.1177/1012690220919676.

Velema, Thijs A., Han-Yu Wen, and Yu-Kai Zhou. 2018. Global value added chains and the recruitment activities of European professional football teams. *International Review for the Sociology of Sport* 55 (2): 127–146. https://doi.org/10.1177/1012690218796771.

Velema, Thijs A., Han-Yu Wen, and Yu-Kai Zhou. 2020. Global Value Added Chains and the Recruitment Activities of European Professional Football Teams. *International Review for the Sociology of Sport* 55(2): 127–46.

Verdasco, Andrea. 2018. Communities of belonging in the temporariness of the Danish Asylum System: Shalini's anchoring points. *Journal of Ethnic and Migration Studies* 45 (9): 1439–1457. https://doi.org/10.1080/1369183X.2018.1443393.

Warner, Stanley L. 1965. Randomized response: A survey technique for eliminating evasive answer bias. *Journal of the American Statistical Association* 60 (309): 63–69. https://doi.org/10.1080/01621459.1965.10480775.

Young, Christopher. 2007. Two world wars and one world cup: Humour, trauma and the asymmetric relationship in Anglo-German football. *Sport in History* 27 (1): 1–23. https://doi.org/10.1080/17460260701231026.

6

Identity Work in Online Fan Forum Discussions

6.1 Introduction

Our first empirical chapter describes and analyses the discourses among fans of the eight selected clubs. Based on the results of a thorough qualitative discourse analysis of relevant articulations and posts on online message boards, we aim to discern variations in how fans position themselves towards the Europeanisation of football, as well as the factors which shape such positioning. Our enquiry is structured around three sets of four paired comparisons of clubs in four different European countries. This research design allows us to control for three main conditioning factors influencing fan attitudes towards the supposedly more Europeanised aspects of the game: the club level (sporting success), the league level (Europeanisation of player markets) and the embedding societal context (extent of Euroscepticism).

Our analysis reveals that the factor which carries the most explanatory power is the extent of the fan's chosen club's participation in, and exposure to, European-level competition. Other variables—that is different degrees of a Europeanisation of player markets (and consequent varying normalisation effects stemming from cosmopolitan squad composition) and especially the extent to which the surrounding societies are

Eurosceptic—seem to matter less. For European identity studies, the work corroborates that a lifeworld arena such as football can foster Europeanised identifications, even in the face of, for instance, strong anti-EU sentiments in the embedding sociopolitical environment.

6.2 Structured Paired Comparisons of Football Fan Discourses

As elaborated in Chap. 5, we created a purposive sample of football clubs and their respective fan scenes across Europe. Our choice of clubs was designed to afford leverage to find out which of the presumed drivers of a Europeanisation of mindsets among football fans would have the most shaping power: frequent exposure to European-level football (flowing from their sporting success); normalisation of ever more internationalised and Europeanised rosters and players markets; or the political climate in the societal environments in which particular clubs and fan communities are embedded. Through this purposive sampling we ended up with eight cases: Bayern München (hereinafter Munich) and Hannover 96 from Germany; Manchester United and Newcastle United from the UK/England; Sturm Graz and Wacker Innsbruck from Austria; and Olympique Marseille and Toulouse FC from France.

To discern predictors of Europeanisation among football fans in the above-mentioned sense we first turned to online message boards, taking texts produced by fans themselves—articulations of their patterns of identification, their self-understandings and their delineation of commonalities and groupness—as raw material for our investigation. As sketched out in Chap. 5, such club-related online forums have the advantage of being accessible to anyone who seeks to affiliate oneself with a club. They are publicly available on the internet and readable without registration, and they are independent of the club and other gatekeepers such as editors or journalists. This combination of features makes them particularly promising resources for tapping unfiltered, everyday and even unconscious articulations of Europe among fans.

Based on these preliminary ideas, we identified one online fan forum for each club (usually the largest, and in the case of Wacker Innsbruck two equally small ones) and selected a time frame of two league seasons—2016/17 and 2017/18. From all the text within this time period, we sampled those threads which included discussions about rivals, competitions, players/transfers and sporting performance in particular. As a robustness check of the thread selection, we performed a term search on "Europe", "European", "[*name of respective country*]", but also football-related terms such as "UEFA", "[*name of respective league*]", "Champions League" and "Europa League". In total, our material covered 85 threads across the selected forums, with 74.422 individual posts.

This material we then treated with the help of a refined analytic grid and the software Atlas.ti, a computer-based tool to engage in thorough and systematic qualitative discourse analysis. First, we further operationalised the two lead concepts of "communities of belonging" (COB) and "frames of reference" (FOR) (cf. Chaps. 4 and 5 for more detail). Table 6.1 solidifies these operationalisation efforts. It not only displays the selected categories (horizontally), with which we analysed online fan discourse, but also lists those values which would have allowed us to code references and articulations as "fully Europeanised" (vertically).

Whereas some textbooks hold that Atlas.ti is superior for achieving particular depth of textual analysis—for example, because it allows for implementation of a particularly sophisticated type of qualitative discourse analysis (cf. Woolf and Silver 2018)—in light of our research objectives, we were specifically attracted by three features. First, it not only lends support in collecting and storing relevant data, it supports the user in what is called an NCT approach: noticing, then collecting, then thinking (cf. Friese 2014, 3, 12–22). Second, it allows for the in vivo coding of material in a very intuitive manner (ibid., 92–3); instead of merely searching text for what is expected to be found, the coding scheme can grow organically as the texts analysed produce new yet relevant articulations. Instead of only imposing pre defined categories as such depicted in Table 6.1, it thus allowed for the extension of the analytic grid if necessary. Finally, the visualisation component of Atlas.ti substantially

Table 6.1 The analytic grid for online discourse analysis: categories of comparison

Inclusion	Exclusion	Relation to other Fans	Events as narratives	European competition	National competition	Context (travel, attention, rivals)
The **club** defines "itself" as orientated towards "Europe".	The **club** defines "the other" due to their opposition to "Europe" (Cup, Players, Fans).	There are strong **relations** among fans whose club play (regularly) in ECCs.	There are specific positive Europe related **narratives** constituting the self-understand of the club.	ECCs are more **valuable** than national competitions.	National competitions are less **valuable** than ECCs.	"Europe" (Player, Fans, Cups) attracts more **attention** then national competitions.
Players are included by their good performance regardless their origin.	**Players** are excluded due to their poor performances and under no circumstances due to their origin.			Playing in ECCs is the possibility to **compete** among European top clubs.	National competitions are only a **necessary evil**	Fans do regularly **travel** in Europe for attending away matches.

Fans are included when they show their commitment to their club and its values regardless their origin. There are other criteria related to Europe constituting "us".	Fans are excluded due to their behaviour ("event fans") and under no circonstances to their origin. There are no other criteria related to Europe excluding "them" from "us".	**Representing** the nation in Europe is only a minor incentive while playing in ECCs.	National competitions are considered as **normal**	The main **rival** plays in ECCS.

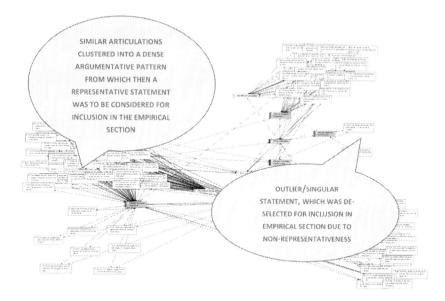

Fig. 6.1 Coded fan articulations, emerging argumentative patterns in our software-based analysis, and the non-random choice of representative examples (here: articulations of ManU fans on a European frame of reference)

supported our search for patterns, or focal points, in debate (cf. Fig. 6.1, see also Konopásek 2007). Using Atlas.ti for a systematic analysis and coding of the large swaths of text and articulations, it was therefore possible to spot recurring argumentative patterns, to visualise clusters of ideas and then also to select quotes *representative* of distinct discourses instead of randomly using supporters' quotes for illustrative purposes.

We are not aiming to merely produce an analysis of eight separate fan discourses, however. To make the most out of our comparative analysis, three sets of four paired comparisons (of fans' discourses and attitudes) have been formed. Structured paired comparisons (Tarrow 2010, 2021) between those sets, making up for twelve pairs in total, have been conducted to identify the (relative) influence of each condition on the dependent variable, that is fans' degree of Europeanisation. We consciously juxtaposed articulations of fans from two clubs in a dyadic fashion, according to a specific variation logic. We thus compared fan discourses along the axes of more versus less Europeanised players markets; more or less/no recent exposure to European-level football; and being embedded in more Euro-friendly versus more Eurosceptic societies, while controlling the variation in the two other domains, respectively. Thus, when we pitched fan discourses against one another along the axis of more or less Europeanised player markets, we formed pairs of teams similarly positioned or shaped in terms of the two other factors. This resulted in the following three clusters of four paired comparisons of fan groups and their discourse:

* 1st Cluster of paired comparisons: variation in Europeanisation of player markets (controlling for: level of participation in European club competitions and public attitudes towards Europe/the EU)
  – For example, fans of Bayern Munich versus those of Olympique Marseille.
* 2nd Cluster of paired comparisons: variation in level of participation in European club competitions (controlling for Europeanisation of player markets and public attitudes towards Europe/the EU)
  – For example, fans of Manchester United versus those of Newcastle United.
* 3rd Cluster of paired comparisons: variation in public attitude towards Europe/the EU (controlling for Europeanisation of player markets and level of participation in European club competitions)
  – For example, fans of Wacker Innsbruck versus those of Hannover 96.

6.2.1 The Europeanisation of Player Markets as a Conditioning Factor

Are fans of highly Europeanised clubs (fielding many non-national European players on a regular basis) embedded in similarly Europhile publics approaching the game differently? We assumed that the composition of player markets in domestic leagues might affect fan attitudes towards "foreign" European players fielded by their respective home team. A high percentage of foreign-born European players, as facilitated in general by the free movement of players within Europe, might mitigate the perception of them being "alien". Have fans of sides in more cosmopolitan leagues thus become accustomed to Europeanised squads in line with the overall composition of the league's player market while nationality plays more of a role in less diverse (Europeanised) league settings?

Bayern Munich Versus Olympique Marseille (OM)

Tracking debates and discussions on player transfers and potential signings, and staff policy in general, revealed interesting differences between supporters of Bayern Munich and Olympique Marseille, though less along the lines of the normalisation thesis. Among Bayern fans, exclusion indeed often happened on the basis of performance, play style (too defensive), a concurring self-definition of attractive (offensive) play and a player's potential to develop and fit into the perceived team structures. Players were more often than not discussed in terms of merit and not origin. Exemplary is a quote from a thread discussing future transfer strategy, which introduces four players and one coach from other European country contexts without referring to anyone's place of origin even once:

> Morata can also play [outside left]. In addition, Lewa may switch to the left and Morata and Lewa practice switching positions. [...] At some point, the time [for coach Ancelotti] will be over and Robberuy's [Robben and Ribery] time can end very abruptly, then every [Bayern Munich] fan would be happy if we had a striker like Morata on board. (ID 154:102, 28.06.2017)[1]

Neither did national origin seem to play a huge role in the case of Olympique Marseille, as players/managers were mostly judged on the basis of their contribution to the team's success in the recent past. More generally, exclusion in the Marseille community was rather based in a certain self-centredness (us against the others), or what could be described as a "siege mentality", which was not grounded in specific references to issues of nationality.

Interesting parallels existed in a shared resentment of the "new rich", "oil rich" or "investor-backed" national and European competitors which was contrasted with narratives of hard work, being pure and authentic or possessing a glorious past and tradition. All in all, national stereotyping

---

[1] All quotes have been translated into English, with the help of DeepL, except for those from the English clubs. Translations have been edited minimally to ensure readability. Quotes from Manchester and Newcastle fans have only been edited to correct typos. The codes indicate the location of the quote in the materials we included in the qualitative discourse analysis.

of unwelcome players and staff from across Europe occurred only rarely. Especially in the case of Bayern Munich, there was a strong streak of meritocratic assessment according to which the value of a player was not dependent on local upbringing, nor the possibility of fielding him for the German national side but in the quality of his play, which was deemed crucially important to remain competitive at *European* level, with the UEFA Champions League (CL) as the premier arena of competition. Hence we find a doubly Europeanised impulse in this line of argument.

As regards any hierarchy of competitions, a clear pattern could be detected in the case of Bayern Munich, according to which the national competition mostly serves as a warm up for "true" and exciting formats at the European level, most notably the CL. Domestic-level matches are seen as a suitable space to let some key players rest and recover, and to let younger players gain experience. In turn, performance in European competition is regarded as the key metric by which to judge whether the season can be counted a success or not. And if not, success at home in no way compensates for this:

> We dutifully take our place in a vacuum again: two classes above our own league. One class below [European-level champion] Real Madrid. (ID 63:124, 26.04.2018)

Such a sentiment is much less pronounced in the case of OM, in part due to the fact that Marseille faces a strong (often times unmatchable) national opponent, the "new rich" Paris St.-Germain/PSG. Hence, where Bayern fans measure their team against foreign rivals such as Real Madrid, Barcelona and the like, and appreciate the pursuit of the best and most talented players across Europe if possible, OM supporters prefer to dwell on past successes at European level and would have their club regarded as a "French representative" throughout Europe, even if more for historical reasons.

In terms of rivalries, Bayern fans seem to have developed two tracks. In addition to national rivalries (Borussia Dortmund being the principal antagonist during the period under study), there was a significant element of perceived rivalry with the European sides with which Bayern Munich competes for the CL trophy. This was especially pronounced with the aforementioned "oil-rich clubs" (such as Manchester City or

PSG), as well as to Real Madrid as a frequent opponent at CL level. Lacking competitiveness to challenge its domestic rival PSG, Marseille fans have come to focus their attention to AS Monaco and Olympique Lyonnais:

> Between Lyon and its referees, Monaco and its tax regime and Paris with its petrodollars [...] we are leading the league of clean clubs! (ID 322:482, 12.09.2017)

In comparison, "second tier" clubs throughout Europe such as Borussia Dortmund, Atletico Madrid and FC Seville are occasionally regarded as role models for resurgence rather than "rivals" in the traditional sense. Talks about such rivalries, however, do not carry any references to nationality/diversity issues in terms of players' origin or similar.

All in all, a somewhat more Europeanised set of attitudes is revealed in the case of Bayern fans (from a league with a more Europeanised player market), but the differences with Marseille fans were neither substantial nor explicit enough to confirm the expected effect.

Hannover 96 Versus Toulouse FC

When comparing the two relegation battlers Hannover 96 and Toulouse FC in the German-French dyad, the perceptions, attitudes and narratives of both fan bases proved similar, despite the differing of the respective national player markets.

In the case of Hannover 96, debate in the forum appeared markedly self-centred: topic-wise (as regards a checkered relationship between fans and the then-investor Martin Kind), in terms of style (a big community of friends well known to one another with hardly much outside input over time), but also as regards horizons of attention (national competition, fear of relegation to the second league, lamenting the poor performance). "Europe" as such—any discussion of players and potential signings throughout Europe, any attention to other European leagues—seemed rather marginal (or even "alien") topics in such an environment. Participation in European competition was fondly remembered but largely disconnected from the experience of the club's current plight. In terms of signing players in the future, the focus was clearly on German clubs from the lower ranks of the league, or even promising young talent from the second league, without particular attention being given to questions of origin, heritage or ancestry:

> Kostic, Ito and Müller would be interesting from [Hamburg]. [...] Heintz would be an option from Cologne. Bittencourt is probably going to Hoffenheim. Otherwise, we could still think about Osako and Cordoba. Yurchenko's contract with Leverkusen runs out. He could be an option [...]. (ID 167:103, 13.05.2018)

In comparison, the fan discourse among Toulouse supporters seemed broadly similar, with parallels outweighing any differences, in particular as regards which topics were considered important, and the overall low incidence of "nationality issues" popping up. The bulk of debate was on the self-perception of being an under-performer, accompanied by myriad posts of concurrence and confirmation. Resentment for this poor performance was directed at locally headquartered global enterprises such as Airbus refusing to step in as sponsors. It also evidenced a degree of jealousy of similarly positioned yet more successful clubs such as FC Nantes or Girondins Bordeaux, rather than blaming the club's own players (or their origins).

In terms of possible future signings, the debates did not include a significant amount of talk on players or staff coming from another *European* or neighbouring country. However, some remarks referred to players' originating from Africa and South America, at least in passing, yet without much judgement:

> How can we not take a guy like Marvin Martin, why not try the [Brazilian] Wellington Silva who was supposed to go to Bordeaux, a good 10 from National [...]? Many African or North African players are also looking to break into Europe or even France!!! (ID 142:62, 27.07.2017)

Broadly speaking the composition of the squad and the nationalities/origins of players in general seemed to be of comparatively minor importance to Toulouse fans, to the point of being neglected altogether. Even highly unusual events such as the stabbing of a Toulouse supporter during a Europa League match against Partizan Belgrade did not incite long-standing debates in the forum under study. The sole interesting articulation as regards "Europe" mentioned the Bosman ruling, which was identified as initiating the demise or disintegration of "modern football" of which Toulouse FC is understood to be a victim rather than having benefitted from the growing gap.

The overarching conclusion of this paired comparison was that no huge argumentative differences could be ascertained between Hannover and Toulouse fans, certainly not as regards the inclusion and exclusion of foreign-born players. To the contrary, questions relating to player nationality and international contexts of the game seemed to be absent, or not an urgent matter most of the time.

Manchester United Versus Sturm Graz

It has become conventional wisdom that the English Premier League (EPL)—not just in terms of global appeal and marketing—has become a "global league" (cf. Millward 2011). Part of this narrative is the wide-ranging liberalisation of the player market, which may have thus had a greater effect on the discourse among Manchester United (ManU) fans than among Sturm fans from Austria.

Comparing those two clubs in two different leagues, the respective online forum threads do not seem to be "on different planets", even though the space reserved for discussing nationality issues, or topics pertaining to the domestic/European competitions-divide, is much bigger in the case of ManU fans. As the predominant way of defining the in-group, transfer targets were judged primarily based on individual performance, with Englishness being of no or distant secondary relevance. The following quote is typical of such a sequencing:

> I think Keane is basically an option to get a young English defender at a far cheaper cost in the squad to replace an injury prone one, while if Rojo comes back strong it's likely he and Bailly to be first choice. (ID 14:21, 26.05.2017)

Rojo's (Argentina) and Bailly's (Ivory Coast) respective nationalities were not specifically foregrounded since preference was given on merit. Additionally, such success-based understanding of the in-group included strong references to Europe. Several fans expressed the self-understanding that Manchester United must be counted among the elite *European* football clubs. As regards the composition of the squad, a recurring topic was the need to integrate younger players into the professional team. In a few cases this was connected with the desire that the squad should feature *a few English (or at least British) players*. If not for success, team spirit and coherence, this was rather deemed relevant to create authentic linkage points for identification.

This self-depiction as a club that integrates players from their own academy also seemed to serve as a distinction from the local rival Manchester City, "against" which it was argued that "belonging" includes values such as hard work and *local* embeddedness through youth football. The construction of belonging was consequently conflated with references to both Europe *and* locality. Europe gets a positive imprint as the place where the adequate competition is taking place. At the same time, the local connection (more than abstract "Englishness") matters as well.

Playing at the European level is also brought up in discussions among ManU fans as a means of attracting good players from abroad, such as a French star striker: *"Now that we are in the [C]hampions [L]eague, the prospect of Griezmann feels real and I am allowing myself to get excited" (ID 14:11, 25.05.2017)*. In such exchanges about players and potential signings from other European countries, many debaters commanded some sound knowledge about foreign leagues, the players and their play style, which implies that they pay a reasonable amount of attention to football across Europe. In this context the EPL is identified as overpriced, players are too expensive for their quality and (continental) Europe serves as a positive contrast.

Compared to this rather complex and multifaceted debate among ManU followers, the online discussion of Sturm fans rather lacks any traces of Europeanisation of communities and frames of reference. In general, the fan articulations seemed to centre on what is going on at the national level, focusing on players predominantly playing *in* Austria (no matter where they originate from). Low levels of attention were paid to other European leagues, and even less interest in other player markets across Europe could be found.

Most transfer discussions indicated a shared understanding of Sturm Graz as a club that develops young players and sells them to clubs in more prestigious leagues abroad, most notably the German leagues. In turn, rumours about any incoming players were mostly limited to the Austrian Bundesliga (ABL) with no particular reference being made to the origin of potential recruits. The only exception was a few positive references to the ABL's incentive scheme for the fielding of young Austrian talent. This positive perception of soft forms of discrimination on the basis of nationality also found occasional expression in the criticism of domestic rivals Red Bull Salzburg for having "too many legionnaires" in their team.

To conclude, there is an interesting but not extreme divergence between ManU and Sturm fans. It would certainly be too far-fetched to argue then that the more Europeanised a player market is, the less issues of nationality play a role for fans. True, ManU followers paid more attention to Europe and regarded European football as their habitat; yet a local anchoring was certainly appreciated and traces of "Englishness" were also visible in debates. In contrast, Sturm followers seemed to be more preoccupied with their national competitive context, even though questions of origin did not lead to particular debates on inclusion or exclusion.

Newcastle United Versus Wacker Innsbruck

The discussions among Newcastle fans indicated a self-conception of their club as an antithesis to most clubs in the EPL, given their limited financial means and sporting potential (this has changed somewhat only recently, after the period under study, due to the buy-in of Saudi Arabian investors). Good players are expected to sign elsewhere ("I just can't see him coming to us without at least trying at a bigger club here or abroad first, for financial or ambition reasons", ID 33:26, 10.04.2018), whereas European competitions were considered out of reach, and their rivals exclusively other English clubs.

In contrast to the otherwise nationally, or even regionally focused set of narratives and debating points, Newcastle fans displayed an unusual degree of interest in developments in several European leagues and player markets in the transfer discussions, even though they did not seem to define the peer group for their club at the European level. The main arguments for or against potential signings were based on quantitative data, for example on goals and assists, from online databases (such as those on transfermarkt.co.uk). Players were thus judged on performance, with little to no reference to these players' home leagues. One of the rare occasions where nationality came into play was the signing of a player to a club in the second Chinese league, which was brought up later as a negative example in other transfer discussions:

> We also don't know what his motivations and ambitions are. Maybe he feels ready to test himself at a club the size of Bayern where you have to put in a performance more or less every game, maybe he sees someone like Rafa as someone who could really help him to develop and be that player. *Maybe he'll want to do an Oscar and go to China for stupid money.* (ID 33:30, 10.04.2018; emphasis added)

Interestingly, such a debate presented a sharp contrast to discussions about similar signings to other clubs across European leagues (e.g. Italy, Switzerland and France) and indicated that differences are potentially less seen across Europe but rather in relation to other aspiring regions beyond the continent.

The discussions on rivalry were consistent in that the reference points remained always within the EPL, as European football plays no role here. Debates about European-level competitions took place but were separated into threads that bore no connection to Newcastle. Likewise, any discussions on EPL clubs "representing" the UK or England in the CL, or whether one should support another English side internationally, did not suggest a common or even a majority position. The fact that Newcastle United competes in a thoroughly Europeanised environment thus seems to have opened the debate on players and lifted attention barriers to some degree, but has not dragged a current relegation battler (and *former* competitor on the European stage) such as Newcastle United and its supporters into a full-blown Europeanisation of perceptions and attitudes.

The contrast to Wacker Innsbruck, a lower-tier club from a less Europeanised league, is instructive. For fans of the Austrian club, the "European" level—both in terms of attention towards leagues and player markets and any form of appreciation for them—seemed to be *completely* absent. Striking is the focus on local forms of rivalry and regional forms of allegiance, as it is the sub-region of Tyrol which commands most attention. In particular, neighbouring Wattens has been singled out as the object of frequent border work:

I just have to think of that only 58% of the players used by [Wattens] are Austrians […] there is not much room left for the "young, wild Tyroleans" who are supposedly so enthusiastic in Wattens. (ID 21:7, 17.07.2017)

Nationality issues, despite not dominating the debate, do show up occasionally, mixed into an appraisal of regional, Tyrolean, talent. As the Wacker supporters express a strong identification with their region, some debaters even suggested that the club needs primarily Tyrolean players to be(come) more authentic. Overall, foreign players were frequently referred to as "legionnaires" (and clearly distinguished from Austrian players).

Synopsis—First Paired Comparison
Taken together, some impact of the degree of Europeanisation in different player markets on the mindsets of football fans was discernible, even though it proved differently pronounced in the dyads under study. Whereas it seemed to be rather modest in the first two cases, it was more pronounced in the comparison of similarly situated clubs from Austria and the UK. However, it must be mentioned that even in the case of thorough internationalisation such as the EPL and Manchester United, in this context notable *local, regional and national* identity anchors continue to exist for their supporters.

On the other hand, as the case of Newcastle United makes clear, even for a club a long way from European competition, the context of a Europeanised league may still draw fan attention abroad, that is to European leagues and players. More closed leagues such as the French and Austrian ones, with their comparatively less internationalised player markets, in turn seem to breed more appreciation for national and local talent, or regional orientations such as in the case of Wacker Innsbruck and Tyrol.

By far the most visible effect in terms of a weakening of national ties and frames is visible in the case of Bayern Munich—an effect which is, however, not replicated in Hannover fans, at that time competing in the same fairly Europeanised context as regards players and squad compositions.

6.2.2 The Level of Participation in European Club Competitions as a Conditioning Factor

It should be immediately noted that this comparative dimension yielded the most meaningful results. The dividing line, introduced here for analytic purposes, also seemed to be felt and reflected upon by the football supporters themselves, especially in view of a growing perceived gap between the European top performers (the haves) and the smaller regional clubs competing and often even struggling at national level (the have-nots). It is in that sense that the topic of (a lack of) exposure to European competition also *resonated* in fan discourse and was a frequent point of criticism or lament by the followers of the supposedly "smaller" clubs, those less exposed to European competition (or not standing a chance of participating in any European cup in the near future).

Bayern Munich Versus Hannover 96
Bayern Munich supporters are accustomed to seeing their club compete at the highest level of European competition, Bayern having played in each CL edition since the 2007/2008 season. The club's record between 2008 and 2018 is remarkable: reaching the semi-finals seven times, making it to the finals thrice and finally claiming the trophy in 2012/12. Considering that the 1992/1993 season was the last time in which Bayern Munich was absent at the European level, it is not unreasonable for fans to see Bayern as the sole German club among the European elite, on a par with European giants such as Real Madrid, FC Barcelona or Juventus Turin. In this regard they consider Bayern to be the principal German club on the European stage, without necessarily seeing that role as one of "national representative".

Such a self-perception is only occasionally challenged in case of an early elimination at the European level (e.g. 2018/19). Such an incident is then explained with reference to the different financial opportunities of clubs backed by financial investors ("oil-rich clubs"). In contrast, Bayern is seen as competitive in spite of the limitations imposed by domestic regulation. The CL is thus considered to be the "main" or "natural" proving ground for Bayern to test themselves, the club's "true" competitive arena and thus both expected and "exceptional", but the latter only in the sense that domestic-level competition is pedestrian in comparison. Elite competition against other top-level European clubs is a key point of reference for the majority of Bayern fans, and the European frame of reference consequently accorded prime importance.

In comparison, national league participation, while not being entirely irrelevant, is rather taken for granted, in particular that Bayern Munich would finish first: "The problem is the Bundesliga. It is such a weak [competition] that we're never really challenged" (ID 63:86, 25.04.2018). Accordingly, performance at CL level eventually decides whether a season is seen as a success: participation in it is a must, reaching the semi-finals an adequate performance, while winning the competition is seen as a realistic goal. Fans do not shy away from describing participation in the CL as a consolation for having to endure a substandard and at times even tedious domestic competition. The Bundesliga fixtures are seen as little more than an opportunity to test and season young talent and acclimatise promising rookies to on-field pressure.

The lack of serious competition at the domestic level is often blamed for the (perceived) decline in Bayern's competitiveness in Europe, and arguably a disadvantage. Consistent with their high regard for European competition, many Bayern fans monitor the European player market for potential transfer targets, both young and old, judged on the basis of skill, play style and how well they might fit into Bayern's plans. National origin does not appear to be a primary concern, though German and locally developed players are thought to contribute to team cohesion.

Unsurprisingly, the sentiments and preferred topics among Hannover fans are quite distinct. Given the very different position in domestic-level competition, the debate foci and hot issues under consideration in online discussion differ(ed) markedly. Hannover 96, who were relegated from the top tier of the Bundesliga during the course of the study, have only occasionally made it to the European stage in the past. The most recent occasion was over a decade ago, a period remembered fondly by fans as a heyday for the club.

In contrast, during the period under study the debate primarily revolved around the impending risk of relegation in the here and now. Exemplary of this break between past and present are statements such as

"[Just to be clear]: We are here in the 2nd league [now], not the Champions League" (ID 53:99, 05.02.2017). Coming from such a perspective, a detailed discussion of any merits of "European competitions" would have been absurd. Consequently, the topic of European football comes up in the discussions of Hannover fans only indirectly. First, perhaps rather ironically, the focus of top German clubs on the CL is seen as affording Hannover a better chance of scoring an upset in their domestic fixtures against such otherwise unreachable rivals. Such observations nonetheless only serve to underscore the domestic competition's status as the main frame of reference.

Similarly, references to previous European competition were to be found through the backdoor of harking back to past glories, as well as in relation to the debate surrounding polarising investor Martin Kind. Yet even then the debate focused primarily on Kind's ideas about financing and steering the club more generally, not any implied chances of making a comeback in Europe due to the investor's money.

There is here an interesting and perhaps instructive distinction that emerges from the comparison between how fans of Hannover and Bayern view communities of belonging and questions of nationality. While for fans of Bayern issues around national ties seemed to have lost salience in the context of a Europeanised arena, Hannover fans seemed similarly agnostic on such questions primarily out of a preoccupation with more pressing concerns.

Manchester United Versus Newcastle United
The discussions among supporters of Manchester United suggested that the concept of the club as top club in a top league was not uncontested, at least in the former regard, given that ManU has not won the EPL since 2013. The club's domestic struggles in the face of strong rivals colour fan's perceptions of both the national league and European competition. Participation in the latter is seen as a must if only to remain an attractive destination for top talent, but also a potential arena for failure. Conversely, the strength of ManU's rivals in the EPL and the limited domestic success also lead to Europe being seen as an attractive alternative route to silverware:

"I think our best bet is the Europa. Keep ticking away at the PL no doubt, but I would concentrate seriously on the Europa" (ID 17:14, 19.11.2016), and three months later through the season: "We have a great chance of winning the EL. We need to make it a priority." (ID 4:24, 17.02.2017)

Such observations illustrate the inclusion of the Europe League into fan narratives as an acceptable alternative to the CL, where ManU had not been competitive during the period of study. In light of this, what may be here reflected is less a "normalisation" effect where habituation through frequent participation drives the growing perception of Europe as a natural arena for the club, and more a "crowding out" dynamic where strong domestic rivals and consequent lack of success in national competition push fans' attention towards Europe.

In contrast to previous studies which have suggested a growing cosmopolitanism among supporters of UK elite clubs which regularly participate in European competition (e.g. King 2000), we observe the orientations and attitudes to be firmly rooted in local or national frames. Regional rivalries with the nearby Manchester City and Liverpool FC continued to be accorded pre-eminence despite frequent exposure to European clubs. Discussions revolving around the Manchester City rivalry did contain references to Europe, albeit largely concerning City's comparative success in that arena, success often seen as being bought at the cost of selling the club to "an oil rich Middle Eastern country".

Discussions relating to transfers and the search for and evaluation of potential signings did not evidence the same parochialism, however, excepting a particular resentment of former ManU players who moved to local rivals, where signing for Liverpool or Manchester City was regarded as a betrayal. Broadly speaking, there was little role for nationality or ethnicity in labelling players "belonging to us" or "them" and indeed ManU fans showed an expansive interest in football across Europe, and extensive knowledge of foreign-based players, exhibiting no notable preference for British or English players.

Meanwhile Newcastle fans conceived of their clubs as a perhaps plucky but ultimately realistic underdog in a major European league, serving as an antithesis to the richer EPL top-flight. Other European leagues drew interest to Newcastle fans primarily in terms of potential signings for the club, and the cross-national attention associated with such transfer speculation was the exception rather than the rule for an otherwise largely domestically oriented fan-base. Fitting the mould of "relegation-battler" discussions revolved around avoiding relegation from and later securing promotion back to the EPL, while European competitions were remote to the point of irrelevance. Rivalries focused exclusively on other English clubs, West Bromwich and Brighton & Hove Albion for example identified as "authentic competitors":

> It's safe to say that the wins we do get will be more Stoke or West Brom style than Man C[ity] level! Always keep an eye out for Stoke results [...]. (ID 30:50, 10.04.2018)

In summary, the comparison of the English dyad is similar to the German one. This means that the level of exposure to European-level competition does seem to condition the main frames of reference of debate among fans. That is not to say, however, that fans of lower-tier teams who rarely qualify for European competition remain entirely oblivious to domestic football in other European countries. Conversely, regular participation in European-level competition does not necessarily cause fans to de-prioritise local rivalries. Also notable was the general absence of explicit reference to nationality markers of exclusion and inclusion in the online talk of the English fans under study.

Olympique Marseille Versus Toulouse FC
Marseille supporters demonstrated a markedly European outlook, with the clubs' eight appearances in European leagues between 2008 and 2018 producing a notable accustomisation to European competition. In several cases, European fixtures were also held up as more exciting and relevant than domestic matches. For a good number of Marseille fans, competing the French league lacked for jeopardy and excitement owing to the club's consistent position between the over-dominant Paris Saint-Germain and the rest of the league.

Where Marseille fans regarded their side as a solid "second best" in the French league, this sentiment was often accompanied by arguments that accentuated the relevance of European competition. In a clear example of a specific event being incorporated into a narrative, memories of Marseille's success in the 1993 edition of the CL, and the final in particular, are a regular touchstone for fans seeing Marseille as "real European side".

> One evening in May 93 on the pitch in Munich. OLYMPIQUE DE MARSEILLE climbs on the roof of Europe! In front of the Milan of Donadoni, Rijkard, Maldini, Papin and Van Basten! (ID 129:8, 10.09.2017)

Additionally, a significant number of Marseille supporters shared evident ambitions for a European resurgence. The so-called Champions Project envisions a focus on European competition as a way of eclipsing local rivals AS Monaco, Olympique Lyon or even PSG specifically by means of renewed European success:

> The pretentious Parisians, the Lyonnais lecturers as well as those self-righteous journalistic [expletive] who mocked Marseille's 'Champion Project' at the beginning of the season can watch the European Cup matches quietly on their sofas, with a Kleenex in their hands. (ID 132:27, 16.03.2018)

With the single exception of a run to the Europa League final in 2018, however, Marseille's on-field results in European competition have not realised that strategy. Stuck in the tier both domestically and in Europe, there is division among fans as to which arena matters most. Many Marseille supporters continue to devote most of their attention to the French competition, while others see European participation in largely instrumental terms. The latter see European competitions as a means to greater revenue streams and as necessary to attract the best talent. In particular, a reputation for consistent European performance was seen as a means to pick up top players *for less money* by making the club a more attractive destination.

In contrast, Toulouse fans dedicate little attention to European competition. As expected, domestic competition is the locus of their main frame of reference. Inevitably there are occasional references on the relevant online boards to the faint hope that Toulouse might win through one of the national cup competitions to secure a one-off appearance on the European stage, but there is little in the way of substantial or sustained discussion on the possibility or its potential implications.

The club's limited exposure at the European level seems to also have narrowed supporters' horizons when it comes to potential transfer targets, with speculation and debate largely limited to French and African football. Potential *European* signings are rarely discussed, with the exception of occasional interest in EPL players. As was the case among Newcastle fans, high-profile players from top leagues are mentioned from time to time on the forums, but such references are isolated and rarely connected to Toulouse itself.

While European-level competition was treated as irrelevant, occasional references to other European clubs were to be found, though only in the form of comparably placed clubs in other leagues, parallels being drawn with the likes of AEK Athens or Stoke City. All told, it appears that the striking discrepancy in exposure to European competition, and the structural divide that prevents any credible promotion to European-level competition, act as barriers to the attention of many Toulouse fans. That divide itself, however, is subject to occasional discussion, especially as regards the role of financial inequalities in perpetuating the gap both between and within different leagues. As a result of such financial inequities, it is argued that for a poorer club such as Toulouse pursuit of European ambitions can be seen as a potentially dangerous gamble:

> If your hobby is to spend money on names without any guarantee [...], it's a gamble that can cost the club too much, with consequences more disastrous than sporting. (ID 142: 81, 24.06.2017)

Sturm Graz Versus Wacker Innsbruck
Both Sturm and Wacker supporters share the view of the ABL as a peripheral, second-tier league. Differing level of exposure to European competition nonetheless seems to have a marked impact on their respective fans' attitudes.

Sturm fans' online discourse reveals a consistent perception of the side as a *top* club in an underdog league, yet discussions are embedded in a distinctly "Austrian frame of reference". Both in terms of transfer talk and rivalries, references to other Austrian clubs predominate. Participation in European competition is seen as a rare opportunity for the club, and with rival Red Bull Salzburg dominating domestically, Sturm Graz fans are aware that such opportunity is somewhat contingent on their rival's success on the European stage:

> Sturm only has a chance to play [the Champions League qualifiers] because RBS scored enough, everyone should be that honest. (ID 67:47, 26.02.2018)

Despite being the principal focus of discussion on Austrian football, the ABL is itself not highly regarded (though this deprecation does suggest an implicit comparison to other European leagues). The dominance of Red Bull Salzburg seems to contribute to the low estimation in which the league is held, similar to the effect seen in Marseille fans who view their domestic league as something of a foregone conclusion owing to PSG's supremacy. Strum fans make frequent reference to the club's limited financial means as a constraint on the side's potential performance, especially compared to richer clubs such as PSG or Real Madrid, belonging to the European elite.

In this regard, elite European football comprises the "other" against which the identity of underdog (at least in terms of the Austrian league) is defined. Despite Sturm Graz regularly competing in European competitions over the past decade, fixtures against top sides, such as the match against Ajax Amsterdam in 2018, remain the exception rather than the rule, the latter being the regular domestic competition or fixtures in the qualification rounds of European competitions.

The comparatively recent "Ajax match" is an instructive example, with related discussions among Sturm fans revolving around a feeling of representing Austria both for pride and potentially "stealing points" from the Dutch in UEFA's rankings system, which orders top-performing countries and determines the allocation of future qualification berths (ID 41:69, 19.07.2018). This predominating *national* frame of reference was again discernable in discussions of domestic rival Red Bull Salzburg's European outings, where the typical hostility of Sturm fans towards the Salzburg side at times relented, to the point of dubbing their rivals "heroes that score for Austria" (ID 67:43, 26.02.2018).

Nonetheless, comparatively frequent participation in European competition (though in this case on the fringes thereof) did not necessarily lead to a more cosmopolitan attitude when it came to interest in and evaluation of potential signings, as is evident in the Sturm Graz supporter discourse. Foreign players are rarely considered, with a marked preference for Austrian players and incentives that encourage fielding them. Conversely, the stereotyping of players from abroad as "foreign mercenaries" is prevalent and universally derogatory.

The most pronounced distinction between the respective discourses of Sturm and Wacker fans is thus not in their attention devoted to the European transfer market or competitions, with neither set of fans showing substantial interest in foreign players and both principally preoccupied with domestic competition. Rather the striking contrast is that while references to Europe remain frequent on Sturm fan boards, it is almost *entirely absent* from discussions among Wacker fans. The focus of Wacker fans is more narrowly parochial, focused in large part on their home region of Tyrol, with local rivals Wattens the principal object of attention. The ABL is regarded as Wacker's natural habitat, with two seasons spent in the second division seen as a temporary aberration. Wacker fan's attention is thus firmly rooted in a national reference frame, with only their low regard for the ABL hinting at an implicit comparison to other European leagues.

Only in a handful of cases do the Wacker fans look beyond Austria, and when they do it is generally to compare their club to, or distinguish it from similarly situated sides, for example looking to the EPL in a discussion on the financial impact of relegation. Likewise, players outside of Austria (bar those in the German second or third division on occasion) attract little attention, with a few fans expressing a desire to see a more "Tyrolean" squad composition. In an interesting parallel, the few references to foreign-born players often also carry the derogatory label of "mercenaries" in both Austrian fan discourses analysed, hinting at a pattern of identification (exclusion), which is not substantially mediated through different levels of exposure to European competitions.

Synopsis—Second Paired Comparison
The second four pairs of comparisons suggest that Europeanisation of the attitudes of clubs' respective supporters does indeed seem to be influenced by regular and especially successful participation in European competitions. This tendency is not uniform however, and may be as much driven by instrumental considerations as by a cosmopolitan outlook, yet most supporters of top-level domestic sides seem to define their clubs as being, or aspiring to be, top-level clubs at the *European* level, too.

The exception here proved to be Sturm Graz, with the ABL being too peripheral to ever transcend its underdog status. Even though there were local points of reference in the cases of fans of Bayern Munich, Manchester United and Olympique Marseille (as evidenced in narratives of local rootedness and rivalries, storied and successful domestic history and aversion to foreign "oil-funded" ownership), these teams' supporters seemed more open to a broader European vision and focused on continental developments. These fans generally appraised players on skill over nationality, follow foreign leagues and regard European competition as more appealing or as their club's natural environment.

This attitude was most pronounced in the case of Bayern Munich fans, who regarded European competition as the club's chief enterprise, while the attitudes of ManU and Marseille fans to Europe were in part instrumental. There also seemed to be a weakening of national reference frames among these fans in terms of what they perceived to be the purpose of participation in European competition, whether their respective clubs also serve as national representatives and whether it is fitting to follow or support rival sides from their own country in European competition—again with the notable exception of Sturm fans.

In contrast, fans of the "relegation battlers" did not concern themselves with European competitions. With the exception of Newcastle fans, they paid scant attention to football in other European countries. Overseas leagues and elite European football simply had little bearing on their club's fortunes, except insofar as European developments such as growing financial disparities or structural changes affect them. Such effects were generally seen as negative, for example perpetuating their side's underdog status. In this regard fans of lower-ranked clubs perceived the European club game as divided into two tiers, with their own club excluded from the elite *European* tier.

This perceived distinction is underscored and reinforced by the use of ironic, sarcastic or even abusive language directed at elite clubs, from which "underdog club" fans wish to distinguish themselves (while simultaneously also lamenting their exclusion). The acceptance of an inferior role in the game and league breeds a sense of fatalism that occasionally also gets re-labelled (and made a virtue) as a preferable and "more authentic form of otherness".

6.2.3 Public Attitudes Towards Europe/the EU as a Conditioning Factor

This section contains four comparisons of fan discourse from otherwise similar clubs which are embedded in societies and publics that differ in their degree of Euroscepticism.

Bayern Munich Versus Manchester United
First, it is striking that in a broad comparison—taking a holistic look at different indicators of identities in terms of both COB and FOR—fans of both clubs tend to have rather Europeanised attitudes. However, in nearly all subcategories (and also overall), the analysed online discourse among Bayern supporters has echoed the ideal type of Europeanised perceptions more strongly than that of ManU fans. As for similarities concerning COB, it can be noted that in both fan communities the national background and ethnicity of the players rarely play a role, while in discussions around potential transfer targets, views of players based abroad are generally (very) positive. For example, players from other European countries are seen as valuable and necessary for the success and development of the clubs. At the same time, both fan communities emphasise the importance of developing home-grown players.

As for the similarities concerning FOR, both fan forum discussions attributed significant value to European-level competitions. The CL as the major competition is regarded as extraordinarily valuable in terms of both general prestige and their respective clubs' fortunes. This is particularly pronounced in the case of Bayern Munich, where CL success is *the* defining criterion for the club's future. The following exchange is indicative of this central position of the CL competition in discussions among Bayern fans, here on the occasion of yet another walkover in the domestic league:

> "The *best* thing we can do is win the CL [...] Then we have done everything right [...]" (ID 152:9, 25.02.2017), which is responded to later on, in the same thread: "If we *don't win* the CL, things will get [more difficult ...] I think that's very thin ice anyway, because you can and must never expect to win the CL". (ID 152:46, 25.02.2017)

In that sense, European competitions—and the CL arguably more so than the Europa League, at least in the case of Bayern Munich—are viewed as the norm in terms of where fans see their club competing on a regular basis. As the "natural habitat" of top performers, both fan scenes consider European competitions as the appropriate competitive environment for their clubs, rather than an arena where their national league or country is to be represented.

The differences between the two fan communities suggest that Bayern fans' attitudes are still more Europeanised than those of their ManU counterparts. As for the differences regarding COB, Bayern fans neither tend to be too enthusiastic about the club's (implicit) policy of signing the best German players, nor about the so-called Stallgeruch-Policy.[2] For some ManU supporters, though, the club's self-understanding is occasionally also one of incorporating *English* players into the team/squad (even if such sentiment is not dominant in the debates analysed).

As far as differences in terms of FOR are concerned, it seems that European (as compared to national) competitions are regarded as even more important by Bayern fans compared to those of ManU. While winning the domestic league seems less rewarding for Bayern supporters,[3] they tend to measure the success of a season by performance in the CL. For ManU supporters, the European competitions are important not only as an end in themselves, but for the purpose of attracting better signings in the future. In addition, Bayern fans (more so than ManU supporters) often tend to view Bundesliga games as warm-up matches or test runs—where younger players can rotate into the team—prior to (important) CL games. Finally, while both clubs regard other (big) European clubs as important rivals, this is more pronounced among Bayern supporters. At the same time, the main rival for ManU fans is the local neighbour Manchester City. Interestingly, though, in both instances the respective local/national rivals are often evaluated according to their

---

[2] A term denoting the preference given to insiders, people from within the club or former players, in hiring and recruiting staff for higher positions in the club. Both policies are seen as being in the way of the necessary optimisation of the club for competing successfully at European level among Bayern fans.

[3] For Bayern fans, the Bundesliga is often seen as a fairly weak competition and as a necessary evil, while for most ManU supporters, the EPL is an important and strong league.

performance at the *European* level, as is indicated by this quote from a discussion among ManU supporters:

> The more [Man City coach] Pep spends the more pressure he will be under. Yes, we spent a lot, but we won trophies. They won nothing, failed in the PL and the CL. Their owners will be expecting the league and especially the CL, the latter is the holy grail for them. (ID 14:25, 26.05.2017)

As we would argue, such articulations further hint at an overall solidified "European" frame of reference, in sporting terms, among both fan communities.

Hannover 96 Versus Newcastle United
Moving on the two smaller clubs in Germany and the UK, respectively, the broad comparison between Hannover and Newcastle fans' perceptions and assessments again reveals that varying "public attitudes" in their home societies might be less of a conditioning factor for their mindsets. There seems to be little difference in terms of the various COB- and FOR-related indicators; if anything, Newcastle supporters, as fans from a more Eurosceptic country, tend to hold slightly *more* European(ised) attitudes.

There are several similarities in the two fan forum discussions. First, the value and attractiveness of national-level competitions is emphasised. Both the German Bundesliga and the EPL are appreciated as the appropriate and appealing competition context, with any period in the national second division seen as an unwelcome aberration before being promoted again (as in the case of Hannover 96). In contrast, references to European-level competition are rather sparse, depending on where both clubs stood in the analysed time frame. Second, in strictly sporting terms, rivals for Hannover and Newcastle fans are clubs from the same region or league, often those that also battle for promotion or relegation. However, whether as aspiration or memory, European competitions are generally seen as attractive and desirable.

The slightly more Europeanised outlook of Newcastle supporters, despite their region's comparative societal Euroscepticism, can be illustrated by two aspects. On the one hand, the discussions in the Hannover forum are rather ambivalent about Europe. It is noted, for example, that since the campaign in Europe during the 2010/11 season, Hannover 96 has been on a downward trend in terms of sporting success. In addition, references to professional football in Europe/other European countries in the Hannover forum are at times strongly linked to criticisms levelled at an "undue commercialisation of the game" (and thus not framed positively). This is, for instance, illustrated by references to the CL as the "root of all evil" (ID 158:40, 27.06.2017), or laments about a "likely extension of the CL to include Chinese teams within the next ten years" (ID 168:37, 27.02.2018). On the other hand, in terms of transfer policies and possibilities, Newcastle fans display a more outward-looking attitude, both in terms of potential signings across the continent as well as (other European) clubs they see their club competing with for young talent.

Olympique Marseille Versus Sturm Graz
All in all, concerning the direction of identity-related assessments under both perspectives (COB and FOR), fans of both clubs tend to exhibit a mix of partially Europeanised attitudes and perceptions, a tendency that is nonetheless more pronounced with Marseille fans than those of Sturm Graz. We remain hesitant to see this discrepancy as grounded in different degrees of valuation for Europe or the EU in the embedding wider publics. Such an inference becomes particularly questionable in view of the results of the next and final pair of comparisons (see below). Smaller variations between Marseille and Sturm supporters, however, might link back to more national inclinations in the case of the Austrian club coming from a more Eurosceptic background.

Among the notable similarities between the two bigger clubs from France and Austria are that both fan communities seem to hold European club competitions generally in high esteem. They are valued as exceptional opportunities (Sturm fans) or as places of past glory and commercial survival nowadays (Marseille fans). It is striking that both fan communities use very similar vocabulary in talking about their aspirations, and in describing the European-level as an aspiration:

> "A fixed [seat in the Europa League] group stage would be a *dream* for Sturm and Austria" (ID 40:24, 20.06.2018; emphasis added), reciprocated in a Marseille discussion thread through: "The European Cup is what can make us *dream* until May". (ID 132:1, 12.03.2018; emphasis added)

However, both fan scenes see their main rivals rather at the national level than at the European level. In an interesting parallel, both fan communities seem to suggest that the respective national champions, both frequently competing at the European level (PSG in the case of France, Red Bull Salzburg in the case of Austria), are (almost) out of reach on the field. Consequently, clubs deemed of similar strength nationally are seen as more realistic rivals (Olympique Lyon and AS Monaco; Rapid Wien and Austria Wien, respectively). Finally, extraordinary events and matches in European competition form identity anchors in both fan communities. For Marseille supporters, the winning of the CL trophy in 1993 still serves as key event, around which narratives of past glory are formed, while for Sturm supporters, the more recent tour to face Ajax Amsterdam in a CL qualifier is a main point of reference for narrative-building.

As for the differences which substantiate the overall more Europeanised perceptions of Marseille fans—first, for them nationality and origin of players did not play a role at all, whereas Sturm fans addressed the (lack of) playing time for Austrian players. Second, for the Sturm supporters playing in European Club competitions has been substantially connected to *representing* Austria in Europe and improving the *country*'s UEFA five-year ranking. In contrast to this more national frame of reference, such concerns were not common talking points in the online debates of Marseille supporters. Instead, Marseille followers tended, to a larger degree, to view the European competitions as an opportunity to compete with the *top European* clubs, even though the club was not itself at that level.

Admittedly, one more aspect might have influenced the outcome of this particular comparison, specifically that Olympique Marseille was very successful in European-level competition in one of the seasons under review, while Sturm Graz failed to make it beyond qualification stage in the European level in the same time frame. A higher esteem for the European level of football in the online discussion forums might thus merely reflect sporting success rather than being the product of the diverging opinion climate dominating the respective domestic societal debates.

Toulouse FC Versus Wacker Innsbruck

Our comparison of fan articulations indicated that supporters of both clubs do *not* tend to have substantially Europeanised attitudes, a tendency that is again slightly more pronounced with the fans of the Austrian club. Among the striking similarities are that most of the fans' attention seems to be devoted to national football. Both fan communities are also clear about the fact that they consider European competitions to be out of reach for their club. Hence, there is a uniformity in distance towards European-level football, which is rooted in the sporting performance and assigned opportunities rather than Euroscepticism and friendliness in the respective societies. In a similar vein, rivals are perceived to exist solely at the *regional and national* levels (concerning the latter, especially those national clubs that are considered of a roughly similar weight class).

Much as was the case with the pair of Olympique Marseille and Sturm Graz though, there are some interesting if small-scale differences (their smallness indicating the limited number of discourse incidents, or articulations in this regard). First, Wacker fans did at times refer to foreign (including European) players, managers or leagues in a somewhat derogatory manner; the sacking of a foreign-born coach for instance is discussed with explicit reference to his nationality: "[n]ow he will be gone, the Italo-Swiss" (ID 147:17, 16.09.2016), while such references were absent from the Toulouse FC fan discourse. Second, Wacker supporters tended to be more likely to support fellow Austrian clubs in European competitions because they held these to represent the national league. In contrast, Toulouse fans did not see other French clubs' participation in Europe as furthering a "national cause". Third, both fan communities have reservations concerning European cup competitions and the Europeanisation of football structures: Toulouse fans, for instance, referred to the Bosman ruling as being "dangerous" in terms of driving the (over-)commercialisation of the game. In this regard, the ensuing explosion of salaries throughout Europe is seen as particularly detrimental to their own club's chances of success:

> […] but the inflation of player prices as a result of the £ mania in English football is driving up the price of players all over Europe, and future purchases will be complicated. (ID 142: 87, 27.07.2017)

Consequently, as noted earlier, efforts to play Europe (in case these are discussed at all, even if hypothetically) are found to carry the risk of over-investing/overstretching for any club. Some Wacker supporters, in a similar vein, used examples of top-level clubs which regularly compete in the CL as counter cases, against which they defined themselves as being in a "different game". In general, Toulouse fans seemed to take more of an interest in these matters, though they critically viewed any related developments. In contrast, Wacker supporters demonstrated a certain *regional* (Tyrolean) identity and focus when it comes to rivalry or discussions of players and transfers.

Synopsis—Third Paired Comparison
No uniform pattern could be discerned in how differing degrees of Euroscepticism, or opinions and attitudes towards Europe and the EU prevalent in the respective embedding societies, affected fan attitudes. This would suggest that differences and similarities across fans in different European countries are not primarily due to the overall orientation towards Europe and the EU among the respective publics. This conclusion is reinforced by the lack of contextualisation bringing in the EU, EU politics or any references to wider public opinion on these matters in the fan discourse under study.

There are perhaps two ways of looking at these findings. On the one hand, we might infer that wider public attitudes have not played an important role here. Even though there has been some co-variation between different levels of Europeanised mindsets (expressed in COB- and FOR-relevant talking points) and variation in the overall opinion climate in the embedding societies, this seems to have occurred somewhat coincidentally rather than constituting an important causal factor. On the other hand, it may still be the case that the wider "public attitude" influences the fan discourse in more subtle ways than are recognisable through explicit references and articulations. This however would need to be (dis-)confirmed through other data and further investigation.

6.3 Further Analysis, Discussion and Conclusion

In a final step, we condensed the data points gleaned from comprehensive online discourse analysis and the paired comparisons. Inspired by the method of congruence analysis (cf. Beach and Pedersen 2016), a certain value was assigned to each indicator under both COB and FOR (i.e. to all analytic categories as listed in Table 6.1) for each club and its respective fan community. This value was to express the extent of Europeanisation in any of the dimensions, and for each club/fan community, according to the respective fan discourse analysed over a two-year period.

We used a five-point scale ranging from thoroughly Europeanised (2), moderately Europeanised (1), neutral/mixed (0), not markedly Europeanised (-1) to not Europeanised at all (-2). On that basis, average scores for different clusters of clubs[4] were calculated:

- the four Europeanised squads versus the four more "home-grown" squads,
- the four domestic top clubs, which are frequently exposed to CL/EL competition versus the four domestically oriented relegation battlers and
- the four clubs from more Eurosceptic contexts taken together versus the four clubs from more Europhile contexts combined.

The idea behind this was to ascertain where the variance of average scores would be most pronounced, and hence, in heuristic fashion, to indicate which factor might carry the most explanatory power. This additional type of analysis (see Table 6.2) (also) suggests that it is the extent of participation in, and exposure to, European-level competition which commands the most power in this regard.

The analysis of fan-discourse drawn from the content of online message boards for the eight selected clubs over two seasons showed that the

---

[4] The clubs and fan communities were assigned the following labels: Bayern Munich (BM), Hannover 96 (H96), Manchester United (ManU), Newcastle United (NUFC), Olympique Marseille (OM), Toulouse FC (TFC), Sturm Graz (SG) and Wacker Innsbruck (WI).

Table 6.2 Degrees of Europeanisation among clustered fan communities across Europe

	Communities of belonging				Frames of references			
	Inclusion	Exclusion	Relation to other fans	Events as narratives	European competition	National competition	Context	Ø
Europeanisation of player markets								
Europeanised PM (BM, H96, ManU, NUFC)								
Total avg score	0.81	0.69	0.00	0.00	0.17	0.25	−0.25	0.24
Home grown (OM, TFC, SG, WI)								
Total avg score	0.13	0.63	0.00	0.00	−0.08	−0.33	−0.58	−0.04
Participation in European club competitions: big versus small clubs								
Top clubs (BM, ManU, OM, SG)								
Total avg score	0.81	0.90	0.00	0.67	1.08	0.58	0.58	0.66
Relegation battlers (H96, NUFC, TFC, WI)								
Total avg score	0.13	0.44	0.00	−0.50	−1.00	−0.67	−1.42	−0.43
Europhile versus Eurosceptic								
Europhile								

(continued)

Table 6.2 (continued)

	Communities of belonging			Frames of reference		
	Inclusion	Exclusion	Relation to other fans	Events as narratives	European competition	National competition	Context
Total avg score (BM, H96, OM, TFC)	0.13	0.20	0.00	0.00	0.08	0.02	−0.15	0.04
Euro-sceptical					−0.25	−0.17	Ø
Total avg score (ManU, NUFC, SG, WI)	0.44	0.50	0.00	0.00	−0.25	−0.17	−0.25	0.04

Europeanisation of football structures and governance seems to have left a mark on how fans understand the game and what they identify as in-group and out-group. Even though we witnessed a certain extent of Europeanisation among fan identifications across all clubs, the most significant factor shaping discourse and perceptions appeared to be the degree of exposure to European competition. It suggests itself as the most powerful channel through which football influences how fans attribute meaning to the European level of football in their debates.

These tendencies were not uniform, and at times seemed to derive as much from instrumental considerations as any developing cosmopolitanism. Still, most supporters of the top-level clubs in European football defined their clubs as aspiring to the elite European level. Although in the cases of clubs like Bayern Munich, Manchester United and Olympique Marseille fans valued a sense of local or regional identity (as revealed through narratives of local rootedness and rivalries, storied and successful history in domestic competition, and dislike of "oil-rich" foreign owners), the discourses nonetheless revealed a marked openness of outlook and broad familiarity with the wider game in Europe. Fans principally evaluated players from across the continent on skill and tactical suitability rather than nationality, and followed football throughout Europe more intensely. The most visible effect in terms of weakening of national ties and frames was found in the case of Bayern Munich, whose fans exhibited a greater esteem for European competition over domestic, and saw the former as the club's natural habitat. In contrast, ManU and Marseille fans saw European competition as complementary to domestic ambitions, rather than as a substitute. Given ManU's domestic struggles, its fans saw Europe as an alternative avenue for advancement and competitive resurgence. They thus split their focus across two frames of reference, continuing to devote significant attention to domestic concerns while exhibiting a fairly Europeanised perspective on communities of belonging, especially in terms of player evaluation. For Marseille supporters, memories of past success on the European stage underpinned a similar view of European competition as a possible avenue for competitive revival, with future success in Europe potentially underwriting a domestic resurgence. Among fans of the four national high-performers, the impact on mindset was the least pronounced in the case of the club with the least European exposure, namely Sturm Graz, underlining the impact of repeat, routine (as opposed to occasional and intermittent) participation at the European level on fan identity.

By comparison, fans of relegation battlers displayed significantly less evidence of Europeanised mindsets. Overseas leagues and elite European football simply had little bearing on their club's fortunes. Hannover fans, for example, at that time competing in the same fairly Europeanised player market of the German Bundesliga as Bayern Munich, showed little interest in Europe. Only in the case of the highly Europeanised league context of the EPL was a mild spill-over effect of monitoring European-level developments observable. The degree of Europeanisation of a club's domestic league in terms of cross-border player movements may thus play a role in driving "normalisation" or "acculturation" effects pertaining to the acceptance or othering of players on the basis of national origin. The case of Newcastle, a club which rarely comes close to competing at the European level, suggests that the context of a Europeanised league may encourage even fans of less competitive clubs to pay greater attention to the broader European game. Newcastle fans frequently discussed foreign European leagues and players despite the club generally having little hope of qualifying for European competitions. Conversely, fans of Wacker Innsbruck, whose domestic league is considerably less Europeanised, exhibited a more local and regional orientation.

An interesting side effect of Europeanisation was revealed in the context of Newcastle fans: at least occasionally, from the perspective on an underdog, the Europeanisation of structures of elite football and the growing gulf between top sides and the rest were blamed for the club's difficulties and cast as insurmountable barriers to entry into the top ranks. In this regard fans of lower-ranked clubs perceived the European club game as divided into two tiers, with their own club excluded from the elite *European* tier.

Somewhat surprisingly the degree of Euroscepticism of the embedding society seemed to have little correlation with fan attitudes, as most evident from the cases of Toulouse FC, Hanover 96 and Manchester United. Despite the former two clubs being located in comparatively Europhile societies, there was little evidence among their fans of Europeanised outlook in terms of COB or FOR. Conversely, ManU supporters displayed a greater degree of Europeanisation and cosmopolitan outlook, despite being located in the comparatively Eurosceptic north of England.

More broadly, barely any explicit reference to European politics, EU institutions or policies could be found in the fan discourse under study. Although UK fan message boards did host some discussion of politics (and in particular Brexit), such discussions were generally separate and distinct from those focused on football.

In the context of our overarching theme, we can see that fans' experience and perceptions of "Europe" are not only affected by the act of investing time and emotional capital into following a football club, but also that which club they follow matters, most significantly whether that club has routine and regular exposure to European competition.

References

Beach, Derek, and Rasmus Brun Pedersen. 2016. *Causal case study methods*. Ann Arbor: University of Michigan Press.

Friese, Susanne. 2014. *Qualitative data analysis with ATLAS.ti*. Los Angeles etc.: SAGE.

King, Anthony. 2000. Football fandom and post-national identity in the new Europe. *British Journal of Sociology* 51 (3): 419–442. https://doi.org/10.1111/j.1468-4446.2000.00419.x.

Konopásek, Zdeněk. 2007. Making thinking visible with Atlas.ti: Computer assisted qualitative analysis as textual practices. In *Historical social research supplement: Grounded theory reader*, ed. Günter Mey and Katja Mruck, 276–298. Cologne: GESIS.

Millward, Peter. 2011. *The global football league: Transnational networks, social movements and sport in the new media age*. London: Palgrave Macmillan.

Tarrow, Sidney. 2010. The strategy of paired comparison: Toward a theory of practice. *Comparative Political Studies* 40 (2): 230–259. https://doi.org/10.1177/0010414009350044.

———. 2021. Progress outside of paradise: Old and new comparative approaches to contentious politics. *Comparative Political Studies* 54 (10): 1885–1901. https://doi.org/10.1177/00104140211024297.

Woolf, Nicholas H., and Christina Silver. 2018. *Qualitative analysis Using Atlas.ti. The five level QDA method*. New York: Routledge.

7

Surveying Football Fans: Cosmopolitans and Communitarians

7.1 Introduction

Chapter 5, dealing with online discussions among football fans, highlighted how the Europeanisation of relevant fan experiences in football contributes to the construction of in-group/out-group differences among fans. We saw how such Europeanised football can influence fan attention for football at the national and European level. While the results demonstrated the general role that football can play in shaping identifications vis-à-vis Europe, the results remain fragmented owing to the nature of the data source. This chapter takes a quantitative approach to the question of Europeanisation through football. Based on an online survey of football fans across the four relevant leagues, it establishes a new typology of football fans according to their attitude towards the experience of Europeanisation of football.

The chapter confirms that fans indeed develop certain attitudes and identifications in response and reaction to football Europeanisation, but it becomes clear that there is little uniformity among fans in this regard. Fans were asked about their attitudes towards various aspects of Europeanisation in football and more general political attitudes. The analysis highlights how the Europeanisation of football has influenced aspects of fan identities differently across fans of similarly positioned clubs, distinguishing between cosmopolitan fans for whom any national attachment plays little role in their fandom, and communitarian fans who attribute great import to such a sense of national belonging. The second part of the analysis identifies which factors have a decisive bearing on who is a communitarian and who is a cosmopolitan, showing that both individual level characteristics and club level factors are important.

7.2 Typology of Football Fans

7.2.1 Cosmopolitans and Communitarians[1]

The typology of football fans employed here is derived from latent class analysis (Collins and Lanza 2010). This approach assumes the existence of attitudinally similar respondent groups who will provide broadly similar answer-patterns in response to survey questions. These groups and their characteristics can thus be identified by means of statistical estimation techniques. Combining deductive and inductive approaches, the method departs from the fan typologies elaborated in Chap. 3. Taking as a starting point the characteristics attributed by Giulianotti (2002) and Redhead (2003) to their respective fan types (i.e. active/passive fandom, aspects of local belonging and performance of fandom activities), indicators are derived deductively in order to best differentiate between the thematic clusters of attitudes that distinguish fan categories. Yet these fan types can then be further refined, inductively identifying the number of classes and refining the respective characteristics based on the data. The data-driven enumeration and characterisation of fan types is thus based on statistical indicators rather than predefined categories. This latent class model approach seeks to group subjects together on the basis of observed characteristics, in this case answer-schemes, thus revealing the number and nature of underlying categories and their associated response-patterns.[2] Already a well-established research method in the fields of

---

[1] This section draws on Weber et al. (2022). We thank Florian Koch for his input to that earlier version.

[2] The method uses a maximum likelihood estimation strategy. All estimation is done using the poLCA package in R (Linzer and Lewis (2010)).

psychology and medicine, Latent Class Analysis has increasingly been adopted by the social and political sciences, for example, to identify patterns of political participation (Weerts et al. 2014; Oser et al. 2013) or to empirically test theoretical types of citizenship (Hooghe and Oser 2018).

The analysis makes use of 15 indicator variables to differentiate football fans on the basis of fandom intensity as well as their attitudes towards local, national and European/international aspects of belonging. These items stem from four areas:

- Four indicators assess fandom intensity: match attention (home and away) and connection to the club, grouping respondents by different possible types of affiliation (club membership, official supporter's group, unofficial fan group, season ticket holder, owning club merchandise, receiving official news/magazine, other)[3];
- Two indicators relate to European competition-related aspects (relevance of European competition vis-à-vis the national competition and representative function of European competitions);
- Four indicators are based on attitudes towards the player transfer market (relevance of local, national and European background of the players); and
- Five indicators (player, manager and owner characteristics: being native, having native language knowledge) measure team and club functioning.[4]

Figure 7.1 shows the frequencies for all items in the model.

The frequency analysis in Fig. 7.1 reveals a broad range of both fandom activity (measured as match attention) and degree of club affiliation among survey respondents. Nonetheless the distribution largely

---

[3] These different forms of affiliations differ in their intensity. Due to the different structure of football in the four countries, there are also differences in what it means to have a certain affiliation (e.g. being an official club member has different meanings). As a result, out of many options to operationalise affiliation, a simple addition of the different types of bonds between the fan and the club was used as a measure in the graph on "How affiliated with the club" as part of Figure 7.1.

[4] The words "native"/"language" were replaced in the questionnaire with the respective language/nationality of the clubs' countries, namely German in the case of Bundesliga (DE) clubs, Austrian/German in the case of Bundesliga (AT) clubs, English in the case of Premier League clubs and French in the case of Ligue 1 clubs. Same applies to country name.

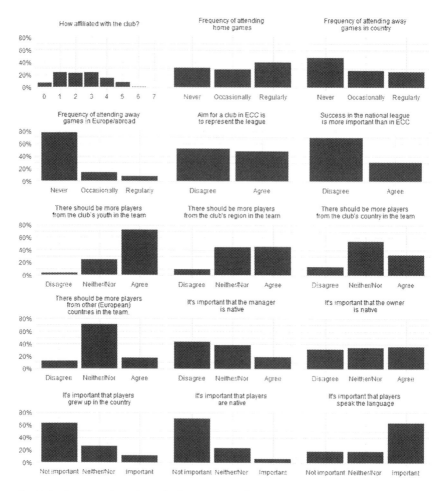

Fig. 7.1 Frequencies of the indicator items for the latent class analysis. N=2950, missing values for the whole data are imputed with the R-package mice

conforms to expectations in terms of fan involvement: home match attendance is common, away matches in the same country are less frequently attended, and only a small minority—22% of fans—have ever attended an away match abroad.

Fans see European competitions (Champions League and Europa League) as at least as relevant as the national league, but their role is contested: opinions differ as to whether European competition is a platform on which to represent the national league as a whole or merely an arena for competition between the best teams in Europe.

The questions concerning the transfer market likewise reveal a range of attitudes among fans which may provide a basis for differentiation and classification. While most fans agreed that contracting players from their club's own youth system is important, there was otherwise a spectrum of opinion with regard to the ideal criteria for signing or retaining (foreign) players.

Respondent attitudes towards aspects of national belonging proved complex. While on average fans were not overly concerned about contracting native players specifically, a majority did attribute importance to players' local language fluency. Interestingly, national belonging was revealed to be of greater salience for fans when it came to owners and managers, with many respondents expressing particular antipathy towards foreign ownership.

While these frequencies show a simple distribution of answers across the sample, the following typology seeks to identify how typical answer-patterns may be grouped together, and thus reveal underlying fan types with regard to football-related Europeanisation.

7.2.2 A New Typology of Football Fans: Making Europeanisation Visible

Our typology takes a two-step approach to the categorisation of football fans: First, we estimate the number of fan types that make up the typology, before analysing the nature of answer-patterns which distinguish these fan types. Based on the survey questions elaborated above, we thus construct our fan typology on the basis of fandom activity and intensity on the one hand, and differing attitudes towards the Europeanisation of football on the other.

How Many Different Types of Football Fans Are There?

The optimal number of groupings within the population is identified in the first stage. Based on indicators measuring incremental improvement to the model compared to the baseline of a single group of fans, the aim of this process is to identify as many types of fans as necessary and as few as possible.

Table 7.1 shows performance indicators for all models from the single-class null model to an over-complex seven-class model. The selection criteria for the optimal number of fan categories in the typology are sparsity, separateness and distinctness of the classes. In other words, we seek the minimum number of types to make the typology feasible, but the types should be as homogeneous as possible to distinguish clearly based on the differences between fan responses.

The optimal model is highlighted above, taking into account the combination of different indicators.[5] Our typology has four different types of football fans.

Essential Features of the Four Types of Football Fans

The four resultant fan types can be distinguished along two basic axes: intensity of fandom and the degree of importance attributed to local and national versus European and international aspects of belonging with regard to the transfer market and club competitions (identity characteristics). We define four categories as follows, starting with the largest group: occasional cosmopolitans (31%), occasional communitarians (29%), frequent cosmopolitans (25%) and frequent communitarians (15%, Fig. 7.2). The sample yields a majority (60%) of occasional fans, which are generally also cosmopolitan, though the difference to the communitarian group is less significant. The frequent fans are also predominantly cosmopolitan, but are more clearly distinguished from the communitarian group.

As our survey utilises a convenience sample, the data is consequently subject to some biases, which may have influence on the sizes of the groups (Cf. Chap. 5). We therefore focus primarily on the underlying structure of fan characteristics rather than on the size differences between the groups. Our main result is that cosmopolitan or communitarian views on aspects of team composition and competitions are found among both frequent *and* occasional fans. The following section details the

---

[5] The methodological steps of the selection process are elaborated in Weber et al. 2022.

7 Surveying Football Fans: Cosmopolitans and Communitarians

Table 7.1 Indicators for the quality of different models, the null model (1-class-model) to a 7-class-model

Classes	Estimated parameters	BIC	Improvement to null model	Improvement to sparser model	Log likelihood reduction	p	R2
1	33	82559.47					
2	67	79256.81	4.34%	4.34%	3574.31	0	0.8
3	101	77541.22	6.76%	2.52%	1987.23	0	0.82
4	135	76897.82	7.87%	**1.19%**	915.04	0	0.8
5	169	76515.11	8.67%	0.86%	654.36	0	0.8
6	203	76244.67	9.32%	0.72%	542.08	0	0.79
7	237	76169.42	9.75%	0.46%	346.9	0	0.79

R^2 is an entropy-based R^2-value using the formula from Oberski (2015, 66).
p = p-value of a Chi²-distribution with the respective degrees of freedom, R^2 = entropy-based R^2-value

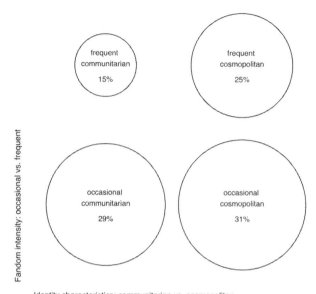

Fig. 7.2 Fan types: Classes of the latent class analysis, group characteristics and sizes. N=2950

precise characteristics of our four groups and how a typical member of each group would answer the indicator items.

The indicators relating to fandom intensity reveal comparatively clear distinctions between the four groups. The two categories of frequent fans and the two categories of occasional fans each return similar answer-patterns to questions measuring match attention and connection to the club. Among *occasional* fans home match attendance is sporadic and away match attendance rare. The *frequent* fans regularly attend home matches and most of them also frequently travel to domestic away matches. Attendance at away matches abroad was rare among all respondents—with few fans, irrespective of their group belonging, prepared to travel internationally to support their clubs with any regularity.

Indicators relating to aspects of Europeanisation of football revealed far more complex differences between the groups. We use the terms 'cosmopolitan' and 'communitarian' to differentiate between fans for whom a sense of national belonging constitutes an important aspect of their fandom (communitarians) and those that accord it little or no salience (cosmopolitans). The latter term has been used by Giulianotti and Robertson (2009, 31–62) in their work on football's globalisation. Communitarianism is used less frequently in football fandom scholarship (but see Benkwitz and Molnar 2012, Abutbul-Selinger 2019).

The groups that we denote as *cosmopolitan* are distinguished by their lack of any preoccupation with notions of national belonging or explicit repudiation of the concept. Conversely, the groups that we call *communitarians* attribute at least some importance to national belonging. The two main most visible aspects of Europeanisation in football are the Europeanised transfer market and the prevalence of European competitions. The fans groups can thus be distinguished by their views on the national origin of players and club owners, and their perspectives on the role of the European competitions (Fig. 7.3).

Players' and Owners' Origin

There is broad agreement across all groups that the development and retention of players from the club's youth system is desirable, while there

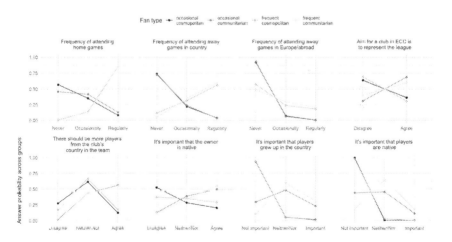

Fig. 7.3 Decisive differences between fan types: predicted answer probabilities of the decisive items at given group membership. Graphs show the answer probability of a certain item conditional on group membership for the four types of fans. N=2950

is little consensus across or among any fan groups regarding the recruitment of foreign-produced players. The clearest distinction between groups we class as *cosmopolitans* and those designated *communitarians* is rather to be found in the prominence accorded to nationality as a reference frame for belonging.

The two *cosmopolitan* groups are broadly unconcerned about the nationality of either players or club owners, and explicitly reject the assertion that players or staff need be nationals of or native to the country of the club that employs them. The two groups here designated *communitarians* differ from the other two groups in that they broadly agree that a club's roster should be made up primarily of local players, ideally hailing from the club's region but at least from the same country, whereas the cosmopolitans are either indifferent on the issue or explicitly repudiate parochial sentiments. The salience of the nation as reference frame can thus be taken as a key point of distinction between cosmopolitans and communitarians.

The varying relevance accorded sentiments of national belonging evidenced by these answer-patterns allow us to discern some distinct category characteristics. For the cosmopolitan groups, the origin of players, managers and owners is irrelevant. For the communitarians, the picture is more heterogeneous. There is a degree of ambiguity regarding the importance accorded player-nationality, but less so when it comes to ownership, with foreign club owners being regarded negatively. This might imply a normalisation of the internationalised transfer market, but less so when it comes to ownership structures, while no patterns implying any generic nationalism can be discerned (even) among the communitarian fans—in this sample at least.

European Competitions

Indicators pertaining to the relative weight placed on European competition vis-à-vis domestic leagues and perceptions of the representative role of clubs on the European stage produced mixed results. While fans across categories almost invariably accorded as much if not more weight to European competition than domestic leagues, a distinction can be made between the groups on the basis of how they understand the role of clubs at the European level. Those fans designated *communitarians* predominantly consider their clubs as representing the national league (and by proxy their country) when competing in European competition, while the *cosmopolitans* see European competition as simply a contest between the best teams on the continent irrespective of the clubs' national origin.

The typology takes the form of a 2 × 2 typology along the axes of fandom activity and attitudes towards localised belonging in a European context. In following section, we seek to specify the relevant characteristics that shape and refine the typology.

7.3 What Shapes the Fan Typology: League, Club and Individual Level Influences

Following the identification of football fan types, the question arises how these types are defined. We refer back to our case selection logic (cf. Chap. 5) that made use of differences between fandom contexts on the country level, on the league level and on the club level. Our potential influencing factors mirror these three levels: the league as such might shape fan types, given the different fan cultures across leagues (cf. Chap. 3). The club might shape fan types as the clubs' participation in European competitions or the share of foreign players might potentially influence attitudes. Where differences between countries in terms of the general public opinion towards Europe was relevant for case selection, we translate this to the individual level of fans. Individual attitudes towards Europe might also shape football-related attitudes. These thoughts shape our model for our further analysis.

7.3.1 Assumed Logics of Influence

We assume three different logics of influence that explain differences between fan types: one logic relates to the league and club level (the exposure logic) and two logics exert influence on the individual level (the spill-over logic and the socio-economic logic).

The **exposure logic** assumes that the more fans are exposed to transnational or cross-border experiences as part of their football fan activities, the less relevant national belonging becomes for them. This is based on well-established research on the subject of the shaping of European identity (cf. Chap. 4): Exposure to and cross-border contact with fellow Europeans can forge and reinforce a Europeanised identity. We model such exposure through three measures: Exposure to European competitions through respective club participation, and share of non-native players on the relevant club's roster, and the prevalence of foreign-born players among other teams in the club's domestic league. . Thus, the exposure logic leads to three hypotheses:

Hypothesis 1a: The more internationalised the respective club squad, the more cosmopolitan fans' attitudes.
Hypothesis 1b: The more prevalent ECC for the club, the more cosmopolitan fans' attitudes.
Hypothesis 1c: The more internationalised the league, the more cosmopolitan fans' attitudes.

The **spill-over logic** assumes that general political attitudes towards Europe and generic European identification "spill over" to football-related attitudes. The assumption is that general attitudes are linked to specific attitudes, that is, it is rather unlikely that fans that are strongly Europeanised in broad political outlook will hold to parochial positions when it comes to football, such as objecting to foreign players on their favoured team's roster. As a consequence, the more Europeanised fans are in general terms, the more they are cosmopolitan in football terms. We measure these general political attitudes by means of related (though non-identical) variables: the individual identification with Europe as compared to national identity, and individual attitudes towards immigration and European unification. This spill-over logic is tested using two hypotheses:

Hypothesis 2a: The more someone identifies with Europe and the less someone identifies with their nation in general terms, the more likely they are to be cosmopolitan.
Hypothesis 2b: The more positive someone's attitudes are towards European unification and immigration, the more likely they are to be cosmopolitan.

Last, the **socio-economic** logic builds on the body of literature that relates national and European identification patterns in individual socio-economic conditions (cf. Chap. 4). We assume, in accordance with past research on this issue, that cosmopolitan attitudes correlate with a higher social status and a higher educational level, but also influenced by age and urban/rural divide. Finally, we assume that a cross-border relation with the own club might make cosmopolitanism more likely: those residing outside their club's home country or those who are not native to their club's homeland might also be more cosmopolitan as investigation into the topic of foreign fandom suggest (Ludvigsen 2019; Kerr and Emery 2011). This logic is tested through four hypotheses.

Hypothesis 3a: The older someone is, the more prone to be communitarian.
Hypothesis 3b: Urban fans are more communitarian than rural fans.
Hypothesis 3c: More educated fans are more cosmopolitan than less educated fans.
Hypothesis 3d: Fans that reside outside the club's country OR are not native to the club's country are more cosmopolitan.

7.3.2 Analytical Model

Our model is a binary logistic regression model with a dependent variable measuring whether an individual has cosmopolitan or communitarian attitudes towards aspects of Europeanisation in football and 11 predictor variables to measure the aspects of the elaborated hypotheses. Figure 7.4 illustrates the analytical model and in particular the construction of the dependent variable. To test the hypotheses along three different logics, each of the three logics are tested separately to identify their individual explanatory power and compare them. Following this, the different logics are combined successively into one model for integration.

Dependent Variable
The dependent variable is derived from the fan typology developed above. As we are mainly interested in the difference between cosmopolitan and communitarian fans, we collapse the 2 × 2 typology into a two-level variable along the axis of attitude towards Europeanisation of the transfer

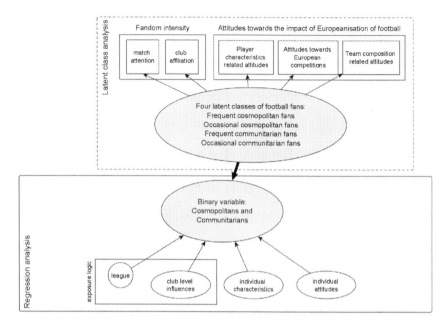

Fig. 7.4 Graphical overview of the analysis and illustrated procedure of constructing the dependent variable

market and competitions.[6] The distribution of the dependent variable is shown in Table 7.2.

Predictor Variables

The 11 predictor variables measure the aspects that were outlined above. The exposure logic covers variables on the club and league level, the socio-economic and the spill-over logics cover variables on the individual level.

Exposure Logic: League and Club Level

The variable set to test the exposure logic includes three variables on the league and the club level.

---

[6] A robustness check was performed using multinomial logistic regression with the four-level variable as dependent variable. The results highlighted that the fan activity is no relevant marker for fans regarding the elaborated hypotheses. As a result of this test, the dependent variable was collapsed to allow for a sparser and less complex model.

7 Surveying Football Fans: Cosmopolitans and Communitarians

Table 7.2 Distribution of the types of football fans, dependent variable for the regression analysis

Type of football fan	n	%	Type of football fan (binary)	n	%
Occasional cosmopolitan	930	31.5	Cosmopolitan	1668	56.5
Frequent cosmopolitan	738	25.1			
Occasional communitarian	854	28.9	Communitarian	1282	43.5
Frequent communitarian	428	14.5			

league The league of the club, a four-level factor covering the four leagues. These leagues can be interpreted as quasi-ordinal in the sense that they represent different levels of league-Europeanisation in two respects: The mean share of non-nationals among players in the participating clubs and past success of clubs of the league in the two European competitions, Champions League and Europa League. The latter is reflected in the UEFA country ranking. Both measures lead to the same order of leagues: Bundesliga (AT) < Ligue 1 < Bundesliga (DE) < Premier League. As the distances between the leagues cannot be understood as equal, the variable is used in the model as a nominal variable with Bundesliga (AT) as the reference category.

clubforeigners A metric variable returning the share of non-domestic players in the first team squad of the club. To account for the significant differences across the four leagues, the value is measured as difference from the league mean, calculated as share of non-domestic players of a club minus the mean share of non-domestic players of all clubs in the league. To account for occasional differences across in certain years, mean of the years 2013–2018 is calculated.[7]

high_ecc A dummy variable indicating whether the club has played a match in any European club competition matches during at least eight of the past ten seasons, which is taken to constitute regular participation in European competitions.

---

[7] All club-level data stems from transfermarket.de. Non-domestic is defined as not having the same nationality as that of the club.

"Spill over" Logic: Individual Attitudes and Identifications

The variables used to test the spill-over logic cover three individual attitudes towards the European integration and domestic immigration as well as general identification with Europe and the nation state.

immigration A ten-scale metric variable capturing the answer to "Immigration made my country" ranging from "a worse place to live …" (1) to "… a better place to live" (11).

EUunification

A ten-scale metric variable capturing the answer to "Unification of the European Union" ranging from "has already gone too far …" (1) to "… should go further" (11).

id_European A dummy variable for those identifying foremost as European. The dummy was created from an item capturing identification with either a) the nation state only, b) the nation state and Europe, c) Europe and the nation state, d) Europe only. 0 is for a) or b), 1 for c) or d).

Socio-economic Logic: Individual Level Characteristics

The variables employed to test the socio-economic logic cover five individual fan-characteristics.

age: the age of the individual in 2020.
education: duration of education in years.
urban: whether the respondent lives in an urban area. The dummy was created from an item capturing whether someone currently lives in a) a big city, b) the suburbs or outskirts of a big city, c) a town or small city or d) a country village, a farm, or a home in the countryside. 1 is for a) or b), 0 is for c) or d).
female: A dummy for those identifying as a woman.
resident: A dummy for those who currently live in the same country where the club is located. For English Premier League clubs, the answer "United Kingdom" was calculated as 1.

Table 7.3 shows the distribution of the predictor variables in the model.

7 Surveying Football Fans: Cosmopolitans and Communitarians

Table 7.3 Overview and distribution of the independent variables. Tables shows exp.(coeff). N=2950

Logic	variable	value	N	%	mean	median	min	max
Exposure	League	Bundesliga (AT)	256	9				
		Bundesliga (DE)	1562	53				
		Premier League	627	21				
		Ligue 1	505	17				
Spill-over	high_ECC				0.46	0	0	1
	Club foreigners				0.01	0	−0.25	0.53
	Immigration				7.43	8	1	11
	EUunification				7.87	9	1	11
	id_European				0.36	0	0	1
Socio-economic	Age				35.9	32	14	91
	Education				15.49	16	1	30
	Urban				0.52	1	0	1
	Female				0.09	0	0	1
	Resident				0.82	1	0	1

7.3.3 Results

Model Performance
In the first step of the analysis, we check how the individual logics perform (Table 7.4). As elaborated above, the leagues differ significantly regarding the share of foreign players and the chances they offer for clubs to play in European competitions. Model 1 thus includes only the league as independent variable. As described above, the leagues can be understood as being quasi-ordinal according to their level of Europeanisation. Here, the results show that the likelihood of having a cosmopolitan mindset is greater for fans of the German Bundesliga and the English Premier League compared to the (least Europeanised) Austrian Bundesliga, but lower for fans of clubs from the French Ligue 1 compared to the Austrian Bundesliga.

The *exposure logic model* builds both on the league and club differences. Within the same league, some clubs have more non-domestic players than other clubs and participation in European competition also differs across clubs. As we assume football fandom to be driven by a strong emotional attachment to a particular club, the frequency of a club's participation in European level competitions and the share of non-domestic players on their roster were hypothesised to be relevant for the degree of cosmopolitan versus communitarian attitudes among its fans. This exposure model performs only slightly better than the league-only model.

The *spill-over logic model* was based on the hypotheses that positive attitudes towards European integration, towards immigration and a European self-identification contribute to a football-oriented cosmopolitan mindset. Model 3 shows that this is indeed the case, all three variables correlate positively with cosmopolitanism. The model performs slightly worse than the model testing the exposure logic.

The *socio-economic logic* assumed a connection between football-related cosmopolitan attitudes and individual characteristics such as age, education, or an urban/rural divide. The model comparison shows that this model (Model 4) performs the worst of the three logics. Except for residency in the club's home country, all variables have the assumed effect on the probability to be cosmopolitan.

7 Surveying Football Fans: Cosmopolitans and Communitarians

Table 7.4 Regression coefficients and performance indicators for the logistic regressions. Reference group of the dependent variable: communitarian fans; shows exp(coeff) and SE in brackets. [1]Reference category: Bundesliga (AT)

Binomial regression – All models						
	League	Exposure	Spill-over	Socio-economic	Individual level	Combined
	(1)	(2)	(3)	(4)	(5)	(6)
Bundesliga (DE)[1]	1.340**	1.339**				1.133
	(0.137)	(0.138)				(0.146)
Ligue 1[1]	0.189***	0.194***				0.217***
	(0.168)	(0.171)				(0.179)
Premier League[1]	1.659***	1.727***				2.049***
	(0.153)	(0.154)				(0.174)
high_ECC		0.958				0.953
		(0.083)				(0.088)
clubforeigners_diff		4.641***				5.362***
		(0.415)				(0.436)
id_European			1.326***		1.384***	1.535***
			(0.086)		(0.088)	(0.094)
Immigration			1.196***		1.192***	1.148***
			(0.017)		(0.017)	(0.019)
EUunification			1.089***		1.059***	1.064***
			(0.015)		(0.016)	(0.018)
Age				0.986***	0.988***	0.987***
				(0.003)	(0.003)	(0.003)
Education				1.081***	1.068***	1.058***
				(0.009)	(0.010)	(0.011)
Urban				1.413***	1.242***	1.279***
				(0.077)	(0.080)	(0.085)
Female				1.329**	1.154	1.137
				(0.136)	(0.142)	(0.148)
Resident				0.927	0.959	1.375***
				(0.100)	(0.105)	(0.117)
Constant	1.306**	1.301*	0.162***	0.577***	0.104***	0.117***
	(0.126)	(0.135)	(0.140)	(0.188)	(0.236)	(0.292)
N	2950	2950	2950	2950	2950	2950
Log Likelihood	−1841.37	−1834.63	−1869.97	−1952.57	−1833.05	−1693.06
AIC	3690.77	3681.25	3747.95	3917.13	3684.09	3414.13
R^2 (Tjur)	0.12	0.12	0.1	0.04	0.12	0.21
RMSE	0.46	0.47	0.46	0.48	0.46	0.44
Correct predictions	57%	57%	56%	53%	57%	61%

*p < 0.1; **p < 0.05; ***p < 0.01

Two further models combine the logics: If the variables measuring the *spill-over* and the *socio-economic logics* are combined, we can see how powerful the variables on the individual level are in explaining the differences between communitarian and cosmopolitan attitudes in football fandom. Model 5 shows that the two logics complement each other to a large extent, although the combination of the two logics reduces the effect of gender to insignificance.

The full model combining all logics (Model 6) performs best in explaining the differences in attitudes. This model will be described in more detail below, using marginal effects and predicted probabilities.

Looking at the marginal effects of the different indicators in model 6 (Fig. 7.5), we see how the indicators differ in their explanatory power and how the effect of the different factors work when the other aspects are normalised. Marginal effects show how a particular indicator influences the likelihood for an individual being identified as cosmopolitan fan (rather than a communitarian fan) given that all other indicators remain constant (at mean, Fig. 7.5).

Verification of the Assumed Logics of Influence

While the model performance focuses on the explanatory power of each of the logics of influence, the substance of the logics needs a more fine-grained analysis. The following section discusses the results in relation to the hypotheses formulated above.

Exposure logic The assumption of the exposure logic was that the more fans get to experience "Europe" through football, the more they perceive it as normal. By this logic, the more Europeanised or internationalised clubs (in terms of the share of non-native players in their first team's squad), the more cosmopolitan their fans are. This can result from exposure at the league level (average share of non-native players across all clubs) or at the club level (share of non-native players at the fan's home club).

Regarding variation across leagues, fans of Austrian Bundesliga clubs are taken as the reference group in the model. The results show that fans of Premier League clubs are far more likely to be cosmopolitan fans than

7 Surveying Football Fans: Cosmopolitans and Communitarians

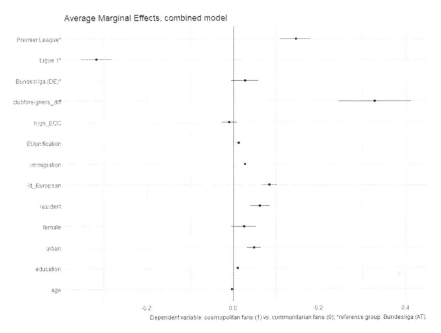

Fig. 7.5 Average Marginal Effects of the covariates in the combined regression model. Graph shows the change in predicted probability of cosmopolitan attitudes as the covariate changes by a 1-unit change

ABL fans no matter how different their clubs, their attitudes towards Europeanisation and their socio-economic status are. At the same time, Ligue 1 fans are more likely to be communitarian. German Bundesliga fans differ little from the ABL-fan baseline, a result which is somewhat remarkable given the differing levels of Europeanisation of the two leagues themselves. Thus, while the greater cosmopolitanism of fans of the internationalised and highly cosmopolitan EPL conforms to expectations, the similar attitudes of German and Austrian fans, as well as the communitarianism of Ligue 1 supporters, suggests league-level exposure may not be a powerful explanatory factor.

Conversely, the results confirm the exposure logic at the club level. No matter which league, the more foreign players a club has (compared to the other clubs in their respective national league), the more likely its fans are to have cosmopolitan attitudes. Yet once again, the exposure effects are not straightforward. We assumed that clubs that play regularly at the European level have a more cosmopolitan fan scene. But the effect of a high number of European appearances proved to be non-significant. This might hint at very different influences of the player and competition factor: While players are often the source of emotional attachment for fans, European competitions can still be seen as competitions between clubs as representatives of their respective nations.

Spill-over logic The spill-over logic assumes that generic attitudes toward Europeanisation spill over to football-related questions. In particular, we assumed that those who had pro-European and pro-immigration attitudes and self-identified with Europe would also be cosmopolitan. Irrespective of league and club, this is still true: there is a positive correlation between supporting EU integration and immigration and football-related cosmopolitanism, but the effect is very weak. Only those who identify first and foremost with Europe and only second with their nation-state are somewhat more likely to be football cosmopolitans.

Socio-economic logic Neither are the socio-economic explanations for the divide between communitarian and cosmopolitan fans confirmed in the combined model, though residence in the club's home country correlates weakly with fan cosmopolitanism. There might be explanations for such effect in international fandom and effects of expatriate fans that are beyond the scope of this work. As the effect is comparatively weak it can be seen as a minor factor in explaining differences across fans. Similarly, the lack of strong correlation detected here suggests that a hypothesised effect of social disparity among fans cannot explain why fans are either communitarian or cosmopolitan.

Summing up the results of the combined model, communitarian or cosmopolitan attitudes in terms of football fandom seem to be mostly caused by football itself rather than reflecting other societal influences.

7.4 Conclusions

An important starting point of this chapter was the observation that—despite the enormous body of literature dealing with football fan typologies—these attitudes towards Europeanisation and fan identification patterns have not received proper attention until recently. We draw on a survey across four leagues, covering a heterogeneous picture of football in Europe to develop a data-based typology of fans in Europeanised football. Latent class analysis was used to derive a statistically grounded typology.

The results show that football fans differ regarding their fandom intensity and their attitudes towards aspects that are directly connected with the Europeanisation of football structures, such as the composition of their teams and the perceived status of European competitions. Furthermore, four distinct types of football fans can be distinguished along two axes: fandom intensity (frequent vs. occasional) and attitude towards football Europeanisation (cosmopolitan vs. communitarian). The fandom intensity axis features two groups of fans: active fans with a high level of match attention and a close connection to their club, and occasional fans with a low number of matches attended and a comparatively loose connection with their club. The Europeanisation axis shows that fans also differ in how much importance they attribute to the role of national belonging for their identification with the club. These two axes form a 2 × 2-Matrix of fans (see Fig. 7.2), showing that the attitudes towards the Europeanisation aspects and fandom intensity are not linked. This result contrasts with earlier typologies that often emphasised the connectedness and locality of engaged fans in contrast to casual or less involved fans (cf. the cited studies of Clarke 1973 and Redhead 2003). Our results can be seen as a development and empirical, comparative corroboration of Giulianotti's (2002) *supporters, followers, fans* and *flâneurs* in English football, who were distinct both in their involvement in the game and their local connectedness.

The Europeanisation axis is complex. For the groups that we call the *cosmopolitans*, national belonging is not important, and they dismiss the relevance of nativity and language fluency of players, managers and owners. The *communitarian* groups tend to value such belonging more, especially on the question of club ownership. This shows that the Europeanisation of the transfer market is viewed very differently across different groups of the fans. While the relevance of national belongings differs between the groups, most all fans nonetheless value the development and retention of home-grown players. Such a strategy is often seen as an antithesis to the Europeanised player market: direct access to cheap talent from abroad reduces incentives for clubs to nurture their own talent (Niemann et al. 2011). For fans, these home-grown players matter, regardless of whether they value national connections to their clubs.

Disparate attitudes towards the Europeanisation of competitions also indicates a divide between the fans. In general, fans value the continental competition as being at least as important as national competition if not more so, but for those that we call the *communitarians*, European competitions remain a place of national representation, while the *cosmopolitans* view continental competition from a pan-European point of view, that is as a contest between the best teams in Europe regardless of national belonging.

These results go beyond older typologies which identified a stronger connection between the fandom intensity and their locality attitudes (Redhead 2003; Clarke 1978). The typology of Giulianotti (2002), distinguishing "hot" and "cool" fandom as well as traditional and consumer fan types, aligns more closely with our results, as it also identifies both intensity differences and connection differences among English football fans. Our results support Giulianotti's findings in regard to fandom intensity and complement his work through a quantitative empirical corroboration covering fans across four different European leagues in terms of a Europeanisation of their mindsets. The novel aspect is the complex distinction between cosmopolitans and communitarians in their attitudes towards the player market and European competitions which flow from that. While a local connection, and especially the relevance of home-grown players, is highly valued by all fans, we see that some supporters might be more prone to follow the trend of a Europeanisation of football than others. For some of the fans, the Europeanisation of football structures has a normalising effect as the relevance of national belonging diminishes.

In the second part of this chapter we analyse the factors influencing fans' attitudes at the individual level, with the spectrum of cosmopolitan/communitarian attitudes as the dependent variable. We hypothesise three different logics influencing individual fans' attitudes: (1) an exposure logic, (2) a spill-over logic and (3) a socio-economic logic. Of these logics, the exposure logic was most convincingly corroborated: the more Europeanised or internationalised football clubs in terms of share of non-native (European) players, the more likely that their respective fans hold cosmopolitan attitudes. At the same time, the results of this logic contradict some of our results in the previous chapter. While here, the exposure through participation in European competitions was far less influential than team composition for the cosmopolitan/communitarian divide, our earlier work revealed that the debates among fans in online message boards were strongly influenced by the clubs' European appearances. This leaves room for discussion on *how* the European competitions influence *which* fans in their everyday fandom. While the analysis of message boards focuses on the expressions of a potentially selected group of fans that devote time and energy to discussing football online on a message board that is explicitly related to their club, our survey might have been answered without such a direct connection to European competitions.

However, the most predictive power can be attributed to a combination of the three logics: that is, fans of Europeanised clubs competing in internationalised leagues who want more EU unification and are resident in the club's home country are most likely to adopt cosmopolitan attitudes. For example, this would give UK-based fans of Manchester United—where in 2018/19 60% of the squad was made up of non-native players, 71% of whom were non-native EU nationals—playing in the most internationalised European league, and who voted "Remain" in the Brexit-referendum, a very good chance to display cosmopolitan attitudes.

References

Abutbul-Selinger, Guy. 2019. 'We are not racists, we are nationalists': Communitarianism and Beitar Jerusalem. *Israel Studies Review* 34 (3): 64–82. https://doi.org/10.3167/isr.2019.340306.

Benkwitz, Adam, and Gyozo Molnar. 2012. Interpreting and exploring football fan rivalries: An overview. *Soccer & Society* 13 (4): 479–494. https://doi.org/1 0.1080/14660970.2012.677224.

Clarke, John. 1973. Football hooliganism and the skinheads. *Stencilled occasional paper*. Birmingham: University of Birmingham/Centre for Contemporary Cultural Studies.

———. 1978. Football and working class fans. In *Football hooliganism: The wider context*, ed. R. Ingham, 37–60. London: Interaction Inprint.

Collins, Linda M., and Stephanie T. Lanza. 2010. *Latent class and latent transition analysis: With applications in the social, behavioral, and health sciences*. John Wiley & Sons.

Giulianotti, Richard. 2002. Supporters, followers, fans, and flaneurs. *Journal of Sport and Social Issues* 26 (1): 25–46. https://doi.org/10.1177/ 0193723502261003.

Giulianotti, Richard, and Roland Robertson. 2009. *Globalization & football*. London: SAGE. https://doi.org/10.4135/9781446213544.

Hooghe, Marc, and Jennifer Oser. 2018. Social and political citizenship in European public opinion: An empirical analysis of T.H. Marshall's concept of social rights. *Government and Opposition* 53 (4): 595–620. https://doi.org/10.1017/gov.2017.11.

Kerr, Anthony K., and Paul R. Emery. 2011. Foreign fandom and the Liverpool FC: A cyber-mediated romance. *Soccer & Society* 12 (6): 880–896. https://doi.org/10.1080/14660970.2011.609686.

Linzer, Drew A., and Jeffrey B. Lewis. 2010. PoLCA: An R package for polytomous variable latent class analysis. *Journal of Statistical Software* 42 (10): 1–29. https://doi.org/10.18637/jss.v042.i10.

Ludvigsen, Jan Andre Lee. 2019. Transnational fan reactions to transnational trends: Norwegian Liverpool supporters, 'authenticity' and 'filthy-rich' club owners. *Soccer & Society* 20 (6): 872–890. https://doi.org/10.1080/1466097 0.2018.1448796.

Niemann, Arne, Borja García, and Wyn Grant, eds. 2011. *Transformation of European football: Towards the Europeanisation of the national game*. Manchester: Manchester University Press.

Oberski, Daniel. 2015. *Latent class analysis. European survey research association meeting Rejkjavik, 2015*. http://daob.nl/wp-content/uploads/2015/07/ESRA-course-slides.pdf

Oser, Jennifer, Marc Hooghe, and Sofie Marien. 2013. Is online participation distinct from offline participation? A latent class analysis of participation types and their stratification. *Political Research Quarterly* 66 (1): 91–101. https://doi.org/10.1177/1065912912436695.

Redhead, Steve. 2003. *Post-fandom and the millennial blues: The transformation of soccer culture*. Abingdon: Taylor and Francis.

Weber, Regina, Alexander Brand, Florian Koch, and Arne Niemann. 2022. Cosmopolitans and communitarians: A typology of football fans between national and European influences. *International Review for the Sociology of Sport* 57 (4): 532–551. https://doi.org/10.1177/10126902211028147.

Weerts, David J., Alberto F. Cabrera, and Paulina Pérez Mejías. 2014. Uncovering categories of civically engaged college students: A latent class analysis. *The Review of Higher Education* 37 (2): 141–168. https://doi.org/10.1353/rhe.2014.0008.

8

Football Fans' Narratives of Europe and the Game

Johannes Muntschick, Friedrich Plank, and Regina Weber

8.1 Introduction

Our third empirical chapter focusses on the individual football fan and his or her personal attitudes and self-understandings. As part of a larger group of club supporters, individual fans could ideally typify the attitudes and features of football fandom of their clubs—or at least provide anecdotal evidence thereof. Against this background, the aim of this chapter is to contribute to the overall research question on Europeanisation of fan identities by taking the perspective of individual sense-making. The empirical part follows the volume's analytical scheme of two main dimensions of Europeanised identities: (1) 'communities of belonging' (COB) and (2) 'frames of reference' (FOR). The first combines dynamics of inclusion and exclusion, understandings of in-group and out-group, perceptions of community and discord, and 'narratives' within that context. The second includes preferences and assessments of aspects of football and fandom at the individual level, as well as a wide range of typical fan activities (following football events, travel activities, network building, etc.) in its spatial scope, meaning national versus European-level competitions and the geographic range in which they engage (Weber et al. 2022; see Chap. 5 of this volume).

The chapter is based on qualitative, semi-structured interviews with fans of six of the eight clubs selected for this study from Austria, Germany and England. It is structured in five parts. First, we will outline our database and methodology before we engage with the descriptive findings from the interviews with individual fans. Following the previously outlined logic of our research design (cf. Chap. 6), a set of four paired comparisons in three clusters analyses three main conditioning factors influencing fan attitudes towards the supposedly more Europeanised aspects of the game: the club level (sporting success), the league level (Europeanisation of player markets), and the embedding societal context (degree of Euroscepticism). The findings indicate that the Europeanisation of player markets and the participation of clubs in European competitions engendered positive attitudes in fans towards the Europeanisation of the game, whereas broader public opinion has only a limited effect. Fans' responses in the interviews illustrate these findings with occasionally rough but often very outspoken and pointed statements. Moreover, the analysis reveals that strong local, regional or national identifications of fans go often hand in hand with positive attitudes towards the Europeanisation of the game. Hence, the local, the regional, or the national seems complementary or in some cases even constitutive for the European.

8.2 Database and Methodology

We conducted a total of 63 interviews with individual football fans of different ages, various educational and social backgrounds, and professions between January 2020 and July 2021 (see Table 8.1).[1] Due to travel restrictions and lockdowns during the first two years of the Covid-19

---

[1] We would like to thank Florian Koch for his efforts to act as an interviewer for a few interviews with Bayern Munich and Hannover 96 fans.

Table 8.1 List of pseudonymised interviews

No	Interview ID	Club	Gender	Age	Date	Digital/In person
1	200702_001	Bayern München	Male	41	02.07.2020	Digital
2	200624_001	Bayern München	Male	21	24.06.2020	Digital
3	200711_001	Bayern München	Male	18	11.07.2020	Digital
4	200623_001	Bayern München	Male	58	23.06.2020	Digital
5	8072021	Bayern München	Male	37	08.07.2021	Digital
6	15012021	Bayern München	Male	35	15.01.2021	Digital
7	16012021	Bayern München	Male	33	16.01.2021	Digital
8	09_07_2021	Bayern München	Male	25	09.07.2021	Digital
9	13_07_2021	Bayern München	Female	48	13.07.2021	Digital
10	20_07_2021	Bayern München	Female	26	20.07.2021	Digital
11	30_07_2021	Bayern München	Female	25	30.07.2021	Digital
12	200701_001	Hannover 96	Male	23	01.07.2020	Digital
13	20200112	Hannover 96	Male	29	01.12.2020	Digital
14	2122020	Hannover 96	Male	39	02.12.2020	Digital
15	8012021	Hannover 96	Male	43	08.01.2021	Digital
16	17122020	Hannover 96	Male	69	17.12.2020	Digital
17	27012021	Hannover 96	Female	40	27.01.2021	Digital
18	90321	Hannover 96	Male	65	09.03.2021	Digital
19	180321	Hannover 96	Male	25	18.03.2021	Digital
20	280421_1	Hannover 96	Male	21	28.04.2021	Digital
21	280421_2	Hannover 96	Male	20	28.04.2021	Digital
22	290321	Hannover 96	Male	25	29.03.2021	Digital
23	300321zwei	Hannover 96	Male	21	30.03.2021	Digital
24	300321	Hannover 96	Male	?	30.03.2021	Digital
25	201106_002	Manchester United	Male	28	06.11.2020	Digital
26	201111_001	Manchester United	Male	31	11.11.2020	Digital
27	201111_002	Manchester United	Male	63	11.11.2020	Digital

(*continued*)

Table 8.1 (continued)

No	Interview ID	Club	Gender	Age	Date	Digital/In person
28	201112_001	Manchester United	Male	58	12.11.2020	Digital
29	201113_001	Manchester United	Male	24	13.11.2020	Digital
30	201116_001	Manchester United	Male	30	16.11.2020	Digital
31	201119_001	Manchester United	Male	68	19.11.2020	Digital
32	201204_001	Manchester United	Male	74	04.12.2020	Digital
33	200310_001	Newcastle United	Male	37	10.03.2020	Digital
34	200312_001	Newcastle United	Male	44	12.03.2020	In person
35	200312_002	Newcastle United	Male	27	12.03.2020	Digital
36	200313_001	Newcastle United	Male	21	13.03.2020	Digital
37	200316_001	Newcastle United	Female	22	16.03.2020	In person
38	200917_001	Newcastle United	Male	39	17.09.2020	Digital
39	200922_001	Newcastle United	Male	39	22.09.2020	Digital
40	200922_002	Newcastle United	Male	50	22.09.2020	Digital
41	200924_001	Newcastle United	Male	64	24.09.2020	Digital
42	200929_001	Newcastle United	Male	26	29.09.2020	Digital
43	200114_002	Sturm Graz	Male	34	14.01.2020	Digital
44	200115_001; 200115_002	Sturm Graz	Male	62	15.01.2020	In person
45	200116_003	Sturm Graz	Male	28	16.01.2020	In person
46	200117_001	Sturm Graz	Male	22	17.01.2020	In person
47	200117_002	Sturm Graz	Male	31	17.01.2020	In person
48	200118_001	Sturm Graz	Female	31	18.01.2020	In person
49	200120_001	Sturm Graz	Male	63	20.01.2020	In person
50	200124_001	Sturm Graz	Male	45	24.01.2020	In person

(continued)

Table 8.1 (continued)

No	Interview ID	Club	Gender	Age	Date	Digital/In person
51	200125_001	Sturm Graz	Male	49	25.01.2020	In person
52	200128_001	Sturm Graz	Female	70	28.01.2020	In person
53	200204_001	Wacker Innsbruck	Male	58	04.02.2020	In person
54	200205_001	Wacker Innsbruck	Male	39	05.02.2020	In person
55	200205_002	Wacker Innsbruck	Male	44	05.02.2020	In person
56	200206_001	Wacker Innsbruck	Male	44	06.02.2020	In person
57	200206_002	Wacker Innsbruck	Male	50	06.02.2020	Digital
58	200210_001	Wacker Innsbruck	Male	62	10.02.2020	In person
59	200210_002	Wacker Innsbruck	Male	28	10.02.2020	In person
60	200211_001	Wacker Innsbruck	Male	33	11.02.2020	Digital
61	200212_001	Wacker Innsbruck	Male	50	12.02.2020	In person
62	200212_002	Wacker Innsbruck	Male	36	12.02.2020	In person
63	200213_001	Wacker Innsbruck	Female	52	13.02.2020	In person

pandemic, most interviews took place online through the use of video conferencing tools. These extraordinary circumstances did not have any noticeable negative or positive impact on the quality of our interviews acording to our understanding.

Our attempts to compile as representative a sample of fans as possible is limited by the small n, namely of the individual club samples and possible biases regarding the composition of each of these samples. Taking gender as an example, our total sample of interviewees contains only eight female fans. This is a share of only 12.7%, which is only slightly lower than the share of women interested in football competitions in the French Ligue 1 and the German Bundesliga. The share of women interested in the English Premier League, however, stands at least for 20% and there is evidence that as many as 37% of global football fans today are women (Nielsen 2022, 4). This illustration exemplifies how, despite all our efforts at purposive sampling and greatest possible variation, significant limitations to claiming full representativeness remain.

Using a semi-structured questionnaire, we conducted about ten (+/-) interviews with fans of almost every club of our selection: Bayern Munich (11), Hannover 96 (13), Manchester United (8), Newcastle United (10), Sturm Graz (10), and Wacker Innsbruck (11). Unfortunately, and due to unexpected difficulties and restrictions in the context the intensifying Covid-19 pandemic, only very few interviews with supporters from the two French clubs could be gathered. Given this lack of data we decided that the focus for our systematic interview analysis and the paired comparison mainly rests on the clubs from Austria, England, and Germany.

The interviews with the football fans, conducted in German or English and recorded with the consent of the participants, were transcribed before we proceeded with qualitative data analysis (using MAXQDA software) of the anonymised texts. Our common conceptual framework served as a guide to identify relevant passages, and we applied it to the empirical material by coding inter alia all relevant parts of the interviews into the themes COB and FOR (see Chap. 5 of this volume).

8.3 Description of Interview Findings Across Six Clubs

Before engaging in a detailed analysis of the three sets of four paired comparisons, we outline descriptive findings of the interviews with fans of six clubs: Bayern Munich, Hannover 96, Manchester United, Newcastle United, Sturm Graz, and Wacker Innsbruck.

8.3.1 FC Bayern München: Dahoam[2] in Europe

Fans of Bayern Munich are very proud of their club and express a self-conscious attitude clearly rooted in an expectation of success. This is not surprising insofar as Bayern Munich is the record champion of the German Bundesliga and a frequent participant in European competitions, where the club has won several trophies in recent years. Perhaps as a result, fans of other German clubs occasionally attribute a certain arrogance to Bayern Munich fans, despite Bayern fans frequently recounting friendships and good relations with fans of other Bundesliga clubs. Apparently, celebrating successes (and possibly being spoiled by successes) is one reason why people from all over Germany—and beyond—became Bayern Munich supporters (interview 8). A strong regional connection to Bavaria as *Heimat* is part of the club's identity but does not preclude a pronounced outward-orientation across borders, towards European competitions and successes.

Bayern Munich fans' in- and out-group formation indicates that a local or national background is desirable, notably with regard to recruiting new players, but not a necessary condition to become part of the community of belonging. One fan explains:

> So, it doesn't have to be Germans, but just people who have already played in a German club before. At best, of course, from the own youth, which, well, rarely happens. (Interview 10)[3]

According to some fans a certain German background, not in a tribal sense but rather referring to German language proficiency, is desirable for practical reasons because this is said to make it easier to integrate new players into the team; ideally they are already familiar with the German football system. Most fans argue that a player's or manager's origin is not relevant as long as they fit into Bayern Munich and identify with the club. Others emphasise that they should be likeable, have brains and

---

[2] Bavarian dialect for 'at home'.
[3] All quotes from the German and Austrian clubs have been translated into English with the help of DeepL. Translations have been edited minimally to ensure readability when necessary.

harmonise well. In general, however, quality and performance are decisive factors:

> As long as the player reasonably fulfils his target and he can help the club, I ultimately do not care where he comes from. What I see rather critical is that more and more larger transfer sums are ultimately paid for players. (Interview 8)

Regarding sponsorship, Bayern Munich supporters think practically and critically. They are aware that football is an international business and money matters to success, but not at any price. One fan remarks:

> Of course, they must have money, otherwise they can't give any money. So it should not be anyone who is dubious. Where you think, oh God: What have they done? (Interview 9)

While most fans share the idea that it is desirable to have a Bavarian or German company with a good reputation as main sponsor, they are highly critical of "Russian oligarchs" (interview 9) or businesses such as Qatar Airways who they do not believe share their values (interviews 2, 4 & 5).

In sum, Bayern Munich fans' COB are based in self-identity and for pragmatic reasons (language) mainly located at the regional and national level, albeit also European and cosmopolitan in a sense as they are open-minded towards international players and trainers who could enrich the team and enhance the club's performance. They are sceptical of big international sponsors with dubious backgrounds which might sully the club's reputation.

Regarding frames of reference, the interviews reveal that national competitions are important insofar as winning the German Bundesliga is almost mandatory. This is also reflected in responses when asked about the club's biggest rivals: most refer to Borussia Dortmund and RB Leipzig. Only few have difficulty finding an easy answer—and refer to European clubs:

Nationally, if you have to name one, it's probably Dortmund, but currently I think Dortmund and Leipzig are really good. […] in general, it's just really difficult. But if you win the Bundesliga championship eight times in a row, you can't talk about having a tough rival. Internationally I think there exist a few, so even besides Barca there is City in England. (Interview 6)

Since Bayern Munich has repeatedly won the German Bundesliga and occasionally the German football association's trophy (DFB-Pokal) in recent years, fans seem to be so accustomed to national achievements that their ambitions and frames of reference have become increasingly Europeanised. Winning the 'Meisterschaft'[4] is just a welcome domestic step on the pathway towards European competitions, which are the natural and deserved playground for the best clubs and offer an opportunity to meet opponents of their own class.

The main goal is to win the championship, but that's just the way it's been for the last eight years […] okay, the Bundesliga is a goal, but it's actually just a secondary goal. (Interview 2)

Several Bayern Munich fans account UEFA Champions League (CL) games as their best football experiences. One fan, for example, raves about winning the CL final against Borussia Dortmund in 2013:

I watched the game in public viewing with friends and stuff like that. […] And for the first time after twelve years to see a Champions League victory. And to see FC Bayern back at the top of Europe in the end. That was a very special highlight and very beautiful moment. (Interview 8)

The fan's high regard of this match is interesting insofar as it has been perceived within a European frame of reference although it was an entirely German final between two (rival) Bundesliga clubs.

While most fans admire the level of play in European competitions, there is also criticism—mainly towards the CL. In contrast to the Bundesliga, which fans like because of its down-to-earth character, comparatively low degree of commercialisation and a great atmosphere in

---

[4] The winner of the Bundesliga holds the Meisterschaft title at the end of the annual football season.

many stadiums (interview 3), the CL is perceived as too detached from the fans despite its obvious attractiveness.

> For me it just goes too much in this direction of commerce. The fan doesn't play a role. [...] That maybe they're considering holding the Champions League final in Qatar or Beijing. Where I think to myself, that's just a European competition. I don't have to play the final in Qatar because I can pocket a few more millions there. (Interview 5)

Some Bayern Munich fans fear that European football and the transfer market are unfair in a sense as they favour only the few big and wealthy clubs in Europe, which causes further concentration effects.

> I think that Europe is already quite unfair and very focused on the top [...] money is spread over two or actually one club in Germany, one club in England and two clubs in Spain and maybe one in Italy, which of course also leads to the fact that the excitement in the Champions League is terribly low now [...] and also the player market is in such a way [...] that makes it not really diverse and very boring in my eyes. The money is simply distributed very unevenly. (Interview 7)

Notwithstanding such sporadic complaints, most Bayern Munich supporters do actually follow the matches on various media channels and would travel to away games if possible. Among our selection of interviewed fans, however, only a minority had travelled abroad to watch Bayern Munich play. The self-understanding as a European top club is nonetheless reflected in positive references to big teams from other European countries and many Bayern supporters follow other European top leagues (mainly the French and English).

In sum, the analysis of the FOR shows that the national level is important, and the Bundesliga is a good place for demonstrating performance and (re-)establishing superiority over domestic competitors. Achievements at the European level are realistic and form a regular part of the club's seasonal goals, often referred to as 'the triple'.[5] Bayern Munich fans are

---

[5] The triple includes winning the German Meisterschaft, the DFB-Pokal and a European competition.

self-confident and aware that their club is one of the few big clubs in Europe who have the ambition and capacity to win European competitions on top of the national championship.

8.3.2 Hannover 96: Playing National, Dreaming Europe

Hannover 96 is a German football club with a long history and its fans draw part of their self-esteem and love for the club from its bygone golden past. National competitions and domestic issues are highly relevant, as are questions of club management and key investors. Hannover 96 fans regard European competitions as desirable but currently out of reach for their club. Besides a decent interest in European football, however, bitter criticism often prevails against an alleged de-coupling and over-commercialisation of European competitions.

Interviews reveal that Hannover 96 supporters' in- and out-group formation has a regional focus with some features that go beyond national borders. Many consider a regional or local connection to players with 'football origins' in Hanover or the club's youth important, believing that this provides for stability in the team, makes players stay longer due to their regional connection, and strengthens the bonds between fans and the squad:

> I would find it very cool if a player comes from the Hanover region. That is pretty much currently the top priority [...] players who burn for the club, identify with the club rather than players who come from far away, cost some money, who have names, but just do not identify themselves very much with the club. (Interview 23)

This demand for a local or regional connection need not imply a tribal parochialism, however. Another fan highlights several advantages of a regional connection for the club but emphasises that the nationality and origin of the players is not important:

Of course, it's nice when players are [...] from Lower Saxony, maybe even trained at home. That implies that you don't have to spend a lot on transfers, the player knows the club very well and the people and this includes possibly also a bit of a feeling of guilt to do their part, I would say, about wanting to continue playing at the club, but I don't really care about nationality [...] that never played a role as long as the players are willing to integrate. (Interview 13)

Many fans display a very pragmatic attitude in this regard: local or regional connections are assumed to make it easier for players and managers to adapt to Hannover 96, become an integral part of the team and thus perform better. One fan emphasises when asked about the importance of the origin of trainers:

It does not matter. So, I'll put it this way, if he can speak German well, I think it's best; would make everything a lot easier. But well, if there is no other way, then you just make the compromise, you'll definitively get there somehow. (Interview 21)

While most fans deny the significance of nationality, good language proficiency is considered instrumental to harmonise with(in) the squad. Apart from that, Hannover 96 supporters prioritise that players, trainers, managers and newcomers identify with the club, are down-to-earth, approachable and show good character traits. Other factors, however, seem to have a distinctly excluding impact. One fan emphasises "that the player is not just coming for the money [...] and is not one of those, shall we say, mercenaries" (interview 20). Another fan adds that a player should not "come to the first training session completely extroverted with his leopard Lamborghini. Moreover, he shouldn't come from Braunschweig [the local rival; the authors]" (interview 24).

Regarding the in- and out-grouping of sponsors, Hannover 96 fans likewise consider regional connections important as local sponsors could better identify themselves with the club and vice versa. Equally important seems to be that potential sponsors have a respectable reputation, including their products and working conditions. This goes hand in hand with critical remarks towards international sponsors from Qatar or Saudi Arabia where the human rights situation is questionable.

In sum, the COB of the Hannover 96 fans focus on the region, but primarily for pragmatic reasons and certainly not in a sense as to exclude newcomers and outsiders. Nonetheless actors who are seen as too aloof or obviously money driven are seen by many fans as incompatible with the club's identity.

Regarding frames of reference, talks with Hannover 96 supporters indicate that national competitions are considered key.

> I only watch Hannover, I don't watch the UEFA Cup, I don't watch the Champions League, because it's just […] so far away from me […] only Hannover 96, but that's the most important thing, of course. (Interview 14)

Such statements indicate that European football is too distant for some Hannover 96 fans—obviously in terms of performance gaps or simply because their club has not played European competitions in over a decade (interview 20). Most supporters value national competitions as the remaining arena where their club plays—or in case of the first Bundesliga: used to play. Given this situation, fans settle for focussing on national competitions, despite admitting (implicitly) that other (European) leagues and competitions offer better quality football. One fan highlights:

> For me, it's not about Hannover being the best team in Europe, it's more about being able to watch soccer in Hannover. Bundesliga, at best. So that is high level, but it doesn't need to be the best in the world. (Interview 21)

This is corroborated by the fact that the biggest rival of Hannover 96, Eintracht Braunschweig, is a German club within regional distance. Some fans, however, look beyond regional rivalry and also refer to European competitions as highly valuable and exciting. They dream of Hannover 96 playing against European top-level clubs, again, possibly remembering of a few seasons of the club's 'golden past' where it participated in European competitions. One fan explains:

For me personally, as a Hannover 96 fan, it was more exciting internationally, because it was then completely new clubs, completely new countries that you could explore, so to speak, and the international competitions still have a completely different, I'll say, charm. So [...] it's really a highlight when 96 plays against a club that you only know from TV. (Interview 22)

During the few years when Hannover 96 participated in European competitions, a remarkably large share of fans took these competitions—and even the preceding test matches—as an opportunity to travel around Europe and visit cities and stadiums abroad. Football-related experiences in West and East Europe were predominantly positive. Moreover, they were often perceived as more nail-biting than regular Bundesliga matches, even when 'only' watching via television as this fan recalls:

The two years in Europe, yes, that was a gift, yes, those games. [...] I was only in front of the TV [...] the Sevilla game, the first one. I died a thousand deaths. (Interview 14)

Appreciation and admiration of European football is often combined with a very critical attitude towards an alleged over-commercialisation of football in general and of European competitions in particular, specifically the Champions League. According to many fans, there is an alarming influx of big money and too much influence of wealthy sponsors in top-level European football. One fan remembers:

When Hannover was in the Europa League, it was a completely different experience, because they played internationally. That was something cool and something attractive, but it was all about the money in the end. (Interview 21)

Such grievances do not prevent Hannover 96 fans from following European football, although their top priority is definitively the national-level competition. This is because the club's relegation to the second Bundesliga a few years ago and the (so far unsuccessful) quest to return to the first German league is important and a burning issue for many fans. This is also reflected in many supporters' references to domestic and club-related issues, often including comments about their president (and key sponsor) Martin Kind whose ambitions and actions regularly raise mixed feelings and conflicting sentiments among Hannover 96 fans (interview 14).

In sum, the analysis of the FOR shows that the main frame is the national level and fans regard as crucial that their club becomes more stable and successful, with a view to regaining a place in the 1. Bundesliga. European football is an object of nostalgia for Hannover 96, but its fans are realistic enough to recognise that European competitions are currently out of reach.

8.3.3 Manchester United: Local at Heart— International in Ambitions

Manchester United (ManU) supporters show an attitude that emphasizes the club's local connection, but their community of belonging is certainly not national. Many admire players who play attractive football irrespective of their origin and background. ManU fans are proud of their club, which they regard as rich in tradition, and are confident about its successes, (past) international trophies and overall reputation. One fan remarks that "Manchester United's reputation for me as a big club depends on us winning trophies. We can't go three, four, five, six, seven years without winning a trophy because that would be horrendous" (interview 8), which gives good reasons to assume that (inter)national success forms part of the club's and supporters' identity. It is therefore not surprising that many fans of the 'Red Devils'[6] show interest in European football and follow matches and competitions at the European level.

The ManU fans' in- and out-group formation indicates that a local background or connectedness with the region is important to some extent because it strengthens the bonds between the team and its supporters and makes players more loyal to the club and its values—and ideally stay longer. One fan mentioned:

---

[6] Red Devils is a common nickname of Manchester United.

> United have always got a history of having our home-grown players [...] To me it's important to be able to see local players like Brandon Williams who was recently coming to the team for United. His mum runs a market stall, it's just down the road from me. So, it's nice to have that little touch and that connection. (Interview 30)

While several fans share these thoughts on the benefits of home-grown players for practical reasons, there is no evidence of tribalism or exclusion because of ethnicity or foreign nationality. In contrast, there is strong evidence for a clear transnational outlook that goes beyond borders and reflects an appreciation of universal values and characteristics that have little to do with personal background.

> But above all, I think what's more important to me is that they fit in with the thoughts of the club. The club have always been known for playing attractive football. So, I like to think that we're buying players who can excite the crowd. The United fans traditionally in my view have always liked players who take risks [...]. (Interview 32)

While this suggests a recognition of the benefits of the international transfer market for a club with sufficient financial resources such as Manchester United, a view shared by several supporters, there are also voices who are ambivalent about this business, referring to a player "being forced to move to a club he doesn't really like. He doesn't want to move to the cold north-west of England and he never settled" (interview 26). In general, however, ManU supporters are inclusive towards players and managers who share the values and ideals of the club and, more importantly, who are hungry for victory and perform, irrespective of where they come from. One supporter emphasises:

> Of course it needs to be a manager that is qualified to win. [...] Although the nationality of the coach doesn't matter, I think for this [the identity of the club; the authors] he needs to embrace some of the particular values either of the club or of the city or of the country as well. (Interview 25)

This rather meritocratic point of view corresponds with an occasionally pragmatic attitude towards club owners and sponsors. One fan argues

"A good owner for me would be one that puts playing success first, winning trophies first, rather than what they can take from the club" (interview 32). This attitude seems to be well justified in light of EPL (English Premier League) club owners who have taken money out of their clubs over the past couple years. These are negative examples, of course, but several ManU fans seem to be generally critical—or even dismissive—of international ownership in club football (interview 28).

In sum, ManU fans' COB are rooted at the local and regional level, yet extend to the European and international level, as expressed through a cosmopolitan, pragmatic worldview that apparently values performance over local roots and sensitivities.

Regarding frames of reference, interviews with ManU fans show that most see national competitions as important. When asked about the club's biggest rival, for example, virtually all supporters referred to Liverpool or other teams in the Premier League (e.g. Manchester City or Leeds). Only one fan requested clarification on the question "In Europe or in Britain?" (interview 31), which suggests that two important levels of reference can prevail in parallel; even though the eventual answer was "In general? Liverpool" (interview 31).

Most ManU fans perceive the EPL as a strong league, at least compared to other European football leagues, and attribute a certain quality and toughness to English football. This seems to make national competitions particularly attractive.

> I do think the significance of winning the English Premier League – again, with two of the United's most important rivals have been the champions for the last couple of years – would have a very important, symbolising role as opposed to winning the Champions League which can be resolvable pure luck, but you can be lucky in who you draw the particular matches that are played. It is a cup tournament. But in the Premier League in order to win you have to be good throughout the whole season for 38 matches. (Interview 31)

Many supporters share this attitude, highlighting that

> The Premier League is number one. The Premier League, which is the Golden Fleece. When you go to the Premier League, you've got to show you real colours by winning a championship. The Champions League is the icing on the cake. First is the Premier League. Home grounds, you got to win it there. (Interview 27)

It seems, again, that valuing the EPL as important frame of reference is compatible with a strong interest and ambitions in European competitions. However, several ManU supporters share an attitude that the domestic league comes first. They love to see their club winning the Premier League over/before winning international competitions. The latter are seen as an additional nice-to-have, along the lines of 'dry bread at home is better than roast meat abroad'. Unsurprisingly, the Europa League (EL) is perceived less relevant and prestigious than the more competitive Champions League (interview 25).

However, fans' admiration of international competitions and their prestige goes often hand in hand with criticism on the business and institutions behind such events. Ambivalent attitudes also exist towards the transfer market, which offers opportunities for wealthy clubs but seems to be hyped up by money. Fans are aware of a division in European football which gives advantage to big clubs with good infrastructure and sufficient (financial) resources to participate in premium football and top-level competitions. Although Manchester United is obviously part of that group, several fans express mixed feelings about the CL and its current structure:

> I think that it's kind of premium competition, especially Champions League, of course, because they try to make it as competitive for the biggest teams as possible. Obviously, it's getting harder and harder to get to Champions League, even group stage for smaller teams from weaker leagues […]. (Interview 29)

Nevertheless, several fans welcome ManU matches in such competitions as an opportunity to travel around Europe and beyond. This makes them exceptional compared to 'ordinary' EPL games because international away games offer insights in different (football) cultures.

What we usually do is we'll travel for the match and then we might stay an extra day to have a look around the place and take in some of the scenery and the culture and what-have-you. So, quite enjoyable, really. Lisbon, Belgrade was nice to do that. (Interview 32)

In sum, the analysis of the FOR shows that the national level is important as a measure of the club's quality and competitiveness and to celebrate success, while achievements in European and international competitions are more prestigious and 'nice to have'. Fans usually perceive Man United as one of the big clubs in Europe which not only plays attractive football but also has defined ambitions to participate (and succeed) in European competition.

8.3.4 Newcastle United: Local Working-Class Identity with Interest in Europe

Fans of the Newcastle United Football Club (NUFC), often nicknamed the 'Toon Army', show strong emotional connections to their club and are proud of its long history and local (also social) rootedness. Many fans have supported NUFC since childhood, irrespective of whether the club achieved successes at national or international level during that time. The supporters embrace their underdog status and cultivate the self-image of a small, down-to-earth working-class club. Their attitude towards European football is that of mostly positive interest; although they are aware that participation in European competitions is ambitious and probably currently out of reach.

NUFC fans' in- and out-group formation has a focus on the local, specifically the city of Newcastle, or the surrounding region (Tyne and Wear). This is, however, neither tribal nor exclusive in terms of origin. NUFC fans emphasise repeatedly that their—and the club's—identity is rooted in social class and Newcastle United's historical background as a working-class club, as one fan highlights:

Newcastle United have been an important club in English football since the 1900s when the football league was started. It was all built up around industrial heartland and we're a working-class city, we're working-class region with coal mines and shipyards, we have steel works. [...] The point I'm making is we're proud of our working-class area. (Interview 38)

Several fans emphasise that they are hard-working people from the working class, which, they argue, reinforces the self-image of the club and its supporters. It also explains the strong bonds between them and the team as well as the particular NUFC spirit:

> I think the type of clubs that are working class and work hard you always see that correlation with the stadium and the fans and the club itself, you always see that kind of connection. (Interview 36)

To be part of the in-group implies subscribing to this image and adhering to traditional—possibly even stereotypical—working-class values. This is reflected in many supporters' statements when asked what they value in players and trainers, as one fan remarks:

> I want someone in the Newcastle team who would be like that [a working man like me; the authors] and would nurture the younger players and get a little bit more fight out of them because they're not the best players in the world. [...] someone who was more level-headed and sensible and just a good solid professional, not necessarily the most fancy. (Interview 40)

Several fans express the wish and need for more player from the club's own youth (academy) because they assume that they will easily fit to the team and strengthen the club's identity due to their local connection. Moreover, "there's always been this thinking that it's important that the local working-class lads make good" (interview 39), which implies sentiments of class-consciousness combined with a solicitude and 'supporterly care' towards fellow Geordies.[7]

Being a born Geordie, however, is not required. In general, NUFC supporters deny the importance of ethnicity or nationality, but instead

---

[7] Geordies is the nickname for citizens of Newcastle and the surrounding area. Several fans made use of this term in the interviews.

demand strong commitment, a hard-working attitude and good performance, as this fan highlights:

> I don't care where you're from or the colour of your skin or anything like that as long as you're a good player and have a good attitude. The only thing Newcastle fans want is effort. If you give 100% effort week in and week out, the fans are going to applaud you even if you lose. (Interview 34)

The same applies for managers, as emphasised by another fan:

> I want a manager who's hard-working and driven [...] who can recognise honesty and to recognise the chemistry of the team and be respectful and hard-working like our past two managers have been [...] not like José Mourinho who's just me-driven and just constantly likes to have a chip at the media and stuff like that and will badger his players in public [...]. (Interview 36)

Becoming or being part of the in-group is obviously strongly connected to the above-mentioned shared values, while egocentric behaviour, lack of solidarity or being seen as aloof can see one placed in the out-group, at least with respect to players and managers, as is also reflected in many fans' views of the European transfer market: They look at it from a business perspective and as an opportunity to recruit high-performing employees. Likewise, fans think practically when it comes to sponsors and their background, as one fan bluntly stated: "As long as he's got money, no. It doesn't matter" (interview 40).

In sum, the NUFC fans' COB is mainly local or perhaps regional, yet open to any who share the club's traditional values and working-class ethics.

Regarding frames of reference, Newcastle United fans in our interviews expressed a rather detached interest in European football and international competitions, appreciating the top-level and high-quality football, while recognising that NUFC is not currently at that level.

> The Champions League football is lovely. [...] it's brilliant watching well-played and well thought out, well strategized, well-executed football. It's

just wild. I don't care who plays it. It makes no difference. If Newcastle would play in that I'd be over the moon but they're not. So, I have no problem watching other clubs. (Interview 33)

One fan notes that the CL is the top tier and "the best way to prove who's the best European club out there" (interview 35). Others refer to other European leagues and clubs when talking about their interest in European football (interview 36).

Most fans rate the strength of the Premier League highly compared to other leagues and some fans admire its generally tougher style of play compared to continental Europe (interview 42). But the quality of football played in the premiership is not the principal reason they value the league, rather they often simply recognise it as the current arena in which their club competes. One fan expresses the dream to see the NUFC play in European competitions (again), but argues that stability and performance in the national league must come before for going European:

> [...] we did so well in the 2011-2012 season and got inside Europa League but on top of that really good running in the Europa League. I really like to taste that again but with a little bit more stability in the Premier League this time, maybe. (Interview 36)

The importance of the regional and national level is also reflected in the markedly congruent answers of most fans when questioned about Newcastle United's main rivals: Virtually all refer to Sunderland "that's to do with proximity, that's to do with them being forty miles down the road and something that you're brought up with" (interview 39) or other PL clubs like, for example Brighton or Crystal Palace.

In sum, a closer look at the FOR shows that the Premier League is the main frame for Newcastle supporters. Patterns of Europeanisation are nonetheless clearly visible as many admire the quality of football in European competitions. Interviewees generally saw being an NUFC fan as entirely compatible with enjoying football as played in leagues or clubs across the North Sea in Europe.

8.3.5 Sturm Graz: Regionalised Europeanisation and Embedded Within Europe[8]

Sturm Graz supporters' perception of European football locates Austrian football on the outside, but at the same time their community of belonging is by no means national. The fans' in- and out-group formation has a regional focus with transnational features that go beyond national borders. The local (or regional) connection to players with origins in Graz and Styria is considered important and assumed to guarantee stability in the squad, with the expectation that locally rooted players stay longer due to their regional connection:

> A regional footballer, a Styrian [...] who comes from the national league and who is able to establish himself and plays once and then really is awarded a place in the team, he won't go away so quickly. (Interview 44)

This demand for a regional connection should not be taken for tribalism. As another fan emphasises, one need not be interested in the nationality or a possible migration background of the players, but in their local connection to the club:

> Where they actually come from in the sense of migration background, I don't care at all, just to state it clearly, but it would be important that they were trained in the club. Whether they have an Austrian passport or not, is not even of second, but last, interest for me. (Interview 45)

Other fans show similar attitudes. The club's regional embedding is defined as including the Balkans. They refer to "a very successful history with players from the Balkans, and coaches from the Balkans" (interview 47) or highlight the integrating effect of football for society in general, "especially in a city like Graz, where a lot of people live who fled from the Balkan wars" (interview 48).

Not all fans definitively deny the significance of nationality. A few articulate the need for (more) Austrian players, mainly because the

---

[8] Major parts of the findings on Sturm Graz have been published before by Weber (2022).

Austrian Bundesliga awards money to clubs based on the share of Austrian players.[9] These considerations can be considered instrumental because when explicitly asked whether it matters that a player is Austrian or not, a fan emphasised the financial interests of the club:

> No, that doesn't make any difference to me [whether someone is Austrian; the authors], it's just that because of the legionnaire regulation for TV revenues, the places for non-Austrians are more or less limited for a club like Sturm, that's why there's something like this, that you always have to think about who you can get with a non-Austrian passport. (Interview 43)

Some Graz fans also argue pragmatically, stating that it is imperative to employ the best players no matter where they come from, despite financial losses. One fan stresses that player nationality is less important than competing successfully both on the national and European level (interview 46).

In sum, the COB of the Sturm Graz fans are located between the regional and the cross-national in Europe. They focus on their region, but do not limit their self-understanding to national borders—except for practical reasons.

Regarding frames of reference, fan interviews revealed that the Austrian Bundesliga is the prime focus. This is nonetheless occasionally combined with a perception that the league is not very prestigious, not least due to limited financial and infrastructural opportunities. Other European leagues are seen as far away in these terms, as are European competitions. Fans argue that such division in the game makes European football less relevant for them:

> Champions League, Europa League [...], it's not really interesting for me now. Simply because in the Champions League you can see it now, all the clubs in the round of sixteen come from the top five nations, in the European club rankings. There's no variation anymore, simply because the top clubs are already drifting so far away from the rest. A club from the

---

[9] This fund is referred to as 'Österreichertopf' ('Austrians pot'). It involves the provision of subsidies for clubs of the Austrian Bundesliga who promote the use of football players from Austria and limit the share of foreign players.

Ukraine, Turkey or Austria can never keep up with clubs from Germany, England, Italy or something like that, so it's just not attractive for me anymore. (Interview 46)

This attitude is corroborated by another fan who expresses no interest in participating in European competitions, seeing no value in sporadic qualification only to lose most matches. This negative attitude towards the top European leagues is combined with fears that Sturm Graz would lose its character when being too successful on the European level:

To go back to the successes we had back then, to win the group or to be promoted, I think that is completely unrealistic and I don't know if I would want that for my club today, this kind of success, because it always also implies a kind of distance to the values of your own club - and you can see this with all the clubs that play up there a lot. (Interview 47)

Fans therefore see the main potential for success on the national level. They value a national win (league champion or cup win) higher than playing at the European level. However, not all fans have a negative attitude towards European competitions. While the CL is generally seen as out of reach and a closed-door event for a few clubs, the Europa League (EL) is seen as a potential alternative. Accordingly, negative attitudes are mainly directed towards the CL. What fans associate with 'European football' in general, however, is not that bad and does not reduce their football interest to the national level (interview 47).

One fan articulated the self-understanding of playing in a minor league in combination with a strong interest in European competitions, which is seen as attractive occasion for fan travel:

It would be nice if we'd play in a European competition, don't talk about a title anyway, but it would be nice to play in Europe, just because of the travels, so I would like that again, to travel somewhere with Sturm [...] so if I had the choice between titles in Austria or European competitions, I'd prefer European competitions. (Interview 50)

This indicates that some fans see football matches as an opportunity to travel around Europe. Moreover, it also shows how exceptional the European competitions are compared to 'normal' national league matches. Cross-border regionalisation also appears within the frames of references and is namely related to travel. Fans recount how their football-related travel focuses on the neighbouring countries, often because of short travel distances and easy access to matches. While several fans express support for clubs in the Italian Serie A, the interest in smaller leagues in neighbouring countries is more remarkable and seems directly motivated by regional connections and short travel distances:

> Yes, I already have a good knowledge about the leagues that are located around Austria, I always check whether I could watch a match somewhere, Also, when I make an away trip to Altach, I maybe also try to see a game at St. Gallen, it's just across the border, and also Slovenia is half an hour south of the border, there you always get to watch games. (Interview 46)

In sum, the analysis of the FOR reveals a pattern of a regionalised Europeanisation reflected in how fans refer to the different leagues on different levels. While the main frame for potential success is the national level, European football on the level of the Champions League remains a dream. However, at the same time, many Sturm Graz fans critically assess current European top football and more regional and cross-border references are made towards leagues and clubs in neighbouring countries.

8.3.6 Wacker Innsbruck: A Flagship for the Region, an Eye Towards Europe

Wacker Innsbruck fans often demonstrate very strong (emotional) connections to their home region of Tyrol. Some express a distinct local patriotism when talking about their club and many see Wacker Innsbruck as a flagship for the region (interview 57). Fans seem to be fine with the underdog self-image (interview 53) of a small, non-commercialised club (interview 56). National competitions and the Austrian Bundesliga are important insofar as they are the main (and only) stage for their club.

8 Football Fans' Narratives of Europe and the Game

Their attitude towards European football is a mixture of (critical) interest and a certain disregard. Several fans show transnational sympathies or connections to fellow small clubs in other European leagues, mainly in the German Bundesliga. However, they perceive their own club somehow as an outsider to the European theatre of football (interviews 58 & 59).

The fans' in- and out-group formation often has a focus on the home region of Tyrol or on Austria. While some emphasise that they do not care where the players come from, as long as they can play well and fit into the club (interview 54), there are more voices that argue that the local (or regional) connection to players from Austria—or preferably Tyrol—is desirable and important for the club:

> Ideally, and really nice, that would be if there were eleven Tyroleans. That's not possible, of course. But this Austrian way, which they also have there, from certain subsidies, I think that's good, but that's also dreaming. If a black African scores all the goals, that's just as okay. But now, for example, to have a squad that consists only of eleven legionnaires would bother me. (Interview 57)

Another fan expresses concerns that foreign players, often referred to as 'legionnaires' in a slightly derogative tone, may not develop a strong connection to the club as to really identify and 'live' with it:

> If a player comes from Serbia or Norway or somewhere else, then that's a player who you know will maybe play there for a few years and then is gone again. [...] If I could choose [...] I give a native player a chance. (Interview 59)

The preference for Tyrolean or Austrian players does not imply a general disregard for foreign players. One fan made it clear that she is

> pleased when young people from immigrant backgrounds join us from time to time. And they demonstrate their skills. And I think that soccer connects and has an integrative effect. (Interview 63)

Nonetheless, Wacker Innsbruck fans assume that players with a local connection contribute to the stability of the squad (as players stay longer) and to the club's identity. Several indicate an instrumental stance in this respect and highlight the practical benefits of a larger share of Austrian players in the context of the so-called 'Österreichertopf' (interview 62).

The attitude towards trainers and sponsors is slightly different. Most fans do not see a need for regional connections but demand technical competence and good leadership in coaches—no matter where they come from. Regarding sponsors, they are more sceptical of rich investors from abroad—and apparently frustrated over nearby sponsors, as this fan highlights: "Of course, the more local the better, but if it doesn't work, it hasn't worked for so long with the local economy, nor with local politics" (interview 59), which indicates that local networks and regional entanglements between club and political/business elites are viewed critically by some (interview 55).

In sum, the COB of the Wacker Innsbruck fans are mainly located at regional and to a lesser degree at the cross-national European level. They focus on Tyrol and highlight the regional identity of their club but also look beyond borders with particular interest in other (small) clubs in neighbouring European countries.

Regarding frames of reference, virtually all interviews with Wacker Innsbruck supporters point to the importance of national competitions. This is corroborated by the fact that the majority of fans identify a domestic arch-rival in Austria Salzburg. When questioned about rivalry, one supporter elaborates further:

> Austria Salzburg historically, of course. Not the 'Dosenkopie' [derogative term referring to Red Bull Salzburg; the authors] of it, but the real Austria Salzburg at that time. Rapid Vienna, of course. In the meantime, Sturm Graz, too […] These are the typical competitors. But all on a national level. (Interview 60)

The value of the Austrian Bundesliga, however, is rooted not in its prestige or the quality of matches, but rather in its practical relevance: national competitions and the national title are important "given the condition that we often don't play internationally in Austria" (interview

60). Fans highlight that national competitions are indeed relevant for clubs that lack financial capabilities and infrastructure to play internationally (interview 54).

Many Wacker Innsbruck fans favour a national success of their club over participation in European competitions (interviews 54 & 58). The value of the national championship is based on a realistic assessment of the club's current capabilities and the welcome implication that winning the national title implies beating rival Salzburg (interviews 60 & 63). One fan recounts:

> Definitely a national title. Absolutely. For me, that's the highest. [...] Experiences like that bring tears of joy to my eyes. Still do. I'll be honest with you. For me, that's the highest thing ever. A national title. Definitely, definitely. (Interview 54)

However, valuing national competitions can go hand in hand with a general interest in European football, which offers entertainment and insights beyond the gameplay, for example, opportunities to get to know different countries (interview 57). While Wacker Innsbruck fans have had few opportunities to watch their own club play in European competition, several interviews point to cross-border regionalisation within the frames of references because supporters often follow leagues and clubs in other, mainly neighbouring European countries. Such fans took occasional opportunities to travel abroad and watch their club play away games, mainly in nearby Italy, Germany or Eastern European countries such as Croatia or the Czech Republic (interviews 55, 56, 58 & 60).

In contrast to a generally positive attitude towards the Europa League, most fans have a critical or even negative attitude towards the Champions League. The latter is seen as "closed club where we were left out" (interview 60) or as big business, which is boring because it is allegedly always the same teams of a few rich clubs playing there (interview 58). The fans' critique on a division in European football, which is also reflected in frequent critical remarks about the European player market, seems to be driven by the perception of Wacker Innsbruck as a non-commercialised underdog club that neither has the means nor a realistic chance to successfully participate in the European competitions, nor benefit from the common transfer market.

In sum, the analysis of the FOR shows that the regional and national levels are clearly dominant. Certain patterns of Europeanisation, however, do exist as many fans follow clubs in other European leagues, occasionally travelling there. While Wacker Innsbruck supporters are often interested in European competitions, they nevertheless critically assess international top-level football against the background of their own regional club identity and underdog self-perception.

8.4 Paired Comparisons of Results

Having described in detail the expressions of specific supporters in terms of communities of belonging and frames of reference, the following analysis seeks to engage in a cross-case analysis. Our inquiry is structured around three sets of four paired comparisons (see Tarrow 2010) of clubs in four different European countries. This research design allows us to control for three main conditioning factors influencing fan attitudes towards the supposedly more Europeanised aspects of the game: the club level (sporting success), the league level (Europeanisation of player markets), and the embedding societal context (extent of Euroscepticism).

As already elaborated in Chaps. 5 and 6, these structured paired comparisons should allow us to identify the (relative) influence of each condition on the dependent variable, that is, fans' degree of Europeanisation.

This resulted in three clusters of four paired comparisons of fan groups and their discourse (Table 8.2). In contrast to the analysis of these paired comparisons in Chap. 6, which engages in a detailed assessment of the clusters on a club-to-club basis, this chapter will analyse general patterns expressed by supporters of the clubs along the lines of the three clusters.[10]

---

[10] It should be noted that this chapter focuses on the fan scenes in Austria, Germany and England, so unlike the previous chapters, not all areas of the analysis matrix are considered equally.

Table 8.2 Three clusters of paired comparisons

Cluster of paired comparisons	Variation	Control 1	Control 2
1: league level	Europeanisation of player markets	Participation in European club competitions	Public attitudes towards Europe
2: club level	Participation in European club competitions	Europeanisation of player markets	Public attitudes towards Europe
3: country level	Public attitudes towards Europe	Participation in European club competitions	Europeanisation of player markets

8.4.1 Assessing the League Level

It was assumed that the differences in Europeanisation of player markets across our four leagues would be mirrored in how 'normalised' foreign players are for the fans: Those fans from leagues with more Europeanised player markets should be enframed in more Europeanised communities of belonging and vice versa.

The comparison of supporters of Bayern Munich and Hannover 96 gives only limited support for the thesis that the varying composition of the player market in the Bundesliga influenced views among the interviewees on the normalisation of European squads. For fans of Bayern Munich and Hannover 96 alike, 'communities of belonging' are not bound to nationalities but to more pragmatic reasons and, to some extent, reasons related to the perceived identity of the club. This finding is to a lesser extent also evidenced when comparing the supporters from Manchester United, Newcastle United, Sturm Graz, and Wacker Innsbruck, although these clubs are clearly active in different player markets, and varied in terms of Europeanised squads. Just as the fans from Germany, they want a player to accept and perform in his role (interview 8), identify with the club (interviews 5, 10), play attractive football (interviews 18, 32), and have a strong attitude (interview 34).

Differences across clubs are found in the details: For Bayern Munich supporters, the inclusion of players from the club's youth programmes is important irrespective of the players' nationality (interviews 8, 9, 10). Hannover 96 fans describe successes with a multinational squad (interviews 13). Specifically, the education of players within the clubs' structures is seen as important in that it fosters faster integration, tactical education, or a higher probability to stay with the club.

The EPL and Austrian fans also emphasised the relevance of local and home-grown players. Newcastle supporters underline the importance of a strong identification with the club's' background as working-class team (interviews 34, 39). While the nationality of a player is not important for many supporters, fans from Wacker Innsbruck place a greater priority on the inclusion of local players from Tyrol. Some fear that foreign players might be less bound to the club (interviews 57, 59), an advantage of local players that is also identified by fans of Sturm Graz (interviews 44, 45). In contrast, Newcastle United supporters tend to be less interested in the origins of a player, with competitiveness in the EPL given greater priority (interviews 33, 35). Supporters of Manchester United also care less about the origins of players (interviews 27, 32) and praise the international character of the youth teams, from which they hope to see more players progress to the club's first team (interviews 30, 31). This quote from one interviewee is a case in point: "now I think it has become more globalised or Europeanised that as long as this player comes through the youth system, it doesn't matter where this player is from" (interview 25). This approach is also supported by some Sturm Graz fans (interviews 43, 44, 52), though the latter are slightly more favourable towards players from the region, to represent Styria and Austria (interviews 44, 49). But again, it is more important for supporters that players come from the club's youth system. Fans state that this creates more chances for Sturm as club (interviews 46, 48), strengthens the identity of the club (interview 47), fosters the links to the city (interviews 50, 51), or increases identification with Sturm Graz (interview 49).

These assessments of Europeanised player markets reveal a degree of normalisation of European. The findings of the paired comparisons here equally show no specific preferences for coaches in terms of nationality. Likewise, supporters emphasise the performance of a coach (interview 8), his or her competence (interview 55), interaction with the media (interview 47), or leadership skills (interview 29) over other considerations. Some fans nonetheless value a boundness to the identity of the club in a coach (interview 36). Overall, the nationality of a coach is even less important for the interviewees than those of players, regardless of the Europeanisation of the league in terms of player markets.

Overall, the first cluster of paired comparisons indicates that differences in the composition of player markets of the home league have only a limited effect on fan attitudes. The analysis reveals that supporters do not distinguish much between foreign and local players, so long as they perform well. This pragmatic attitude exhibited by many fans is also expressed by Austrian supporters, although to a lesser extent. For fans of Wacker Innsbruck and, to a lesser degree, Sturm Graz, the local origin of players is more important than it is for the supporters of other clubs, based on the belief that local roots foster identification with the team, resulting in players staying longer with the club. The nationality of coaches is even less important for the interviewees, regardless of the nature of player markets in the respective leagues. It is worth noting, however, that similarly to the findings of Chap. 6, for fans in strongly internationalised markets such as the EPL local anchors and identity are still very important considerations. In terms of Europeanisation, more closed leagues such as the Austrian Bundesliga might provide a context in which supporters pay more attention to local and regional players and foster a regional orientation of the club. In contrast, fans of clubs active in Europeanised player markets tend to engage more often with European leagues and players, and even fans of clubs such as Newcastle United that rarely participate in European competitions tend to be shaped by these contexts. The emphasis on internationalised squads made by Manchester United and Bayern Munich fans shows considerable evidence to suggest that very Europeanised player markets are different to more closed markets. This finding, however, does not completely mirror the examination of interviews from Hannover 96 and Newcastle. Likewise, there is some evidence to suggest that the closeness of a player market plays a role, but this effect might be more limited than assumed in the context of the league.

8.4.2 Assessing the Club Level

The second comparison analyses the extent to which the frequent exposure to and (successful) participation in European-level competition engenders Europeanising tendencies among the respective supporters. It thus engages at the club level and pairs those clubs that play in the same league and qualify for European championships with varying frequency and success. It was assumed that more frequent participation in European competitions produces more Europeanised frames of reference.

The analysis reveals a tendency for supporters of clubs that frequently participate in European championships to become more Europeanised than those fans whose clubs rarely engage in international tournaments. However, interviewees showed a degree of interest in European-level competition regardless of their own club's success and participation. This mirrors a football setting that has become increasingly Europeanised. The fans that refer most frequently to the European level as main area of competition are the interviewees with affiliations to Bayern Munich. They regard the European championships, notably the CL, as most important tournament (interview 2), generating better fan experiences than national games (interview 10) and reference the various successes the club had in recent years as best experiences they had as fan (interview 8). Interestingly, some supporters of Bayern Munich refer to European clubs such as Real Madrid or Liverpool as the club's main rivals which suggests a very Europeanised outlook (interviews 5, 6, 7, 10). This also relates to a view of the Bundesliga as boring for the club, which clearly dominates the league (interviews 5, 11). In contrast, fans of Hannover 96 for which European championships are very distant, still see the national level as key, also in terms of rivalries (interview 21). Compared to Bayern Munich fans, supporters of Hannover 96 praise the Bundesliga as more interesting (interview 19) both in terms of competitive and social aspects of fandom (interview 21). While the interviews suggest that they view the CL as rather boring and less relevant for their football experiences (interview 23), they have more positive perceptions of the Europa League (interviews 13, 19). Despite rarely participating at the European level, Hannover 96 fans refer to Europa League experiences as "highlights" (interview 23) and "gifts" (interview 14). Common to both fan groups is the rather critical view of the CL as over-commercialised and dominated by wealthy investor-backed clubs (interviews 5, 7), and being "all about the money" (interview 21). Overall, the first paired comparison indicates substantial differences between fans of Bayern Munich and Hannover 96. However, these distinctions were less marked in the other paired comparisons.

The difference in views on the participation on the European level and the importance of the national level is only marginal between supporters of Manchester United versus Newcastle United fans, or fans of Sturm Graz and Wacker Innsbruck. For instance, both Manchester and Newcastle supporters view the EPL as the key competition for their clubs and the national level as the main frame of reference (interviews 27, 31, 39). The European level is mostly viewed as prestigious and a 'nice to have'. Fans refer to the CL as "premium competition" (interview 29), as fascinating (interview 30), and "the best way to prove who's the best European club out there" (interviews 33, 35). Others praise the "quality of football being played" as "just superb" (interview 34). To some extent, interviewees supporting Newcastle United are less interested in the CL (interviews 37, 39) and view the CL as boring since only a few teams repeatedly make up the winners (interview 40). These differences, however, provide only limited evidence for significant variation for the proposed process. Likewise, the differences between supporters of Sturm Graz and Wacker Innsbruck are marginal. Both fan groups have the Austrian Bundesliga as main focus (interview 54). The European level, however, is viewed equally as "exciting" (interview 57) and an opportunity to travel abroad, a behaviour both fan groups also engage with by watching other clubs, most notably from near Austria. Supporters from both clubs also express limited interest in European competitions (interviews 43, 48, 50, 54). What both fan groups have in common with German supporters is the more critical view of the CL as competition for the big clubs (interview 46), as "closed club where we were left out" (interview 60), or as commercialised and repetitive in that it continual featured the same wealthy clubs (interview 58). A further interesting finding was that some supporters of Austrian clubs which are less involved in European competitions are interested in leagues of the neighbouring states such as Germany, Switzerland, Slovakia or Slovenia (interviews 46, 56, 59) in part because those leagues are perceived as less commercialised.

Overall, the analysis of the second set of paired comparisons indicates that the extent to which supporters are exposed to a frequent and (successful) participation in European-level competition can set in motion specific Europeanising tendencies among the respective supporters. Some paired comparisons such as in Germany and, to some extent, England show a greater difference between fans of clubs that participate in European competitions and those that do not. Although these differences are not in evidence in all paired comparisons, with Austria showing only a limited effect, there is some explanatory power for the proposed link. Overall, supporters show a high level of positive attitudes towards playing European, although the tournaments have been also criticised in terms of commercialisation and closed character for some clubs.

8.4.3 Assessing the Country Level

The last cluster focuses on comparisons of fan discourse from otherwise similar clubs which are embedded in societies and publics that differ as regards their degree of Euroscepticism. It thus engages with the country level and pairs those clubs that are in different environments in terms of public attitudes towards Europe and the EU. It was assumed that a more positive public attitude toward Europe would be reflected in fan perspectives on football.

The analysis of this last cluster indicates that differing public attitudes towards Europe and the EU might be less of a conditioning factor for fan attitudes than expected. These findings mirror to some extent those of Chap. 6. Across the interviewed fans, there seems to be little difference regarding their communities of belonging and their frames of reference. Just as in the other two clusters of paired comparisons, it is worth highlighting that the fans of Bayern Munich in particular rarely attribute a specific importance of the nationalities of players and coaches. For most of the fans pragmatic considerations, most notably the performance and the fit of a player to the team, are the most relevant. This was also reflected in discussion of young players from the youth academies, where nationality does not seem to be important (interviews 8, 9, 10, 25, 52). Fans of both Austrian clubs were outliers to a degree in their greater emphasis on the value of local origin for players, largely due to such players' perceived loyalty to the club (interviews 44, 45, 57, 59). Likewise, differences in the way fans of English clubs Newcastle United and Manchester United view their communities of belonging in terms of players are only marginal when compared to those of their German counterparts. As for the supporters of Bayern Munich and Hannover 96, nationalities are not considered important (interviews 32, 34).

In terms of FOR across the clubs, a same finding can be drawn. Overall, the perception of European competition is rather positive across all fans. They view the competitions as key levels for their clubs (interviews 27, 31, 39), as great experiences (interviews 8, 23, 57), or the most important tournaments in football more generally (interviews 33, 35). Common to many fans is criticism towards the CL as commercial platform for only some clubs with money as biggest influencing factor (interviews 5, 7, 21, 29, 46, 58).

Overall, the analysis of the third cluster does not indicate that public attitudes towards Europe and the EU play a significant role in conditioning perceptions of communities of belonging and frames of reference for the interviewees. Although some fans are more positive towards the European level, such as the fans of Manchester United and most notably Bayern Munich, such a positive attitude is common across almost all the interviewed supporters. It is thus rather likely that differences across fans in different European countries are less due to the overall orientation towards Europe among the publics, but more to specific fan cultures.

8.5 Key Findings and Conclusions

Aiming to focus on the individual fan in more detail, this chapter engaged in the analysis of the 63 interviews conducted with supporters of Bayern Munich, Hannover 96, Manchester United, Newcastle United, Sturm Graz, and Wacker Innsbruck. First, we outlined in detail the views expressed in the interviews in terms of communities of belonging and frames of reference, before we embarked on the analyses of three sets of four paired comparisons across the clubs.

This analysis led to the following main findings. First, the first cluster of paired comparisons analysing the variation in Europeanisation of player markets indicates that differences in the composition of player markets and more Europeanised squads as consequence of an increased inclusion of foreign players have some effect on fan attitudes, though to a limited extent. Overall, very Europeanised player markets create some divergences when compared to more closed markets. Second, the second set of paired comparisons analysing variation in level of participation in European club competitions indicates that the extent to which supporters are exposed to a frequent and (successful) participation in European-level competition can indeed drive specific Europeanising tendencies among the respective supporters. Although fans generally exhibit of positive attitudes towards playing European, there is considerable evidence to suggest that the frequent exposure of Bayern Munich and Manchester United fans is key to the very positive views which the fans of these clubs have of European competitions. Conversely, supporters of clubs that rarely participate in the CL and EL highlight the relevance, quality, and key role of the European competitions, while also criticising their closed character and commercialisation. Third, the third cluster, analysing variation in public attitude towards Europe/the EU, does not indicate that public attitudes towards Europe and the EU play a significant role in shaping the perceptions of communities of belonging and frames of reference of the interviewed fans. Mirroring the analyses of the first and second cluster, fans across all clubs show rather positive attitudes towards playing at the European level.

Finally, the looking at the individual, ordinary football fan with his or her personal attitudes and understanding of football and the Europeanisation of the game has led to important insights on how supporters across different leagues, clubs and countries view the European approach to football in terms of player markets, European competition, and public attitudes. The chapter has analysed in depth the several communities of belonging and frames of reference for those supporters and thus generated important and relevant examinations of European fan culture, inclusion and exchange.

References

Nielsen. 2022. What fans want. The 2022 world football report. https://global.nielsen.com/wp-content/uploads/sites/2/2022/07/Nielsen-World-Football-Report-2022.pdf. Accessed 6 Dec 2022.

Tarrow, Sidney. 2010. The strategy of paired comparison: Toward a theory of practice. *Comparative Political Studies* 40 (2): 230–259. https://doi.org/10.1177/0010414009350044.

Weber, Regina. 2022. Becoming European through football? The case of Sturm Graz. In *Considering Europeanization: Ideas and practices of (dis-)integrating Europe since the nineteenth century*, ed. Florian Greiner, Peter Pichler, and Jan Vermeiren, 235–262. Oldenbourg: De Gruyter.

Weber, Regina, Alexander Brand, Florian Koch, and Arne Niemann. 2022. A European mind? Europeanisation of football fan discussions in online message boards. *European Journal for Sport and Society* 19 (4): 323–346. https://doi.org/10.1080/16138171.2021.1974220.

9

Conclusions

9.1 Introduction

The idea for this book was conceived about a decade ago. From the perspective of 2023, the world— not only that of football—seems to have changed profoundly. Our EUFOOT[1] project idea happened to be shaped significantly by the football-related discourses that had dominated the first one and a half decades of the twenty-first century: the ongoing commercialisation of professional football, the growing Europeanisation of the governance structures of football, as well as the concomitant internationalisation of football player markets, leagues, teams and ownership structures.

On a more general level, the transformations football seemed to take place against the background of a generally advancing transnationalisation of politics, which was accelerated by the digitisation of communication. Our project, running from 2018 to 2021 (gathering and processing data from the years 2016 to 2021), meanwhile seemed to face ever-growing disruptive change: the reality of Brexit with its multifaceted impact on European integration, the rise of populism in Europe and

---

[1] See: https://eufoot.github.io/

beyond, and not least the Covid-19 pandemic and the resulting regulation and responses have contributed to making the world a different place. Or have they really? Inasmuch as the Covid pandemic also spurred a new round of debate on a European breakaway 'super league' (ESL) of top performers, while at the same time distancing quite a few supporters from their formerly beloved sport, it also left its mark on football. In addition, online streaming of football events has moved from the fringes to the mainstream, with the likes of DAZN and Amazon Prime Video becoming important providers. At the same time, social media channels seem to have supplanted more traditional online communication channels (such as e-fanzines and message boards) among fans and spectators. Against the background of such fast-paced and profound disruptions, our main questions did nevertheless prove both resilient and of enduring relevance.[2]

Our two main research questions have been: (1) To what extent are identities of football fans across Europe 'Europeanised'? (2) What factors condition the level of Europeanised identities of football supporters across different contexts? We have approached these questions through an analytical framework that fits our special football context: based on a tripartite understanding of identity as identification, self-understanding and communality (or groupness, Brubaker and Cooper 2000), we developed a framework with two dimensions. In terms of football fandom-related identity, we ask which 'communities of belonging' fans adhere to and which 'frames of reference' they consider relevant (cf. Chap. 5).

Our comparative research design included eight select clubs and adjacent fan scenes in four countries (Austria, France, Germany and the UK/England). The cases had been purposefully sampled to cover three nested contexts of football spectatorship: the *country* (differing degrees of Euroscepticism within the respective societies), the *league* (differing levels of Europeanisation of the respective player markets), and the *club* level (differing degrees of involvement in European club competitions). This ensures variation among clubs across these contexts. As part of our

---

[2] This is also demonstrated by a new string of studies on the ongoing structural Europeanisation of the game (cf. Meier et al. 2022b) as well as its ideational repercussions among its fans and followers (cf. De Witte and Zglinski 2022).

mixed-methods research design, we conducted (1) a qualitative discourse analysis of fan articulations in online message boards, (2) a quantitative survey of approximately 3000 fans in the four selected leagues/countries, and (3) 63 in-depth interviews with purposively sampled fans from six of the eight fan scenes. Our analysis at all stages was informed by the idea of systematic comparison, and the logic of paired comparison in particular, to ascertain which factors might shape identifications with Europe through football fandom more than others (cf. Chap. 5).

In this chapter we proceed as follows: in part two, we analyse and discuss the main findings within and across the different methodological steps. In the third section, we report some experiences and observations that go beyond our scientific results (strictly speaking) and discuss some lessons learned from this project. Finally, we make suggestions for future research.

9.2 Results

At the most fundamental level, we can deduce from our analysis that the Europeanisation of football has left a mark on the mindset of a substantial share of football fans. Both our analysis of fan forums and our semi-structured interviews suggest that especially fans of the high-performing clubs in the respective leagues and those of clubs in the more Europeanised leagues tend to attach high value to European competitions (often higher than national ones). They also tend to have inclusive attitudes towards non-native European and international players and managers (cf. Chaps. 6 and 8). But even fans of the unusual suspects (e.g. Wacker Innsbruck: relegation battler in a less Europeanised league in a rather Eurosceptic country) seem to generally consider players' nationality insignificant as long as they add value to the team (cf. Chap. 8). While our survey suggests that exposure to European-level competitions may not correlate with cosmopolitan attitudes, factors like Europeanised player markets, support for European unification, and especially a Europeanised squad of the own beloved club seem to foster cosmopolitan mindsets—with a combination of these factors providing the greatest prognostic leverage (cf. Chap. 7).

In what follows, we concentrate on five main insights into identity formation through followership of football at different levels. These concern the following aspects: (1) fandom intensity; (2) fan identity as a differentiated spatial process subject to conditions; (3) inconsistent, conflicting and/or contradictory results; (4) fans' criticism of current (Europeanisation of football) trends; and (5) the link between Europeanised attitudes and potentially shifting political mindsets.

9.2.1 The Smaller Role of Fandom Intensity

Our cross-country online survey unsurprisingly revealed that football supporters differ regarding their fandom intensity as well as attitudes towards aspects that are directly connected with the Europeanisation of football structures, such as the composition of their teams and the perceived status of European competitions (Chap. 7). The fandom intensity line features two groups of fans, frequent vs. occasional ones. While the former can be considered active fans with a high level of match attention and a close connection to their club, the latter include occasional fans with a low number of matches attended and a rather loose connection to their club.

The Europeanisation line shows that fans also differ in how much importance they attribute to the role of national belonging for their identification with the club: this relates to the background from which players are recruited into their team as well as the level of appreciation of European-level football competition. Here, a fault line between cosmopolitan and communitarian mindsets becomes visible. In all of this, attitudes towards the Europeanisation aspects and degrees of fandom intensity are not systematically linked.

This finding contrasts with earlier typologies of football fandom (cf. Chap. 3) that had emphasised the connectedness and locality of engaged fans in contrast to the more fluid, or less well-developed, identification patterns of casual or less involved fans. While we clearly saw the main elements of Giulianotti's (2002) four-pronged typology in action in all our four country contexts under study, the degree of fandom involvement, or intensity, was not the determining factor in view of more or less

Europeanised forms of identifications and mindsets. As our 2*2-matrix demonstrated, different degrees of emotional and resource investment into following the sport (and a beloved team in particular) can co-exist with either more *or* less cosmopolitan—and hence: Europeanised—perspectives. This might be an insight which also invites a fruitful exchange with those who have recently started exploring more deeply how football fandom translates into collective action (cf. Cleland et al. 2018), or the very foundations of collaboration and solidarity among football fans (cf. Brandt et al. 2017; García and Zheng 2017).

9.2.2 Spatiality: Between the Local and Europe

As our results indicate, identity formation among football fans is a spatial process in which both the Europeanisation of football and the locality of the clubs play a huge role. In comparison, the national level seemed to move more to the background. With the exception of Bayern Munich, even fans of national champions with frequent appearances at the European top level do define their main rivals at least to some extent as locally or regionally grounded. In a similar vein, interest in signing the best players from all over Europe often goes hand in hand with an appreciation of local talent. At the same time, the national level remains the dominant area for competition and the national championship a wishful target (again, probably with the exception of Bayern Munich). It is in this sense that, despite clearly detectable Europeanising influences, the term 'post-national identity' (King 2000) should be used with care in this context. While fans of a European top club such as Manchester United might express self-understandings that highlight the local embeddedness *also in a European competition context*, with a comparatively lower emphasis on the national resulting from this, any such Europeanisation of reference frames cannot be generalised as a phenomenon valid across clubs and leagues (cf. Chaps. 6 and 8).

Still, those following big (and Europeanised) leagues and supporting Europeanised squads/teams, with routine participation in top-level competition and a huge cross-national media presence, may have indeed shifted fans' attention and also their rivalries *somewhat* to the European level. This is partly due to the perceived lack of true domestic competitors (such as in the case of Germany's Bayern Munich). Alternatively, it might also be the case that a once locally and regionally anchored rivalry has subsequently been transposed to the European level. Arguably, this seems to be true for many Manchester United supporters, who seek to challenge their traditional counterparts of ManCity and Liverpool, but with reference to superseding them *at the European level*, not 'only' nationally (cf. Chap. 6). One of the most interesting insights in this regard is that the idea of representing one's home nation in Europe seems to have become less important than being the best in a meritocratic selection process.

The analysis of online message board discussions and semi-structured interviews further revealed that the degree of exposure to Europe via football influences *how* fans attribute meaning to the European level of football (cf. Chaps. 6 and 8). Even in the case of Newcastle United, a club (during the time of our investigation period) unlikely to participate in European competitions—which is arguably a fairly widespread condition for supporters throughout Europe—the very context of a heavily internationalised/Europeanised player market in the home (i.e. Premier) league seems to contribute to a normalisation of Europe among fans. Increasingly Europeanised leagues and squads seem to have triggered, to some extent, more inclusive perceptions of the in-group, with the home league not primarily regarded as a place over-populated by some 'suspicious others' (e.g. foreign players who may crowd out home talent). In comparison, clubs in the Austrian leagues with comparatively less Europeanised player markets (cf. Chap. 6) or individuals supporting clubs with a smaller share of non-native (European) players in their team (cf. Chap. 8) have bred more, and more openly articulated, appreciation for (national and) local talent among fans. Especially in the Austrian league, where special regulations enforce the contracting of Austrian players, local belonging and a decisively local identity of the clubs are of substantial importance to the fans (cf. Chaps. 6 and 8; Brand et al. 2023). The construction of in-groups and out-groups with regard to a European vs. a national belonging hence seems to be significantly shaped by the amount of exposure to a Europeanised player market and/or Europeanised squads.

9.2.3 How to Deal with Inconsistent/Conflicting/Contradictory Results?

Our mixed-methods approach yields partly diverging, conflicting and inconsistent results regarding the role of the different influence factors for the Europeanisation of fans' identities. This can be seen as a feature rather than a bug of a mixed-methods study (Knappertsbusch et al. 2023). Meta studies of mixed-methods research have put the share of such studies to constitute between 7% and 17% (Pluye et al. 2009, 64–65). And given the bias in academic publications towards reporting "positive" findings—rather than insignificant ones or non-results—with a view to higher acceptance rates (Coursol and Wagner 1986), there is reason to suggest that the actual share of diverging, conflicting or inconsistent findings in mixed-methods research might be even higher. Nevertheless, such results require a thorough discussion and integration.

Our discourse analysis of online fan forums (Chap. 6) clearly suggests that a club's participation in European-level competition is the factor carrying the most explanatory power for Europeanised fan identities. This broadly confirms the 'contact hypothesis' (cf. Allport 1954), according to which the more fans are exposed to cross-border contacts, the less relevance they attribute to aspects of national belonging.

However, our survey analysis rather hints at a combination of various other factors—for example, the degree of internationalisation of a league, attitudes towards European unification, and the degree of Europeanisation of a club's squads—as providing the greatest predicative power concerning cosmopolitan attitudes. Among these, we could identify the degree of Europeanisation of a club's squad as the single most powerful factor in correlating with cosmopolitan—and hence: more Europeanised—attitudes. By contrast, according to our survey findings, affiliation with a club competing at the European level does not increase the likelihood of cosmopolitan fan identities (cf. Chap. 7).

In this context, our analysis based on the semi-structured interviews takes a somewhat intermediate position. While attributing slightly more importance to the club context (i.e. whether clubs regularly compete at the European level), both the club level and the league level (i.e. how

Europeanised the leagues' player markets are) seem to have some, but no overwhelming, bearing on whether fans tend to have Europeanised frames of reference and communities of belonging.

How can these findings be squared? There is some literature suggesting how to proceed in case of such findings. Drawing on Moffatt et al. (2006) and Pluye et al. (2009), we have identified four strategies of dealing with diverging, conflicting or inconsistent findings: (1) bracketing, (2) exclusion or weighting, (3) reconciliation and (4) initiation. Subsequently, we will describe these strategies, followed by a discussion of their application and their relevance to our specific research context. Our discussion reveals that there may be scope for combining some of these strategies.

'Bracketing' describes and accounts for conflicting evidence by suggesting that different methods are measuring different phenomena or different aspects of phenomena (Moffatt et al. 2006, 6). Rather than indicating differences in reality, different methods tend to reflect different epistemologies. Hence, it is not surprising that methods corresponding to positivist/objectivist epistemologies tend to produce a different account of social reality than more post-positivist/interpretative methods (Harrits 2011, 160). Studies using one particular method may reveal dimensions of a research object not measured by another method. Datasets emerging from different methods are thus viewed as complementary (Moffatt et al. 2006, 7). There is scope for making use of bracketing in our case: our various methods may reveal different types of Europeanised mindsets or rather different fan types and their Europeanised (fan) identities. While the analysis of message boards focuses on the expressions of a potentially selected group of fans that dedicate time and energy to discussing football online in a message board that is explicitly related to their club, less devoted supporters might also have participated in our survey. In fact, about 60% of our survey respondents have been classified as 'occasional' supporters; among the cosmopolitans, this share is even higher. In addition, interviewees who tend to be rather highly devoted fans confirm their club's (non-)participation in European-level competitions matters, at least to some extent. It is interesting to note here that the two methods that deviate from strict positivist/objectivist epistemologies—the qualitative (discourse) analysis of fan forums and the semi-structured interviews—generated relatively similar results. An alternative (albeit not so convincing) explanation for the different outcomes across methods are the different times the analyses were conducted: the analysis of online message boards was carried out for the seasons 2016/17 and 2017/18; the survey was conducted during the spring/summer 2019; and the interviews were carried out between fall 2019 and fall 2021. Yet, apart from the ESL proposal of April 2021, there seems to be no single intervening variable that may have substantially affected the strength of our explanatory factors. The ESL initiative, however, may have had a somewhat negative impact on the value of European club competitions as a frame of reference during the last part of the interview phase. Yet, whether this had a negative bearing on club participation in European-level competitions is doubtful because this arguably is likely to have "turned off" Bayern and ManU fans just as much as those of the underdog clubs, at least according to media coverage (cf. Dawson 2021; Mathers 2021; Ramsay 2021).

'Exclusion' or 'weighting' questions that data generated by different methods is equally valid in the face of conflicting evidence and investigates the rigour and weaknesses of each method. Different outcomes are viewed as non-complementary and the data produced through the seemingly more deficient method is excluded or devalued. This strategy tends to be informed by the positivist propensity to identify a singular truth as a result of which qualitative data is more likely to be downplayed (Creamer 2018; cf. Giddings and Grant 2007). Pluye et al. (2009, 63ff.) found no evidence for this strategy explicitly reported in publications based on mixed-methods research designs, which they explain through the publication bias mentioned above. We tend to ascribe less bearing to this strategy for dealing with our diverging findings. It is true, however, that our methods have their weaknesses. (Semi-structured) interviews, for example, may entail the risk of interviewer biases, differences emanating from different interviewers at work, as well as a (too) narrow and specific sample. In our case, there was also a shortfall in terms of French fans and potential biases in fan recruitment for our study as well as fan responses due to the specifics of the pandemic situation. Analysing message boards carries the potential deficiency of leaving substantial room for interpretation when it comes to the utterances of individuals, often in the absence of the provision of necessary context. And although the survey may be the most 'scientific' of these methods, it has its shortcomings, especially regarding a biased sample resulting from a self-selection online survey, which is visible, for example, in the unequal participation of fans from our four countries. Having said that, we much doubt that any of the methods—in the way conducted in this project—carries such flaws that it disqualifies the obtained results in favour of another method. Similarly, we do not think that one of our methods is 'more equal' than others and that certain results of our study can be ignored.

'Reconciliation' as a strategy suggesting that diverging findings can be interpreted, that is, reconciled, in a plausible, sense-making manner. In order for this to potentially happen, a re-analysis of the existing data is necessary. As a result of reconciliation, a new and/or more comprehensive explanatory framework—encompassing different components of conflicting evidence—may be developed (Pluye et al. 2009, 59). There may be some potential for employing a reconciliation strategy in view of our conflicting evidence. Key here may be the re-analysis and re-interpretation of what a Europeanisation of player markets means for our analysis. Does it really matter in terms of fan attitudes whether an *entire league* is Europeanised or might it not be more important whether *one's own club's squad* is Europeanised? The latter may have a greater impact on fans' mindsets in the end, given that it is here where most of their emotional investment lies. And as pointed out in Chap. 7, the share of non-native (European) players among one's own club's players has been identified as the single most powerful factor correlating with cosmopolitan attitudes. Hence, it seems promising to take another look at our eight clubs in terms of the composition of their squads. In doing so, it becomes apparent that each of the top clubs in the four leagues also has a higher share of non-native EU nationals than that of the relegation battlers (cf. Chap. 7, Table 7.2). Thus, an important component of the causal mechanism leading from participation in European club competitions to Europeanised mindsets might be that there tend to be more non-native EU players in those teams. However, this reconciliatory explanation needs to be qualified: first, the share of non-native EU players is only slightly higher when comparing top teams in France, England and Austria with the relegation battlers in those counties (only in Germany this difference is significant). Second, the share of *non-EU* foreigners is even higher among the smaller clubs in England and France compared to the respective national top performers. Hence, if at all relevant, the causal mechanism at play here may be the *Europeanisation* rather than the *internationalisation* of relevant teams.

'Initiation' entails the collection of additional (i.e. new) data and further analysis in order to arrive at a plausible explanation of diverging research findings. This often goes beyond the scope of the original research undertaking and may thus require embarking on the initiation of a follow-up research project (Pluye et al. 2009, 63). As not all of the above-described inconsistencies can be conclusively settled through bracketing, exclusion or reconciliation, the collection of new data seems to make sense. In fact, funding for a follow-up research project has been successfully acquired, involving the authors of this book in different capacities as well as additional researchers in key functions. The project FANZinE[3] allows for the collection of substantial data in order to further explore the above-mentioned ambiguities and to advance research in important additional dimensions: first, we seek to take into account the diversity of Europe through the selection of a broader spectrum of countries, thus also including an Eastern European country (Poland), a Southern European country (Spain) and a northern (non-EU member) country (Norway). Second, through the comparison of fans and non-fans, we intend to contrast the effects of the lifeworld football with the rest of society in order to explore if football has a particularly strong potential for the Europeanisation of identities, also in view of building (social) cohesion in Europe. Third, by broadening and deepening our mixed-methods tool-box—through the inclusion of a quantitative analysis of sports media reports along with a (larger representative) survey and interviews with key fan representatives—we hope to shed new light on the above-mentioned inconsistencies and generate robust novel insights.

Hence, while acknowledging the fact that our project has generated some conflicting evidence, we propose a complementary strategy—involving bracketing, reconciliation and initiation—to make sense of these inconsistent findings.

---

[3] https://fanzine-research.github.io/

9.2.4 Fan Criticism of an Increasingly Inaccessible European Football

The identification of fans with European football is likely not isolated from individual and further contextual factors. Rather diverging patterns of identification with Europe co-exist in the same fan communities: some see Europe as the natural football habitat (normalisation of Europeanised players rosters, expectation of, or longing for frequent participation in the Champions League etc.), others perceive 'European football' as a hyper-commercialised, partly inaccessible event alien to the 'true spirit of the game'. It is in this sense that the structural Europeanisation of football may not only contribute to fans becoming European, but might also foster a divide between fans and their clubs (cf. Weber et al. 2020; Chaps. 6 and 8).

Secondly, one crucial aspect of the 'European football experience' (to break up formerly national thinking boxes) is that it remains accessible, and not completely detached from the everyday experiences of regular Europeans. The more the idea of yet another Champions League reform favouring the already richer clubs from the 'Big Five' leagues (or the formation of a breakaway ESL) takes hold, the more European football risks alienating fans in significant numbers. In a similar vein, the more European football—from other leagues, or top-level club competition—vanishes from free TV or other publicly accessible and affordable media and online streams, the less of a *shared*, broadly appealing mass experience football will become over time.

Especially the survey and interview stages of our research uncovered a considerable element of criticism that had developed among fans and those interested in football at different levels. This criticism is not restricted to organised fan groups, Ultras and the likes but has entered the mainstream much more forcefully than a decade ago (also cf. UK Government 2021). This is particularly visible in our interviews with fans at the periphery of European football—followers of Austrian teams, and hence, teams situated in a league outside the 'Big Five' context of top teams populating the elite tiers of European club football (cf. Brand et al. 2023; Chap. 8). Being on the outside clearly does not mean that these fans do not relate to elite competition among European top-level clubs. And quite reasonably, a more general criticism of the overly commercialised nature of modern football blends into their articulations.

However, never did a unidimensional understanding of such commercial trends prevail in our interviews, nor did we find an unambiguous rejection of a nowadays 'hyper-commercialised' sport. Our interviews with Austrian fans exemplify this: when pondering the idea of future developments of the CL and European club tournaments—including the formation of a 'super league' of the richest and (recently) most successful European clubs, for instance—some of our interview partners understandably expressed anxiety that this would only further alienate Austrian fans and strengthen their feeling of being pushed to the margins. Yet, there was also some appraisal of such a development and quite a few interview partners expressed their appreciation of the sporting and entertainment qualities of top-level European football. This fostered the development of secondary fandom or and complementary followership of 'another type' of football. Therefore, rejection of the over-commercialised realities of 'modern football' was not unanimously shared, nor was there a shared perception of Austrian marginalisation.

Our online survey suggests that criticisms of commercialisation, and the elite-level football as detached and aloof, and so on, can go hand in hand with different expressions of fan intensity and different degrees of communitarianism/cosmopolitanism.

9.2.5 Sport and Politics?

In general, the Europeanisation of mindsets among football fans through the football experience seems to be a reality. However, how much of this football-related attention towards the European level (and even appreciation of Europe, not to speak of EU institutions and politics and their role in the reform and governance of the sport, cf. García and Llopis-Goig 2021) really spills over into more conscious political attitudes still needs to be ascertained. For many English football fans, for instance, it is no contradiction to act as a fan in a 'European frame of reference', with a fairly Europeanised notion of in- and out-groups, while nevertheless scathing the EU for all sorts of ills.

We had actually assumed Brexit[4] to be a topic of discussion among English football fans. More specifically, we supposed this to hold true in particular for our selection of online message board threads, as well as when fans were asked about wider societal aspects of their fandom during the interview stage. We were proven wrong, to some extent. While Brexit was discussed in some online forums—albeit in specifically designated threads, not those related to the Europeanised aspects of the game—it rarely featured in the two dozen in-depth interviews. While the latter fact could be explained by a mood of 'getting over it' (by 2020), we found it remarkable that explicit links between the Europeanisation of football governance (partly shaped by the EU) and the assessment of UK-EU relations did not surface prominently in our conversations about fandom experiences. For instance, among ManU fans, 'communities of belonging' were shaped by a dualism between localism and Europe. While the local reference to the city of Manchester proved relevant—both for who is perceived as a good fan and for players—Europe was fans' first reference point for players of high quality. This is contrary to those who perceived Brexit as primarily beneficial for English football, for example, the former England and Arsenal defender Sol Campbell, who stated that "[Premier League] teams load up with too many mediocre overseas footballers, especially from Europe, crowding out young English and British talent" (Gordon 2016). Such a view does not seem to reflect the dominant perspective of fans. Their relation to Europe in this sense was, on the contrary, fairly positive. It is the benchmark against which they judge the quality of players.

Such a disjuncture, or parallel occurrences of normalisation and appreciation of Europe on the one hand and criticisms of some elite football phenomena a/o Eurosceptic positions dominant throughout the embedding societies on the other, at least seemed to be frequent. In a similar vein, Austrian fans remote from European competition and focused on regional identity anchors and talent playing for their club, at times defined their home region in rather non-national terms—even in a

---

[4] On the ramifications of Brexit for sport more generally, cf. Kornbeck (2022).

transboundary fashion, through including portions of Italy or the Balkans. Their strategy for coping with the peripheral status of Austrian football in Europe was to find a niche, a regional-transboundary retreat: especially in neighbouring Germany, Switzerland and Italy as well as Slovenia and other countries on the Balkans. Such an interest appeared to be partly directed towards football below the 'Big Five' leagues, with Italy and Germany being considered as relevant venues for access to high-level European football. This interest was fuelled by local proximity (short car drives or good train connections), and the matches and clubs being chosen for pragmatic reasons. A second motivation, in particular with regard to the Balkans, stemmed from family bonds and ties preserved within former immigrant communities (particularly visible in Graz).

All this also tied with the result that among our hypothesised factors of influence on Europeanised attitudes among football fans, the more conventionally political one—the degree of Euroscepticism in the embedding societies—did not seem to play any explicit role. This somewhat counter-intuitive observation followed from our analysis of the online discussions and was then corroborated by the in-depth interviews at a later stage. It has been most visible with regard to certain clubs: Hannover 96, Manchester United, and FC Toulouse (the latter only as regards the online forums). Although the former two clubs are located in societies that are comparatively Europhile, their fans' articulations have shown only moderate evidence of Europeanised identifications. Conversely, the opposite was true of supporters of ManU who—despite being embedded in Eurosceptic northern English society, particularly outside the centre of Manchester town—seem to have rather Europeanised mindsets. It is in this sense that we could illuminate, through our analyses, the existence of some 'subconscious Europeanisation' of segments of fans through football; a process which, however, seems to unfold alongside—or is even cut off from—growing political Euroscepticism within the respective embedding societies (cf. Chap. 4; Weber et al. 2022).

9.3 (Further) Lessons Learned

In this section, we discuss three lessons we had to learn in our project. They might be interesting or formative for future research on football fans and the nexus of sport-related and political identity formation in particular: a possibly growing resistance of fans to be investigated as objects of study; the impact of the Covid pandemic on football, however lasting and recurring it might be; and debates around the need to reform European-level football, which also carry the flavour of risking more Europeanised identifications and orientations, due to the destructive qualities of rampant commercialisation.

9.3.1 The Football Fan: An Elusive Object of Study

Despite our best efforts, diligent preparation and a multi-pronged strategy, we certainly encountered problems in implementing our project. One of the most surprising (and rather unexpected) of these was that we occasionally faced challenges in recruiting study participants—to a lesser extent at the survey-stage, more forcefully during our interviews. While during the Covid pandemic, shifting priorities and harsh regulation measures (see below) did play a role, we feel that this cannot account for everything. At times, we pondered whether there was even an increasing resistance among football fans—organised and occasional—to be treated and interrogated as objects of study. This was most pronounced in the case of France.

While we cannot ultimately rule out cultural barriers and impeded opportunities for access (through Covid restrictions: empty stadiums, lack of match-day experiences, even temporary curfews) to be responsible for the slow and only partial recruitment in particular of French supporters willing to be interviewed, other factors also seemed to bear significance. It may be true that French football supporter culture has matured into an established object of scientific study by now (Hourcade 2021), and even features big in fan publications across Europe (Erlebnis Fußball 2021). Nevertheless, finding French fans willing to talk to us proved elusive.

We may speculate in this regard whether a decade of harsh restrictions on away fans in particular, and further othering and criminalisation of (intense) football followership in France (Steinberg 2019),[5] has not also left its mark on fan communities of French clubs. Could it not be that the media frames of endemic violence, the travel restrictions on the grounds of curbing match-day violence, and other measures in place in many French municipalities since 2011 have also eroded the willingness to identify with football, or being considered a fan?

Among our eight selected fan scenes, the French supporters proved to be a tough case. Yet, we also sensed a growing disinterest, occasionally even resistance, among football fans in various locations to being included as objects of investigation. While there might also be an element of saturation (having been exposed to too many surveys via Facebook or online message boards, having been contacted too often to voice an opinion on the game and issues surrounding it, and oftentimes for only thinly disguised marketing reasons), there was also another source for non-participation. (We witnessed this, to different extents, both when we sought to disseminate our survey and during the interview stage in our attempts to recruit people who would sit down with us for an hour or so and discuss their fan experience in more detail.) The more organised fans in particular view such studies increasingly as instances which could be used to spy on them and to gather intelligence on them. The case of the German fan researcher Thein, who was exposed in 2015 to have been co-opted by the German Agency of Protection of the Constitution, seems to have left its mark here. It was also in this sense that even sophisticated strategies for enhancing access to and the quality of survey responses (Gibbons and Nuttall 2012) and for recruiting willing interviewees ran empty more often than anticipated.

---

[5] Against the background of what some have dubbed an ambiguous relationship towards football as a sport in the wider French society and among pundits, media and intellectuals in particular (cf. Ranc and Hourcade 2018, 49).

9.3.2 The Covid Pandemic as a Big Disruptor

Such unwillingness only seemed to harden through the Covid pandemic, the fear it generated among people (leading to social *distancing*), and the measures put in place to cope with it (restricting mobility, access, and opportunities to meet in person, around football). Empty stadiums, suspended leagues, disrupted seasons, and the near-complete shutdown of amateur football in many places in 2020 and 2021 might also have a more lasting effect, though. In particular, the parallel appearance of spectacles televised before empty terraces, with staff and players continuously being tested and quarantined to be able to keep the show running while many spectators were put under severe restrictions and threatened with job loss, might resonate much longer. While re-prioritisation away from football concerns might have been enforced (or just reasonable) in the early stages, it remains to be seen whether some distance toward the former leisure-time favourite will persist. Moore (2021, 43) is certainly right in stating that Covid exposed the simple truth that football, in comparison to the pandemic, is "not a matter of life and death"; yet it is far from clear that this disruption will really lead people to "see and value the game in a different, healthier way".

With our interviews set to start in spring 2020, Covid-19 came as a source of disruption to us in many ways. The immersing we had planned—on-site observation and familiarisation, attending matches and contacting fans and supporters in their habitat—all this was no longer possible during the project. Recruiting respondents online in an effort to substitute for the live interviews, recruiting them for another hour long talk through Skype and Zoom and the like, was as tough as progress was glacial. Among many factors, the pressures of the situation seemed to shape not only time budgets and the willingness to converse—it also appeared to distance potential talking partners from football. As one of our respondents, a follower of Hannover 96 in Germany, summed up nicely: "I do follow football with much greater distance since the outbreak of Covid. Priorities just shifted".

From the perspective of 2023, with stadiums re-opened and many aspects of football (attendance) back to normal, it will be interesting to observe how much of a lasting effect Covid will have on football and on the fandom practices surrounding it (cf. Ludvigsen 2022). On the basis of a survey among followers of an unnamed club from the German Bundesliga (statistical data allows for inferring that it could be Borussia Dortmund), Wilkesmann (2022) predicts that the majority of followers have not given up on football and their team, that the match-day experience continues to be important, and that most will return to the stadium. Still, below that drive back to the normal, there was also a noticeable weakening of ties among season-ticket holders and fan club members—rather intense forms of fandom—if compared to pre-Covid levels. In their predictive study on the likely future impact of Covid-19 on the football ecosphere, Beiderbeck et al. (2021), interestingly enough, included only one dimension directly related to fandom: stadium attendance. This is surprising insofar as they start off with the assertion that the number of people emotionally involved in following the sport is much larger than the number of jobs in the related industry. And arguably, the bulk of their 15 projections, which they discuss with the help of experts and the Delphi method, consists of regulatory, economic and technological aspects. In principle, these can and in fact often do become relevant from a fan's point of view. Still, their prime measure of supporters' ties to the match is stadium attendance, which they predict to be slightly decreasing—a tendency in line with pre-Covid trends. But would that indicate an overall bigger distance between fans and the game, one accelerated though not caused by Covid? The verdict on this is still out. Yet, some observers indeed argue that significant numbers of fans and supporters witnessed during the Covid pandemic how big the split between their lives and professional football had become (cf. Lange, quoted in Knebel 2021). Or, as yet another supporter from H96 put it: "During the Covid crisis, sad as it is, it's all about making money. […] The Corona story demonstrates in the end, that it is all about profits, not about the players and the games as such".

9.3.3 Super League Dreams and Nightmares

Finally, even though the latest round of debate on a breakaway league of top-tier European clubs only took place in the final stages of our field work, we think that there have already been signs of how people would possibly respond to such a development in their capacity as football fans and followers. In this regard, it is interesting to observe how studies of the ESL plans in 2021 have treated the voice of 'the' fans so far. Brannagan et al. (2022), for instance, refer to a "universal disapproval of the creation" of such a league by clubs, players, *and fans*. As they assert, the mere plan achieved the creation of an overarching social identity against it. The significance of this is that fans of different clubs usually pitted against one another now seemed to be united in their opposition. In a similar vein, Wagner et al. (2021) emphasise that the announcement "was met with fury, fans' mobilization, severe critique from football fans generally but also from fans inside the 12 clubs". And they declare the ESL dead for now, a development they themselves "cannot mourn". And neither can and do we, from a normative point of view.

Still, the results of our analyses clearly show that, at least before the Covid pandemic hit, significant numbers of those emotionally or otherwise invested in football as team supporters, spectators, and so on also found merit in top-level, elite football in Europe. Could it not be that the very dynamics of the moment—an existential pandemic, disrupted public life, at times bizarre continuity on the pitch and in top-level football, and the move of several elite teams to extract even more revenues from the European football ecosystem—had against that very background galvanised sentiments into a rather strict repudiation? A level of rejection that is not thoroughly indicative of the often not unidirectional, even ambiguous renderings of elite-level European football?

In a similar vein, the analyses of Twitter communication among fans about the ESL plans by Meier et al. (2022a) hint at the fact that, aside from rejecting *this particular plan at this very moment*, most exchanged arguments rather backed the current status quo, advertently or not. This means that the time does not seem to be ripe for a huge and comprehensive fan movement towards a transformative change of the game, aside from networks of activists and transnational supporters' organisations. Even in its current structures, European top-level football—with the CL as the epitome of both Europeanisation, commercialisation and 'modern football'—has found its followers, and fans from different locations and levels of competition do appreciate some of what they are served, at least. Or, in the words of a Newcastle United supporter we interviewed: "It's just wow, wow, wow. This is what European football has to offer at the moment. It's absolutely exciting and breath-taking and it's just (…) something I think (…) hopefully when we passed this, what's going on at the moment with coronavirus, once we hopefully get off this kind of hurdle at the moment it's something I'm very looking forward to watch".

9.4 Further Research

Staying with football fans as (sole) research subjects, our results would be further probed (and possibly corroborated) through the inclusion of countries and leagues that have not yet been part of our analysis, such as Central Eastern European countries/leagues or those of European non-EU members. In addition, it would be very valuable to have data on the same categories of analyses across a wider timespan to establish causal relations between certain changes in the Europeanisation of the governance structure, competitions, and so on, and (potential) changes in fan attitudes. However, since the most substantial changes in European governance and player markets are in the past, one would need comparable historical data that does not seem to exist. Yet, as far as events/ideas like the announcement of the European Super-League project are concerned, it would be possible to conduct a (more systematic) analysis of this proclamation on supporters' identities.

In terms of research methods, a quantitative text analysis (Ignatow and Mihalcea 2017; Lemke and Wiedemann 2016) of representations of national and European competitions (and other aspects) in the respective specialist media of certain countries could be conducted. This would generate an assessment of the visibility of European competitions and (national) leagues to the respective publics, with media consumption as one seemingly important factor influencing fan perceptions. Furthermore, as our online survey cannot be considered 'representative', a similar but representative quantitative survey, taking the form of an online panel, could be conducted via established providers in certain relevant countries.

Our results so far only provide insights into the mindsets of football fans. What they do not shed light on are the perceptions of other sports fans and those of non-fans. As for the first aspect, our findings may be of relevance for investigating similar dynamics in other fields of sport. Patterns of intense fan identification have been ascertained, for example, in sports such as college basketball (Wann and Branscombe 1990) or Aussie rules football (Lock et al. 2014). A key factor seems to be the sense of belonging to a local fan community, including the feeling of making an active contribution by supporting the team but also of contributing to the local community (Heere and James 2007). Crawford (2003), using the example of ice hockey fans, and Heere et al. (2011) on American college football, demonstrate that identification with a team is significantly influenced by local communities. On the other hand, sports other than football display astonishing levels of Europeanisation. A case in point is the Ryder's Cup tournament in professional golf, where a European team competes under the flag of Europe (cf. Harris 2014). In addition, team sports other than football have undergone similar changes towards a Europeanisation of governance structures, competitions and player markets, such as handball, basketball or ice-hockey. Hence, further research could investigate whether the general findings we have arrived and the (particular strength of) influence factors at play may be transferable and comparable to other types of sport fans, and if so, whether and how they may differ from our results.

Another important point of departure for future research is the inclusion of non-fans and the comparison of the attitudes with those of (football) fans. It may well be the case that sport/football provides certain conditions that are particularly conducive to the adoption of Europeanised attitudes, such as the high emotional investment of fans combined with Europeanised governance structures, competitions and player markets. If there is no difference between fans and non-fans, the identity-inducing socialisation function of football (or sports more generally) may be overestimated, and other societal mechanisms may stimulate similar (or more substantial) processes in the direction of Europeanised mindsets. The inclusion of (and comparison with) non-fans also has an important sociopolitical dimension: if fans differ from non-fans in the sense that they have more cosmopolitan or Europeanised mindsets, this would have important (policy-relevant) implications for the social/societal cohesion in a Europe that is becoming increasingly polarised and in which Eurosceptic parties and movements are making significant inroads. Many of the aspects mentioned in this section have been taken up by EUFOOT's successor: a project coined FANZinE, which involves the authors of this book in various functions and—crucially important—a number of fresh minds.[6]

References

Allport, Gordon W. 1954. *The nature of prejudice*. Reading: Addison-Wesley.
Beiderbeck, Daniel, Nicolas Frevel, Heiko A. von der Gracht, Sascha Schmidt, and Vera M. Schweitzer. 2021. The impact of COVID-19 on the European football ecosystem – A Delphi-based scenario analysis. *Technological Forecasting and Social Change* 165: 1–17. https://doi.org/10.1016/j.techfore.2021.120577.
Biel, Jonas, Tobias Finger, Vincent Reinke, Jennifer Amann, Arne Niemann, and Marc Jungblut. 2023. Becoming European through football media? Representations of Europe in German football news coverage. *International Journal of Sport Communication*. Advanced Online Publication. https://doi.org/10.1123/ijsc.2023-0004.
Brand, Alexander, Arne Niemann, and Regina Weber. 2023. Pipe dream or closed shop? Experiencing the Champions League from the sidelines. *Soccer and Society* 24 (4): 520–533.
Brandt, Christian, Fabian Hertel, and Sean Huddleston, eds. 2017. *Football fans, rivalry and cooperation*. London: Routledge.
Brannagan, Paul Michael, Nicolas Scelles, Maurizio Valenti, Yuhei Inoue, Jonathan Grix, and Seath Joseph Perkin. 2022. The 2021 European Super League attempt: Motivation, outcome, and the future of football. *International Journal of Sport Policy and Politics* 14 (1): 169–176. https://doi.org/10.1080/19406940.2021.2013926.
Brubaker, Rogers, and Frederick Cooper. 2000. Beyond 'identity'. *Theory and Society* 29 (1): 1–47.
Cleland, Jamie, Mark Doidge, Peter Millward, and Paul Widdop. 2018. *Collective action and football fandom. A relational sociological approach*. Cham: Palgrave Macmillan.

---

[6] See https://fanzine-research.github.io/; also see: Biel et al. 2023; Finger et al. 2023.

Coursol, Allan, and Edwin E. Wagner. 1986. Effect of positive findings on submission and acceptance rates. A note on meta-analysis bias. *Professional Psychology: Research and Practice* 17 (2): 136–137. https://doi.org/10.1037/0735-7028.17.2.136.

Crawford, Garry. 2003. The career of the sport supporter: The case of the Manchester Storm. *Sociology* 37 (2): 219–237. https://doi.org/10.1177/0038038503037002001.

Creamer, Elizabeth G. 2018. Paradigms in play: Using case studies to explore the value-added of divergent findings in mixed methods research. *International Journal of Multiple Research Approaches* 10 (1): 30–40. https://doi.org/10.29034/ijmra.v10n1a2.

Dawson, Rob. 2021. Man United fans break into Carrington training ground in anti-Glazers protest. *Video* 1: 08. https://www.espn.co.uk/football/manchester-united/story/4366572/man-united-fans-block-entrance-to-carrington-training-ground-in-anti-glazers-protest.

De Witte, Floris, and Jan Zglinski. 2022. The idea of Europe in football. *European Law Open* 1 (2): 286–315. https://doi.org/10.1017/elo.2022.15.

Erlebnis Fußball. 2021. La Saga Supras. Ein Interview. *Erlebnis Fussball* 83: 6–77.

Finger, Tobias, Jennifer Amann, Jonas Biel, Arne Niemann, and Vincent Reinke. 2023. Researching football, identity and cohesion in Europe. *Sports Law, Policy & Diplomacy Journal* 1 (1): 31–57. https://doi.org/10.30925/slpdj.1.1.5.

García, Borja, and Ramón Llopis-Goig. 2021. Supporters' attitudes towards European football governance: Structural dimensions and sociodemographic patterns. *Soccer and Society* 22 (4): 1–16. https://doi.org/10.1080/14660970.2020.1790356.

García, Borja, and Jinming Zheng, eds. 2017. *Football and supporter activism in Europe. Whose game is it?* Cham: Palgrave Macmillan.

Gibbons, Tom, and Daniel Nuttall. 2012. Using e-surveys to access the views of football fans within online communities. *Sport in Society* 15 (9): 1228–1241.

Giddings, Lynne S., and Barbara M. Grant. 2007. A Trojan horse for positivism? A critique of mixed methods research. *Advances in Nursing Science* 30 (1): 52–60. https://doi.org/10.1097/00012272-200701000-00006.

Gordon, James Bridget. 2016. How footballers reacted to Brexit results. *Paste Magazine*, June 24, 2016. https://www.pastemagazine.com/soccer/footballers-react-to-brexit

Giulianotti, Richard. 2002. Supporters, followers, fans, and flaneurs. *Journal of Sport and Social Issues* 26 (1): 25–46. https://doi.org/10.1177/0193723502261003.

Harris, John. 2014. Europeanisation of the Ryder Cup? *Sport & EU Review* 6 (1): 14–19.
Harrits, Gitte Sommer. 2011. More than method?: A discussion of paradigm differences within mixed methods research. *Journal of Mixed Methods Research* 5 (2): 150–166. https://doi.org/10.1177/1558689811402506.
Heere, Bob, and Jeffrey D. James. 2007. Sports teams and their communities: Examining the influence of external group identities on team identity. *Journal of Sport Management* 21 (3): 319–337. https://doi.org/10.1123/jsm.21.3.319.
Heere, Bob, Matthew Walker, Masayuki Yoshida, Yong Jae Ko, Jeremy S. Jordan, and Jeffrey D. James. 2011. Brand community development through associated communities: Grounding community measurement within social identity theory. *Journal of Marketing Theory and Practice* 19 (4): 402–422. https://doi.org/10.2753/MTP1069-6679190404.
Hourcade, Nicolas. 2021. Vorwort. In *ULTRA. Französische Lebensart (Translated)*, ed. Adrien Verrecchia, Bastien Poupat, and Bernoit Taix, 14–24. Burkhardt & Partner Verlag.
Ignatow, Gabe, and Rada Mihalcea. 2017. *Text mining: A guidebook for the social sciences*. London: SAGE Publications. https://doi.org/10.4135/9781483399782.
King, Anthony. 2000. Football fandom and post-national identity in the New Europe. *British Journal of Sociology* 51 (3): 419–442.
Knappertsbusch, Felix, Margrit Schreier, Nicole Burzan, and Nigel Fielding. 2023. Innovative applications and future directions in mixed methods and multimethod social research. *Forum Qualitative Sozialforschung/Forum: Qualitative Social Research* 24 (1). https://doi.org/10.17169/fqs-24.1.4013.
Knebel, Bjarne. 2021. Die Fans wenden sich ab. *11 Freunde*, September 10, 2021. https://11freunde.de/artikel/die-fans-wenden-sich-ab/4496158
Kornbeck, Jacob, ed. 2022. *Sport and Brexit. Regulatory challenges and legacies*. London: Routledge.
Lemke, Matthias, and Gregor Wiedemann, eds. 2016. *Text Mining in den Sozialwissenschaften: Grundlagen und Anwendungen zwischen qualitativer und quantitativer Diskursanalyse*. Wiesbaden: Springer VS. https://doi.org/10.1007/978-3-658-07224-7.
Lock, Daniel, Daniel C. Funk, Jason P. Doyle, and Heath McDonald. 2014. Examining the longitudinal structure, stability, and dimensional interrelationships of team identification. *Journal of Sport Management* 28 (2): 119–135. https://doi.org/10.1123/jsm.2012-0191.

Ludvigsen, Jan Andre Les. 2022. *Sport mega-events, security and Covid-19. Securing the football world*. London: Routledge.
Mathers, Mathew. 2021. European Super League: YouGov poll finds 79 per cent of fans oppose elite competition. *Indeptendent*, April 19, 2021. https://www.independent.co.uk/news/uk/home-news/european-super-league-fans-opposed-yougov-b1834114.html
Meier, Henk Erik, Borja García, Mara Konjer, and Malte Jetzke. 2022a. The short life of the European Super League: A case study on institutional tensions in sport industries. *Managing Sport and Leisure*: 1–22. https://doi.org/10.1080/23750472.2022.2058071.
Meier, Henk Erik, Borja García, Serhat Yilmaz, and Webster Chakawata. 2022b. The capture of EU football regulation by the football governing bodies. *Journal of Common Market Studies* 61 (3): 692–711. https://doi.org/10.1111/jcms.13405.
Moffatt, Suzanne, Martin White, Joan Mackintosh, and Denise Howel. 2006. Using quantitative and qualitative data in health services research – What happens when mixed method findings conflict? [ISRCTN61522618]. *BMC Health Services Research* 6: 1–10. https://doi.org/10.1186/1472-6963-6-28.
Moore, Kevin. 2021. Football is not 'a matter of life and death'. It is far less important than that. Football and the COVID-19 pandemic in England. *Soccer and Society* 22 (1–2): 43–57. https://doi.org/10.1080/14660970.2020.1797496.
Pluye, Pierre, Roland M. Grad, Alissa Levine, and Belinda Nicolau. 2009. Understanding divergence of quantitative and qualitative data (or results) in mixed methods studies. *International Journal of Multiple Research Approaches* 3 (1): 58–72. https://doi.org/10.5172/mra.455.3.1.58.
Ramsay, Gordon. 2021. Football fan groups condemn 'ultimate betrayal' of European Super League. *CNN*, April 19, 2021. https://edition.cnn.com/2021/04/19/football/european-super-league-fan-reaction-spt-intl/index.html
Ranc, David, and Nicolas Hourcade. 2018. France. In *The Palgrave handbook of football and politics*, ed. Jean-Michel De Waele, Suzan Gibril, Ekaterina Gloriozova, and Ramón Spaaij, 39–59. Cham: Palgrave Macmillan.
Steinberg, Arne. 2019. Voyage, voyage. *11 Freunde*, November 12, 2019. http://11freunde.de/artikel/voyage-voyage/564579
UK Government. 2021. Fan-led review of football governance: Securing the game's future. *Gov.uk*, November 24, 2021. https://www.gov.uk/government/publications/fan-led-review-of-football-governance-securing-the-games-future

Wagner, Ulrik, Rasmus K. Storm, and Kenneth Cortsen. 2021. Commercialization, governance problems and the future of European football – Or why the European Super League is not a solution to the challenges facing football. *International Journal of Sport Communication* 14 (3): 321–333. https://doi.org/10.1123/ijsc.2021-0049.

Wann, Daniel L., and Nyla R. Branscombe. 1990. Die-hard and fair-weather fans: Effects of identification on BIRGing CORFing tendencies. *Journal of Sport and Social Issues* 14 (2): 103–117.

Weber, Regina, Alexander Brand, Arne Niemann, and Florian Koch. 2020. Non-elite conceptions of Europe: Europe as a reference frame in English football fan discussions. *Journal of Contemporary European Research* 16 (3): 293–319. https://doi.org/10.30950/jcer.v16i3.1089.

Weber, Regina, Alexander Brand, Florian Koch, and Arne Niemann. 2022. A European mind? Europeanisation of football fan discussions in online message boards. *European Journal for Sport and Society* 19 (4): 323–346. https://doi.org/10.1080/16138171.2021.1974220.

Wilkesmann, Uwe. 2022. Should I stay (at home) or should I go (to the stadium)? Why will some football supporters not return to the stadium after the COVID-19 pandemic in German Bundesliga? *Soccer and Society* 23 (8): 1069–1083. https://doi.org/10.1080/14660970.2022.2033732.

Index[1]

A

Advocacy coalition, 33
Atlas.ti, 142, 155, 158
Austria
  Austrian Freedom Party, 131, 132
  Green Party, 132
Austrian clubs
  Red Bull Salzburg, 166, 175, 176, 183, 248
  Sturm Graz, 21, 138–139, 154, 164–166, 175–178, 182–184, 186n4, 190, 226, 243–246, 248, 251–253, 255, 257
  Wacker Innsbruck, 18, 21, 139, 143n19, 154, 155, 159, 166 168, 175–177, 184–185, 186n4, 190, 226, 246–253, 255, 257
  Wattens/WSG Tirol, 167, 168, 177

B

Banal Europeanism, 51, 52
Banal Nationalism, 51
Bosman
  EU foreigners, 134, 135
  post-Bosman, 42
  ruling, 4, 32, 41–43, 163, 184
Brexit, 12, 15, 19, 131, 134n3, 191, 261, 274, 274n4
Brubaker, Rogers, 23, 87, 88, 91–94, 91n2, 96, 110, 122, 123, 262

---

[1] Note: Page numbers followed by 'n' refer to notes.

C

Case selection, 2, 121, 128–140, 203
Collective identity, 9, 10, 87, 90n1, 92, 94n3, 99, 101, 102, 110
Commercialisation, 22, 43, 45, 69, 77–78, 80, 182, 229, 256, 258, 261, 273, 276, 280
(hyper-)commercialisation, 17, 69, 272, 273
Communities of belonging
  encoding of events in narratives, 125
  inclusion/exclusion, 122–124, 221
  relations between fans – coalitions and networks, 123, 124
Community law, *see* European Union, law
Comparative analysis, 141, 147, 158
Congruence analysis, 186
Contact hypothesis, 267
Cooper, Frederick, 23, 87, 88, 91–94, 91n2, 96, 110, 122, 123, 262
Cosmopolitanism, 172, 189, 205, 210, 213, 214, 273
Council of Europe (COE), 37
Covid-19
  pandemic, 15, 66, 225, 226, 262
  pre-covid 19, 279
Cultural studies, 64, 69

D

DAZN, 262
Discourse analysis, 16, 19, 22, 132, 141, 146, 147, 153, 155–157, 160n1, 186, 263, 267, 268

E

Eder, Klaus, 23, 88, 94, 94n3, 122, 125
England, *see* United Kingdom (UK)
English clubs
  Manchester City, 161, 165, 172, 180, 237
  Manchester United, 7, 19, 21, 22, 77, 108, 140, 154, 158, 159, 164–166, 168, 171–173, 178–181, 180n3, 186n4, 189, 190, 217, 226, 235–239, 251–253, 255, 257, 258, 265, 266, 269, 274, 275
  Newcastle United, 18, 18n4, 19, 21, 140, 154, 159, 166–168, 171–173, 181–182, 186n4, 226, 239–242, 251–253, 255, 257, 266, 280
Erasmus/Erasmus+, 11, 12, 107
EUCROSS, 10n3, 13, 104–106
Eurobarometer, 10, 132, 133
Euro-friendliness, *see* Europhilia
European Club Association (ECA), 3, 4, 40, 46–48
European Community, 98, 131, 132
European competitions, 16, 18, 21, 22, 42, 83, 126–127, 135–138, 144, 145, 161, 162, 166, 168–178, 180, 181, 183, 184, 189–191, 195, 196, 201–204, 207, 210, 214–217, 222, 227, 229–231, 230n5, 233–235, 238, 239, 242, 244–246, 249, 250, 253–258, 263–266, 274, 281

participation in, 16, 18, 130,
  135–136, 162,
  169–178, 203, 204,
  207, 210, 217, 222,
  239, 249, 254, 256,
  258, 265, 267, 269, 270
European Economic Area
  (EEA), 139
nationals, 134, 135
European identity, 1, 9–14, 25, 38,
  80, 97–105, 107, 108, 110,
  125, 154, 204
European integration, 9, 15, 31–51,
  98, 99, 131, 132, 208,
  210, 261
Europeanisation
  bottom-up/uploading, 3, 11, 12,
    36–40, 107
  convergence, 37, 102
  Europeanisation of player
    markets, 1, 2, 16, 18, 22,
    42, 124, 129, 130,
    133–135, 153, 159–168,
    190, 216, 222, 250–253,
    258, 262, 263, 266, 268,
    270, 282
  harmonisation, 37
  subjective Europeanisation, 51,
    52, 122, 125, 127
  top-down/downloading, 3, 11,
    36–38, 40
  transnational/cross-loading, 10,
    36–40, 38n3
European Professional Football
  Leagues (EPFL), 46n4
European public sphere, 8, 99,
  102, 109
European Social Survey, 132, 132n1

European Super League (ESL), 48,
  127, 262, 269, 272,
  280, 281
European Union
  institutions
    European Commission, 3, 8,
      40, 44, 70
    European Court of Justice
      (ECJ), 3, 4, 32–34,
      40, 41, 133
    European Parliament, 12, 34
  integration, 9, 13, 36, 132, 214
  law, 32–34, 42–44, 133
  nationals, 36, 103, 133–135,
    217, 270
  unification, 21n5, 132, 204, 208,
    217, 263, 267
Europhilia, 130, 159
Euroscepticism, 2, 130, 153, 179,
  181, 184, 185, 190, 222,
  250, 256, 262, 275

Fan forum, 14, 16, 18–19, 22, 24,
  121, 132, 142–143, 145,
  153–191, 217, 262, 263,
  266–269, 274, 277
Fans Against Racism in Europe
  (FARE), 124
Fan Supporters Europe (FSE), 124
Fan travel, 2, 67, 245
Fan typology
  communitarians, 20–21, 24,
    193–217, 273
  cosmopolitans, 20–21, 24,
    193–217, 273
FANZinE, 72, 262, 271, 283

292 Index

FIFA, 4, 21, 32, 34, 39, 41, 45–48
Football fandom, 1, 10, 11, 14, 23, 51, 63–83, 108–109, 141, 201, 210, 212, 214, 221, 262–265
Football leagues
  Austrian Bundesliga, 18, 133, 134, 136, 138, 139, 144, 165, 175–178, 195n4, 210, 212, 213, 244, 244n9, 246, 248, 255
  Belgium Pro League, 42
  English Premier League, 5, 8, 14, 19, 44, 49, 82, 134n3, 135, 140, 164–168, 171–173, 175, 177, 180n3, 181, 190, 208, 210, 213, 226, 237, 252, 253, 255
  European level leagues (*see* UEFA)
  German Bundesliga, 18, 44, 135, 138, 144, 181, 190, 195n4, 210, 213, 226–229, 247, 279
  La Liga, 45
  Ligue 1, 18, 134, 136, 137, 144, 195n4, 207, 210, 213, 226
  Serie A, 246
Frames of reference
  context of competitions, 127–128, 130
  European competitions, 126–127, 130, 171, 173–175, 178, 180, 183, 229, 238, 241, 244, 246, 249, 258, 265
  national competitions, 126–128, 174, 178, 180, 195, 228, 231, 233, 237, 248, 249, 255

France
  Front National, 132
  Rassemblement National, 132
Free movement of workers, 42
  Article 48 of the Treaty establishing the European Community (TEC), 41
FREE-project, 14
French clubs
  FC Toulouse, 137, 154, 162–164, 173–175, 184–185, 186n4, 190, 276, 277
  Olympique Marseille, 19, 136–137, 154, 159, 173–175, 178, 182–184, 186n4, 189, 250
  Paris Saint-Germain, 161, 162, 173, 174, 176, 183

G

G14, 4, 40, 45–48
German clubs
  Borussia Dortmund, 48n5, 161, 162, 228, 229, 279
  FC Bayern München/Bayern Munich, 18, 19, 21, 22, 137–138, 159–162, 168–171, 178–181, 186n4, 189, 190, 222n1, 226–231, 251–258, 265, 266
  Hannover 96, 18, 21, 138, 154, 159, 162–164, 169–171, 181–182, 186n4, 190, 222n1, 226, 231–235, 251–255, 257, 278
  RB Leipzig, 228

Germany, 16, 41–43, 49, 128, 131–133, 132n1, 144, 154, 181, 226, 227, 230, 245, 249, 251, 256, 262, 266, 270, 275, 278
Globalisation, 52, 96, 201
Glocalization, 82
Governance (structures) [of football], 1–3, 5, 7, 31, 40, 51, 52, 70, 71, 75, 110, 124, 189, 261, 282

Home Gown Player (rule), 134

Identity
  communality/connectedness/ groupness, 23, 24, 87, 88, 91, 93, 94, 108, 110, 122, 154, 262
  European identity, 1, 9–14, 25, 38, 80, 97–105, 107, 108, 110, 125, 154, 204
  identification, 10, 11, 23, 24, 52, 64, 87, 88, 91, 93, 94, 105, 110, 122, 154, 262
  self-understanding, 9, 23, 24, 87, 88, 91–94, 105, 110, 122, 154, 262
  Social Identity Theory, 88–109
In-group, 13, 18, 23, 90, 123, 130, 164, 189, 193, 221, 227, 231, 235, 239–241, 243, 247, 266, 274
Intergovernmentalism, 32, 33

Internationalisation, 8, 21, 21n5, 42, 128–130, 133, 168, 261, 267, 271
Interviews, 14, 16, 21, 22, 24, 121, 141, 145–147, 145n21, 222–257, 222n1, 263, 266–269, 271–278

Latent class analysis, 194–196, 200, 215
Logistic regression model, 205

Manchester United, 7, 19, 21, 22, 77, 108, 140, 154, 158, 159, 164–166, 168, 171–173, 178–181, 180n3, 186n4, 189, 190, 217, 226, 235–239, 235n6, 251–253, 255, 257, 258, 265, 266, 269, 274, 275
Marketisation, 65, 69, 78
MAXQDA software, 226
Message board, *see* Fan forum
Methodology, 147, 222–226
Mixed methods, 16, 141, 142, 146–147, 263, 267, 269, 271
Multilevel governance approaches, 33
Myth, 12

Neofunctionalism, 32

O

Online message boards, 16, 18, 24, 121, 142–143, 145, 153, 154, 186, 217, 263, 266, 269, 274, 277
Online survey, 16, 24, 121, 141, 144–147, 193, 264, 270, 273, 281
Oulmers case, 46
Out-group, 13, 18, 23, 90, 123, 130, 189, 193, 221, 227, 231, 235, 239, 241, 243, 247, 266, 274

P

Paired comparisons, 14, 19, 141, 146, 153, 158, 159, 164, 168, 177–178, 185, 186, 222, 226, 250–258, 263
Player market, 1, 2, 4, 16, 18, 21, 22, 41–43, 83, 124, 129, 130, 133–135, 153, 159–168, 170, 190, 216, 222, 230, 249–253, 258, 261–263, 266, 268, 270, 281, 282
 Europeanisation of, 1, 2, 16, 18, 22, 124, 129, 130, 133–135, 153, 159–168, 190, 216, 222, 250–253, 258, 262, 263, 266, 268, 270, 282
Political Science, 9, 10, 12, 13, 35, 70, 98, 101, 110, 195
Principal-agent analysis, 34
Professionalisation, 65, 70, 77n3, 80
Public attitude (towards Europe), 16, 22, 128, 131–133, 159, 179–185, 256–258

Q

Qualitative methods, 14, 16, 121, 141, 263, 268, 269
Quantitative methods, 14, 263, 271, 281

R

Red Devils, *see* Manchester United
Refugee crisis, 15
Rivalry, 19, 24, 124, 126, 127, 145, 161, 162, 167, 172, 173, 175, 178, 185, 189, 233, 248, 254, 265, 266

S

Single Market, 34
Social cohesion, 100, 271
Social Identity (Theory), 88–109
Social science, 31, 53, 87, 91, 110, 195
Social transnationalism, 39, 104, 106
Sociology, 23, 51, 64, 68–70, 91n2
Sport Management, 23, 64, 68–70, 96
Sport Psychology, 96
Sport Studies, 5, 23, 64, 68, 69
Structured paired comparisons, 16, 141, 154–159, 250
Subjective Europeanisation, 51, 52, 122, 125, 127
Subjective globalisation, 52
Supporters Direct Europe, 124
Supranationalism, 32, 48, 51, 80, 102

T

Transfer market, 18, 23, 35, 51, 177, 195, 197, 198, 201, 202, 205, 216, 230, 236, 238, 241, 250
Transfermarkt.co.uk, 166
Treaty of Rome, 133
TV spectators, 67, 141

U

UEFA
 association coefficient ranking, 47
 Champions League, 2–5, 7, 12, 18n4, 22, 40, 41, 44, 46–50, 108, 126, 135, 136, 140n18, 143, 155, 160–162, 167, 169–173, 176, 179–183, 185, 186, 196, 207, 229, 230, 233, 234, 237, 238, 241, 242, 244–246, 249, 254, 255, 257, 258, 272, 273, 280
 club coefficient ranking, 47
 Country's UEFA five-year ranking, 47, 183

Europa Conference League, 5, 126–127, 135
Europa League, 4, 22, 49, 50, 126, 135, 136, 138, 143, 155, 163, 172, 174, 180, 182, 186, 196, 207, 234, 238, 242, 244, 245, 249, 254, 258
UEFA Cup, 4, 49, 50, 233
Ultràs, 67, 141, 272
United Kingdom (UK), 14, 16, 19, 41, 43, 48, 67, 76, 82, 107, 128, 131, 132, 132n1, 140, 140n17, 144, 154, 167, 168, 172, 181, 191, 208, 217, 226, 229, 230, 236, 245, 256, 262, 270, 274

W

White Paper on Sport, 4
Working-class, 6, 72, 76, 77n3, 79, 239–242, 252
World Cup, 125